AF600071

THE SIMPLE IMPEDIMENTS TO HOLY ORDERS

THE CATHOLIC UNIVERSITY OF AMERICA
CANON LAW STUDIES
No. 224

THE SIMPLE IMPEDIMENTS TO HOLY ORDERS

AN HISTORICAL SYNOPSIS AND COMMENTARY

BY

HENRY JOHN VOGELPOHL, A.B., J.C.L.
PRIEST OF THE ARCHDIOCESE OF CINCINNATI

A DISSERTATION
SUBMITTED TO THE FACULTY OF THE SCHOOL OF CANON LAW
OF THE CATHOLIC UNIVERSITY OF AMERICA IN PARTIAL
FULFILLMENT OF THE REQUIREMENTS FOR THE
DEGREE OF DOCTOR OF CANON LAW

THE CATHOLIC UNIVERSITY OF AMERICA PRESS
WASHINGTON, D. C.
1945

Nihil Obstat:
CLEMENS V. BASTNAGEL, J.U.D.,
Censor Deputatus
Washingtonii, D. C., die 15 maii, 1945

Imprimatur:
✠ JOANNES T. McNICHOLAS, O.P., S.T.M.
Archiepiscopus Cincinnnatensis
Cincinnati, O., die 17 Maii, 1945.

MURRAY & HEISTER—WASHINGTON, D. C.
PRINTED IN THE UNITED STATES OF AMERICA

 9

To
My Mother and Father

TABLE OF CONTENTS

PART III

IMPEDIMENTS BASED ON THE DEFECT IN FAITH

PART IV
THE IMPEDIMENT BASED ON ONE'S EVIL ACTS

FOREWORD

Under the canon dealing with the simple impediments to Holy Orders the Code of Canon Law lists seven different conditions or states of being, temporary in nature, which make the reception of Orders illicit. Such an arrangement of the simple impediments is of modern origin. An author of the sixteenth century gave over sixty conditions or states of incompatibility with the reception of Orders.

The purpose of this work is twofold. It seeks to trace in a summary form, from its origin down to the promulgation of the Code of Canon Law on May 27, 1917, the canonical legislation on the impediments now listed under canon 987. It then endeavors to present a canonical commentary on the legislation as it has been in effect since May 19, 1918.

The canonical commentary will, for the greater part, be confined to an exploration of the import of canon 987. In the unfolding of the commentary certain definite conclusions will be drawn in consequence of which certain individuals will be regarded as subject to the impediments, and other individuals will be considered as falling outside the scope of the prohibitory enactments of canon 987. It must at the same time be remembered, however, that the exclusion of certain individuals from the comprehension of the canon does not give to the individual the right to receive Orders. Many canons, other than the one under consideration, can through the laws which are enacted in them debar one from the reception of Orders. The writer has no intention to give a complete listing of all of the qualifications demanded of an ordinand. The question which the writer hopes to answer in this work is the following: Who is impeded from the reception of Orders in virtue of canon 987?

The material of this work is divided into four parts. In the first part some preliminary considerations are offered for the better understanding of the subsequent three parts. The impediments are treated in the second, the third and the fourth parts. For each impediment there is given a historical synopsis and a canonical commentary.

The historical development of and the canonical commentary

on four of the listed impediments are contained in the second part. These four are considered under one general heading inasmuch as all of them are based on the direct obligations one has toward physical persons, such as a husband has to his wife, a slave to his master, or a citizen in view of certain civic and contractual considerations, such as military service or the rendering of an account. Although primarily the latter two considerations point to actions which must be placed, yet ultimately they involve the performance of duties to specified persons.

The second part of the dissertation is divided into two chapters, the first of which has two articles—article one, *husband to wife,* and article two, *slave to master.* The second chapter of this part also has two articles—article one, *military service,* and article two, *secular affairs involving the rendering of an account.*

The third part deals with the two impediments arising from a defect in the faith, either in the individual, *the neophyte,* or in the individual's parents, the *non-Catholic progenitors* whose son seeks ordination.

The last part is concerned with the impediment which is based on *infamia facti.* It is regarded as an impediment deriving from one's evil acts. The evil action in this instance does not necessarily postulate any subjective guilt, but only an objective contravention of the positive law or of the moral order, for the stigma of infamy can and does arise from the latter in the judgment and moral reaction which are harbored concerning these acts.

The author takes this occasion to express his profound gratitude to His Grace, the Most Reverend John Timothy McNicholas, O.P., S.T.M., Archbishop of Cincinnati, who provided the privilege of pursuing graduate studies in Canon Law, and who, as a generous patron of the Sacred Sciences, made possible this publication. The writer likewise wishes to express his sincere thanks to the members of the Faculty of the School of Canon Law of the Catholic University of America for their scholarly direction and valuable assistance in the preparation of this dissertation; and, finally, to all those relatives and friends whose interest and prayers have aided in bringing this work to completion.

THE SIMPLE IMPEDIMENTS TO HOLY ORDERS

PART I

INTRODUCTION

CHAPTER I

PRELIMINARY CONSIDERATIONS

Article I. General Reason for Impediments

The phrase "*Alter Christus*" connotes succinctly the dignity of the Sacred Priesthood of the New Testament. This dignity was profoundly appreciated in the very beginning of the Christian era,[1] as was also the dignity of the Priesthood of the Old Testament in the time of preparation and promise.[2] Consequent upon such a sense of appreciation it was to be expected that stress would be laid on certain prerequisites as necessary for those who aspired to such an office, and that certain states and actions of individuals would be classed as not being in conformity with the exalted sublimity and sacred majesty of such an office.

Thus in the Old Testament strict rules were invoked to govern the admission of candidates to the priesthood.[3] The rigor of this legislation became more pronounced in the New Testament, as is witnessed by the letter of St. Paul to Titus,[4] and the second letter of St. Paul to Timothy.[5] Certain actions were branded as incompatible with the functions of the priesthood.

Article II. The Rule of St. Paul

The rule enacted by St. Paul forms the basis for our present-day legislation on the irregularities and impediments to Holy

[1] I Tim., III, 2; V, 22; Titus, I, 6.
[2] Levit., XXI; XXII.
[3] *Loc. cit.*
[4] Titus, I, 6.
[5] II Tim., III, 2; V, 22.

Orders. The present legislation has been developed through the centuries. The various divisions in the law along with the use of more technical terms mirrors this development. The term "irregularity" points but to a deviation from the rule or *regula* as enacted in the writings of St. Paul. A departure from this rule (*in regula*) made one irregular.[6]

Article III. The Distinction Between Irregularity and Impediment

It must be remembered that the term "irregularity" was a general term in the early legislation, and was for the most part interchanged with the term "impediment." The mind of the early legislators may be expressed in the words: "One who is irregular is impeded from receiving Holy Orders," or "One is impeded from receiving Holy Orders because he is irregular."

The list of irregularities was enlarged or curtailed according to the special considerations or needs occasioned in the various periods of the Church's history.[7] In the *Decretum* of Gratian and in the various Decretal Collections irregularities or impediments are the object of legislative consideration in various passages. At times several of these are treated under one division, several under another division, so that one cannot find a treatment in these collections in which *ex professo* all the impediments or irregularities are listed under one heading, such as "*De Irregularitatibus*" or "*De Impedimentis*."[8]

The classification of the departures from the *regula* into irregularities and impediments, based on the consideration of their longer or shorter duration, made its appearance as early as the first part of the seventeenth century. Although this classification was disputed among authors,[9] the terminology employed in indication of this classification was given official sanction with the promulgation of the Code.[10]

---

[6] C. 3, D. XXV; c. 1, D. XLVIII.

[7] Ayrinhac, *Legislation on the Sacraments* (New York: Longmans, Green & Co., 1928), p. 359.

[8] Ayrinhac, *loc. cit.*

[9] Cf. Laymann, *Theologia Moralis* (9. ed., Moguntiae, 1742), lib. I, tract. V, pars V, cap. IV, n. 10 (hereafter cited as Laymann).

[10] Cf. canons 983–991—*Codex Iuris Canonici Pii X Pontificis Maximi*

Among the works of the early legislators and codifiers of law mention can be found of irregularities which today are termed simple impediments.[11] The fundamental basis for the distinction, that of the element of duration, has always been present. There have always been departures and deviations from the rule which could be counteracted with the progress of time, and others which, once they existed, were in no way amenable to alteration over any period of time.

Article IV. The Simple Impediment

A. Definition

The term "simple impediment," the equivalent of which is found in the Code,[12] denotes in general an inability to comply with a rule or *regula* as enacted in the present law of the Church. A simple impediment is specifically different from an irregularity properly so called in this that it is by its nature temporary. It may be defined as a *canonical hindrance, temporary in nature, which of itself prohibits primarily the reception of Orders and secondarily the exercise of Orders already received.*[13] It is

iussu digestus Benedicti XV auctoritate promulgatus (Romae: Typis Polyglottis Vaticanis, 1917).

[11] Ayrinhac, *Legislation on the Sacraments*, p. 360.

[12] Canon 987: "*Sunt simpliciter impediti: . . .*"

[13] Cf. Suarez, *Opera Omnia* (28 vols., ed. L. Vivès, Parisiis, 1856–1861), Vol. XXIII, *De Censuris in Communi*, disp. XL, sect. 1 (hereafter cited as Suarez, *De Censuris*); Schmalzgrueber, *Ius Ecclesiasticum Universum* (5 vols. in 12, Romae, 1843–1845), lib. V, tit. 37, n. 60 ss (hereafter cited as Schmalzgrueber); D'Annibale, *Summula Theologiae Moralis* (5. ed., 3 vols., Romae, 1908), I, n. 399, not. 2 (hereafter cited as D'Annibale); Boenninghausen, *Tractatus Iuridico-Canonicus de Irregularitatibus* (3 fasc., Monasterii: Typis et Sumptibus Theissingianis, 1863–1866), Fasc. I, p. 2 (hereafter cited as Boenninghausen); Gasparri, *Tractatus de Sacra Ordinatione* (2 vols., Parisiis, 1893), n. 157 (hereafter cited as Gasparri, *De Sacra Ordinatione*); Vermeersch-Creusen, Epitome Iuris Canonici (3 vols., Vol. I, 6. ed., 1937, Vols. II et III, 5. ed., 1934–1936, Mechliniae-Romae: H. Dessain), II, n. 252 (hereafter cited as Vermeersch-Creusen); Wernz-Vidal, *Ius Canonicum* (7 vols. in 9, Romae: Apud Aedes Universitatis Gregorianae, 1923–1938), IV (*De Rebus*), pars I, n. 228 (hereafter cited as Wernz-Vidal); Cappello, *Tractatus Canonicus de Sacramentis* (3 vols. in 6, Romae: Marietti, 1932–1939), II, pars III (*De Sacra Ordinatione*), n. 435 (hereafter cited as Cappello, *De Sacra Ordinatione*).

called a *canonical* hindrance not only to show the exclusive right of the Church to establish such an obstacle to Orders, but also to separate it from the prohibitions which are based solely on the natural and positive divine law.[14]

This hindrance includes only those obstacles which are listed in canon 987. There are many hindrances which impede the reception of Orders. However, if the hindrance is not listed in the aforementioned canon, then it is not to be regarded as an impediment in the sense in which impediments to Orders will be considered in this work. The term *canonical* is also employed in the definition to point to the authoritative source from which the impediment derives in its nature of an obstacle to the reception of Orders. It is the Holy See which by way of legislative enactment gives juridical existence to the impediment and causes it to be an obstacle to the reception of Orders in consequence of a universal law of the Church.

An impediment is described as being *temporary in nature* inasmuch as, unlike an irregularity properly so called, it can be obviated with the passing of time through the removal of the cause which gave rise to it.

The remaining part of the definition deals with the effects of the simple impediment. Before any consideration be given to them it is advisable to indicate the number of the simple impediments and to consider what persons are subject to them.

B. NUMBER

At the very outset it must be remembered that an impediment denotes simply an obstacle to the reception of Orders; an impediment is neither a censure nor a vindictive penalty.[15] The number of these obstacles is now established at seven,[16] and

---

[14] Suarez, *De Censuris,* disp. XL, sect. 4, n. 1 ss; Gasparri, *De Sacra Ordinatione,* n. 157; Wernz-Vidal, IV, pars I, n. 228; Cappello, *De Sacra Ordinatione,* n. 435.

[15] Blat, *Commentarium Textus Codicis Iuris Canonici* (5 vols. in 7, Romae: Collegio "Angelico," 1920–1927), III, pars I, n. 336 (hereafter cited as Blat); Wernz-Vidal, IV, pars I, n. 228; Cappello, *De Sacra Ordinatione,* n. 435.

[16] Canon 987.

unless the impediment is expressly mentioned in the law it does not exist.[17]

The axiom accepted by the canonists prior to the present Code was: *Irregularitas non incurritur nisi fuerit in iure expressa.*[18] This axiom is incorporated into the Code in canon 983.

> Nullum impedimentum perpetuum quod venit nomine *irregularitatis,* sive ex defectu sit sive ex delicto, contrahitur, nisi quod fuerit in canonibus qui sequuntur expressum.

As stated before, the distinction between irregularities and simple impediment was not universally accepted before 1918, so that in its application the axiom was not restricted before the Code to refer to only such irregularities as are now properly so called in the Code. Canon 983, however, speaks only of perpetual impediments, so that now the axiom does not directly apply to temporary impediments, but only indirectly in virtue of the general principle, "*Odiosa sunt restringenda.*" [19]

The establishing of any new impediment by written law in the present discipline of the Church is a *causa maior* affecting the universal Church, and as such belongs solely to the Roman Pontiff or an Oecumenical Council.[20] Gasparri (1854–1936), who prior to the Code insisted on a distinction between irregularities properly so called and temporary impediments, presented a discussion of twelve temporary impediments to the reception of Orders.[21]

---

[17] Cf. c. 18, *de sententia excommunicationis,* V, II, in VI°; Cappello, *De Sacra Ordinatione,* n. 437.

[18] Suarez, *De Censuris,* Disp. XL, sect. 4, n. 11 ss; Reiffenstuel, *Ius Canonicum Universum* (5 vols. in 7, Parisiis, 1864–1870), lib. V, tit. 37, n. 67 (hereafter cited as Reiffenstuel); Schmalzgrueber, lib. V, tit. 37, n. 61 ss; Benedictus XIV, *De Synodo Dioecesana* (2 vols., Romae: Typographia S. C. de Propaganda Fidei, 1806), lib. XII, cap. 3, n. 7; Boenninghausen, Fasc. I, 18 ss.

[19] Regula 15, R. I., in VI°, reads: "Odia restringi et favores convenit ampliari."

[20] Cf. Wernz-Vidal, IV, pars I, n. 231.

[21] *De Sacra Ordinatione,* n. 477–614: The twelve impediments considered were: (1) Defectus Confirmationis; (2) turpe mercimonium circa Mis-

No ecclesiastical authority inferior to the Holy See can establish a canonical simple impediment, although it may demand of a candidate for Orders certain requisites not mentioned in the Code. A particular law can not introduce a new impediment.[22] During the time prior to the enactment of the present Code opinions varied on the possibility that a general custom could introduce a new impediment.[23] Those who espoused [24] the opinion that a general custom could not introduce a new impediment based their arguments on the words of Boniface VIII (1294–1303): " Irregularitatis tamen, *cum id non sit expressum in iure,* laqueum non incurrit." [25] They maintained that the Pontiff in the use of the words " *expressum in iure* " understood the phrase as denoting the written common law of the Church. Those who opposed [26] this opinion held that a general custom could give rise to the existence of an irregularity.

Under the present law a difference of opinion still exists. Canon 983 states that no perpetual impediment is contracted if no express mention of it is made in the canons. Cappello interprets this to mean that a general custom can not introduce a new canonical irregularity. He interprets the phrase " nisi quod fuerit in canonibus expressum " as a reprobatory clause.[27] Guilfoyle, however, does not consider the clause as having reprobatory

---

sarum eleemosynas; (3) defectus requisitae aetatis; (4) defectus gradus inferioris et interstitiorum non expletorum; (5) vinculum matrimoniale; (6) militia saecularis; (7) servitus; (8) negotia saecularia et ratiocinia reddenda; (9) defectus debitae scientiae; (10) defectus debitae sanctitatis; (11) sufficientia clericorum in dioecesi; (12) defectus tituli canonici pro ordinatione in sacris.

[22] Cappello, *De Sacra Ordinatione,* n. 437.

[23] Note: The term "irregularity" was used by the authors.

[24] Suarez, *De Censuris,* disp. XL, sect. 5, n. 13; St. Alphonsus, *Theologia Moralis* (4 vols., ed. Gaudé, Romae, 1905–1912), lib. VII, n. 345 (hereafter cited as St. Alphonsus); D'Annibale, I, n. 404, not. 3; Boenninghausen, Fasc. I, p. 19.

[25] C. 18, *de sententia excommunicationis,* V, 11, in VI°.

[26] Laymann, lib. I, tract. V, pars V, cap. I, n. 7; Berardi, *Commentaria in Ius Ecclesiasticum Universum* (Taurinorum Augustae, 1706), lib. V, pars II, cap. 2; Wernz, *Ius Decretalium* (6 vols., Romae et Prati, 1898–1905), lib. II, n. 99 (hereafter cited as Wernz).

[27] Cappello, *De Sacra Ordinatione,* n. 438.

force.[28] However, regardless of the difference of opinions, canon 983 refers only to irregularities properly so called, so that in the law there is nothing which prevents a custom, if it be established according to the norms of canon 25–30, from giving rise to a simple impediment. In virtue of canon 27, § 1,[29] a general usage which has continued uninterruptedly for forty complete years with at least the legal consent of the lawgiver can establish a new impediment, and can extend, limit, or even abolish any existing impediment.[30] There is nothing expressed in the law to indicate the reprobation of such a custom.

There are seven specifically distinct simple impediments. The possible number of these impediments as affecting any one person will increase in proportion to the specific, and not the numerical, multiplication of the bases underlying their existence.[31] Thus a person may have two different offices which are forbidden to a cleric and of which he is obliged to render an account, and yet be bound by only one simple impediment, that of canon 987, 3°. Another person may have two different offices and because of the infamy of fact connected with one of these offices be bound not only by the impediment listed in canon 987, 3°, but also by the impediment mentioned in canon 987, 7°.

C. SUBJECT

Only a validly baptized person of the male sex can be the subject of an impediment to the reception of Orders. Through baptism such an individual becomes capable of validly receiving Orders.[32] Prior to baptism he cannot be impeded from licitly

[28] *Custom,* The Catholic University of America Canon Law Studies, n. 105 (Washington, D. C.: The Catholic University of America, 1937), pp. 107–108.—On these pages he points in an exhaustive list to just 21 canons which contain reprobatory clauses. Among these canons there is no mention of any that deals with the impediments to Orders.

[29] "Iuri divino sive naturali sive positivo nulla consuetudo potest aliquatenus derogare; neque iure ecclesiastico preiudicium affert nisi fuerit rationabilis et legitime per annos quadraginta continuos et completos praescripta; . . ."

[30] Cappello, *De Sacra Ordinatione,* n. 438.

[31] Canon 989; Ayrinhac, *Legislation on the Sacraments,* p. 377.

[32] Canon 968, § 1: "Sacram ordinationem valide recipit solus vir baptizatus; . . ."

receiving that of which he is incapable. Every impediment implies the deprivation of a right, which in turn presupposes that there existed a capacity for the right of which one has been divested. By divine law an unbaptized man is rendered incapable of receiving Orders. A man's right to the reception of Orders cannot exist until the foundation for such a right has been established through the valid reception of baptism.[33]

A fact placed before baptism can however after baptism become and remain the cause of an impediment as long as the fact continues to exist, e.g., the fact of a legitimate marriage which has not been dissolved after the baptism of the husband.[34]

D. EFFECTS

The effects of a simple impediment are expressed in the definition given above in the words: "*primarily prohibits the reception of Orders and secondarily the exercise of Orders received.*"[35]

The direct primary effect of an impediment is the prohibition whereby one is impeded from receiving Orders. The observance of this prohibition is of obligation not only for the person who is subject to the impediment, but also for the minister who confers the Orders. The force of the obligation primarily affects both the recipient and the minister of the Orders, but the prohibition as such affects the minister only indirectly.[36] Some authors[37] maintained that the prohibition directly affected the minister, and only indirectly the one who is impeded from receiving Orders. But such an opinion does not leave room for the universal law to find its proper application in all circumstances whenever an irregularity or an impediment actually exists, even though it be occult both in nature and in fact.[38] Since irregu-

[33] Cf. Suarez, *De Censuris*, disp. XL, sect. 7, n. 1 ss; Wernz-Vidal, IV, pars I, n. 232.

[34] Vermeersch-Creusen, II, n. 254.

[35] Canon 968, § 1: "Sacram ordinationem . . . recipit . . . licite autem, qui . . . neque ulla detineatur irregularitate aliove impedimento." § 2: "Qui irregularitate aliove impedimento detinentur, licet post ordinationem etiam sine propria culpa exorto, prohibentur receptos ordines exercere."

[36] Cf. Cappello, *De Sacra Ordinatione*, n. 440.

[37] E.g., Gasparri, *De Sacra Ordinatione*, n. 166; Wernz, II, n. 103.

[38] Cappello, *De Sacra Ordinatione*, n. 440.

larities and simple impediments are enacted in the law to serve the same end, namely the safeguarding of the reverence and the honor which are due the sacred ministry, it seems indicated that the simple impediments directly affect the recipient, and only indirectly the minister, of the Orders. The law itself in canon 987 uses the indicative mode and with the words "*Sunt simpliciter impediti*" points directly to the prospective recipient of the Orders.

The secondary effect of an impediment is the prohibition of the exercise of the Orders already received, even though the impediment arises after the ordination.[39] If the impediment existed prior to the reception of tonsure, then the conferring of the rite of initiation into the ranks of the clergy would be illicit, but not invalid.[40] If the impediment arose after the licit reception of Orders, then the exercise of the Orders received would be illicit, not however invalid.[41] This is the general rule as enacted in canon 968. Hence it is difficult to see how Cappello justifies the statement: "*Generatim tamen loquendo, impedimenta non secumferunt ipso iure prohibitionem exercendi ordines rite susceptos.*"[42] Other authors do not admit the drawing of such a conclusion.[43]

Failure to observe the prohibition imposed by canon 968, § 2, would not make the offender irregular *ex delicto* according to canon 985, 7°, since there is no canonical penalty attached to the exercise of Orders by one whose status simply implies the presence of a simple impediment. The action however which gives rise to the impediment may be such as in itself to prohibit the exercise of sacred Orders, and the violation of this prohibition in turn can give rise to an irregularity *ex delicto* To illustrate this statement with an example, one may point to a case

[39] Canon 968, § 2: "Qui irregularitate aliove impedimento detinentur, licet post ordinationem etiam sine propria culpa exorto, prohibentur receptos ordines exercere."

[40] Canon 968, § 1.

[41] Canon 968, § 2.

[42] Cappello, *De Sacra Ordinatione*, n. 541.

[43] Blat, III, pars I, n. 354; Wernz-Vidal, IV, pars I, n. 255; Beste, *Introductio in Codicem* (Collegeville, Minn.: St. John's Abbey Press, 1944), p. 515 (hereafter cited as Beste).

in which infamy of fact has resulted from a priest's act of publicly joining a Masonic order, for to such an act is attached a public excommunication.[44] The one so excommunicated also falls under the impediment of *infamia facti*[45] when in the ordinary's judgment the offender has lost his good repute among upright and respectable members of the Church,[46] and in consequence is prohibited from exercising his Orders both by reason of the impediment[47] and by reason of the excommunication.[48] Violation of the prohibition imposed by the canonical penalty of excommunication in the exercise of Orders necessary in the administration of the sacraments would give rise to an irregularity *ex delicto.*[49]

Observance of the prohibition implied by an impediment to the reception, the conferral and the exercise of Orders binds under pain of grave sin.[50] If the observance of this prohibitory obligation would entail a hardship or occasion a predicament whose gravity outweighs the gravity of the prohibitory obligation itself, the observance of the obligation would not be necessary.[51] Thus, if one recalled at the time of his ordination that he still held an office regarding which he had to render an account, but was unable to leave the church without causing a great amount of sinister speculation and adverse wonderment on the part of those present, he would receive ordination licitly, although of course the impediment would remain. When an impediment arises after the reception of Orders, the prohibition which forbids the exercise of the Orders already received extends *solely* to those acts which are reserved to an ordained person, and not to every act which an ordained person can place. There are certain acts, such

---

[44] Canon 2335.

[45] Canon 987, 7o.

[46] Canon 2293, § 3.

[47] Canon 987, 7o.

[48] Canon 2259, § 2.

[49] Canon 985, 7o.

[50] Suarez, *De Censuris,* disp. XL, sect. 2; St. Alphonsus, lib. VII, n. 342; Boenninghausen, Fasc. I, p. 28; Cappello, *De Sacra Ordinatione,* n. 441.

[51] Cappello, *De Sacra Ordinatione,* n. 441.

as serving Mass, ringing the bells, opening the doors of the church and the like, which even laymen are permitted to place. The prohibition would not extend to such acts.[52]

The prohibition which an impediment imposes on one who wishes to receive Orders, or to exercise Orders already received, affects every degree or step in the hierarchy of Orders in a cleric's life, from first tonsure to the episcopacy. Tonsure, the minor Orders and the two major Orders of subdeaconship and deaconship are preparatory steps toward the priesthood, so that he who is prohibited from receiving the priesthood because of an impediment is also prohibited from receiving first tonsure and the Orders leading to the priesthood.[53]

Prior to the Code not all authors accepted the conclusion that those who were impeded from the reception of Orders were also impeded from the reception of first Tonsure. This difference of opinion was occasioned by a response contained in Barbosa's (1589–1649) collection of apostolic decisions. The authenticity of the response, attributed to the Sacred Congregation of the Council, is dubious. There is no date attached to this response, which places first Tonsure outside the extension of the law which deals with irregularities and impediments.[54] According to Gasparri [55] some impediments, e.g., defect in age or knowledge, prohibited the conferral not of tonsure but only of Orders. If the response referred only to such impediments, the response could

---

[52] Suarez, *De Censuris,* disp. XL, sect. 2, n. 8; Gasparri, *De Sacra Ordinatione,* n. 150; Wernz-Vidal, IV, pars I, n. 228; Cappello, *De Sacra Ordinatione,* n. 442.

[53] Canon 973, § 1: "Prima tonsura et ordines illis tantum conferendi sunt, qui propositum habeant ascendendi ad presbyteratum et quos merito coniicere liceat aliquando dignos futuros esse presbyteros." Cf. also canons 949, 950, 968, § 1 and § 2.

[54] Barbosa, *Summa Apostolicarum Decisionum* (Lugduni, 1645), p. 598, n. 1: "Prima tonsura conferri potest illi qui habet omnia requisita *cap. IV, sess. XXIII,* licet ob aliquod impedimentum non possit ascendere ad alios ordines, non obstante *cap. XI eiusd. sess.,* quia hoc loquitur de quatuor minoribus, illud vero de prima tonsura tantum. *S. C. C. teste Sellio in select.* Canon., c. 2, n. 19."

[55] *De Sacra Ordinatione,* n. 167.

be authentic, although most of the authors in forming their opinions disregarded the response.[56]

The effect of an impediment on the acceptance or the retention of an office,[57] or of a benefice,[58] depends on the obligation, incumbent upon the recipient or the possessor of the office or the benefice, to perform acts which are proper to a cleric. If the reception or the exercise of Orders is necessarily connected with the office or the benefice, then the conferring or the retaining of such an office or benefice would be illicit.[59]

Before the Code the effect of an irregularity on the conferral, the acceptance or the retention of a benefice was disputed.[60] The law did not clearly state whether the acceptance or the retention of an office or of a benefice by one who was irregular was only illicit or also invalid. Under the present law there is no question of invalidity, since nowhere in the Code does the law require freedom from an impediment or from an irregularity as a condition for the valid reception, retention or conferral of a benefice.[61] However, the receiving or the conferring of a benefice when an existing impediment makes the exercise of Orders illicit would in itself be illicit if the exercise of Orders was necessarily connected with the benefice.[62]

If the impediment arises after the benefice has been licitly and validly conferred, the retaining of the benefice would not be forbidden, but there would be an obligation to remove the impediment as soon as possible and to supply one who can licitly

---

[56] Reiffenstuel, lib. I, tit. 11, n. 23; Schmalzgrueber, lib. V, tit. 36, n. 90; St. Alphonsus, lib. VII, n. 312; Boenninghausen, Fasc. I, p. 26.

[57] Canon 145 offers the official definition of the term "office.".

[58] Canon 1409 contains the law's definition of the term "benefice."

[59] "Cum quid prohibetur, prohibentur omnia quae sequuntur ex illo."—Reg. 39, R. I., in VIo. Cf. Hickey, *Irregularities and Simple Impediments,* The Catholic University of America Canon Law Studies, n. 7 (Washington, D. C.: The Catholic University of America, 1920), p. 11 (hereafter cited as Hickey).

[60] Cf. Suarez, *De Censuris,* disp. XL, sect. 2, n. 36; Schmalzgrueber, lib. V, tit. 37, n. 46; St. Alphonsus, lib. VII, n. 342; D'Annibale, I, n. 401; Boenninghausen, Fasc. I, pp. 29–38; Gasparri, *De Sacra Ordinatione,* n. 173.

[61] Cappello, *De Sacra Ordinatione,* n. 444.

[62] Cf. canon 991, § 3.

exercise the necessary Orders until the impediment has been removed. When a specific necessity arises, or when there is a legitimate request on the part of the faithful, it would be permissible to exercise one's Orders even though one has contracted an impediment. If the cleric is unable to obtain a dispensation or is unwilling to apply for one, he must renounce his benefice in order to obviate a condition which would *in perpetuum* deprive the faithful of his services as long as they did not specifically request them.[63]

An impediment does not directly take away or necessarily impede the exercise of ordinary or delegated jurisdiction in either the internal or the external forum. Thus a pastor who is bound by an impediment can validly and licitly dispense for a just cause one of his subjects from the observance of the law of fast and abstinence on a particular day.[64]

Article V. Ignorance and Doubt, as They Affect One's Personal Liability to the Simple Impediments

Ignorance of an impediment does not excuse one from the impediment and its effects.[65] One must remember that the simple impediment, like the irregularities, have not been constituted as a punishment or as a vindictive measure, but have been enacted in order to promote the respect and the honor which is due to the clerical state. Thus there is no question of dealing with the conscience of any particular individual, but with the holiness and the dignity of the clerical life itself.[66] The law which governs the effect of ignorance on the impediments applies also to the cases of error and inadvertence.[67]

When a doubt, either of the law or of the inclusion of a fact under the law, arises about the existence of an impediment, proper diligence must be employed in order to dispel the doubt. After

[63] Cf. Schmalzgrueber, lib. V, tit. 37, n. 96; Boenninghausen, Fasc. I, p. 30.

[64] Cf. Suarez, *De Censuris*, disp. XL, sect. 2, n. 45; Boenninghausen, Fasc. I, p. 28; Cappello, *De Sacra Ordinatione*, n. 447; Wernz-Vidal, IV, pars I, n. 234.

[65] Canon 988: "Ignorantia irregularitatum sive ex delicto sive ex defectu atque impedimentorum ab eisdem non excusat."

[66] Cappello, *De Sacra Ordinatione*, n. 455.

[67] Cappello, *loc. cit.*

the use of proper diligence, if the doubt still remains, but merely as a slight doubt, it is to be considered as not existing.[68] A positive and probable doubt of the law regarding an impediment removes the obligatory force of the law establishing the impediment.[69] The ordinary can dispense from those impediments from which the Roman Pontiff is accustomed to dispense, when there exists a doubt of fact which is based on solid reasons, and thus constitutes a positive and probable doubt.[70] However, in virtue of canon 19, the impediment can be considered as non existing, so that the obligation of obtaining a dispensation is in the strict sense of the law not necessary.[71] The doubt of law as affecting the existence of an impediment depends, not on the number of authors who acknowledge the doubt, but on the weight of the reasons which are deduced from the law itself.[72]

Article VI. Dispensation from the Impediments—in General

The seven simple impediments are the result of the enactments of the ecclesiastical law. Accordingly a dispensation from these enactments may be obtained from the authority which enacted the law, the Holy See.[73] Neither the local ordinary, nor the major superiors in a clerical congregation or order, nor any confessor is empowered by the common law to dispense from any impediment, even in occult cases. An exception to this general rule is contained in canon 81, in which ordinaries are empowered to dispense under certain extraordinary circumstances within a limited sphere.

Ordinarily the Sacred Congregation to which one must submit the application for a dispensation from any impediment to Orders

---

[68] Cappello, *ibid.*, n. 439.

[69] Canon 15.

[70] Cappello, *loc. cit.*

[71] Canon 19: "Leges quae . . . liberum exercitium coarctant . . . strictae subsunt interpretatione." Cf. Cappello, *De Sacra Ordinatione*, n. 439.

[72] Suarez, *De Censuris*, disp. XL, sect. 5, n. 7: ". . . non ex auctorum numero, sed ex rationum pondere, et in praesenti materia ex verbis iurium recte expensis et ponderatis colligendum est."

[73] Cf. canons 80 and 81.

is the Sacred Congregation of the Sacraments.[74] However, when a religious is bound by an impediment to Orders, the application for a dispensation is sent to the Sacred Congregation for Religious.[75] The Congregation for the Propagation of the Faith is the competent Congregation for those candidates who are to be ordained for the missions which are subject to the same Congregation.[76]

When there arises a question as to whether a man who is bound by an impediment may be admitted to the seminary, the matter is to be submitted to the Sacred Congregation for Seminaries and Universities.[77] The following of this prescription will forestall many unpleasant difficulties, for "it is more opprobrious to eject a guest than not to admit him in the first place."

> "Everyone knows what a serious and difficult matter it is to dismiss a young man when he has nearly finished his theological studies, not only because of his age, which makes it hard for him to undertake another way of life and plan of studies, but also because of regard for human relations, especially with relatives and friends, who usually attribute such changes of life to a fault committed, or to want of serious purpose, so that one who has got that far leaves nothing undone to continue." [78]

This admonition is especially applicable in the case of the admission of a man to the seminary prior to his obtaining a dispensation from the impediment resulting from his continued marital status.[79] For the internal forum the competent authority to which the application for a dispensation must be sent is the Sacred Penitentiary.[80]

In the application for a dispensation every impediment is to

[74] Cf. Canon 249.

[75] Cf. canon 251.

[76] Cf. canon 252.

[77] Cf. canon 256.

[78] S. C. de Sacr., instr. 27 dec. 1930, n. 3—*Acta Apostolicae Sedis* (Romae, 1909-) XXIII (1931), 121 (hereafter cited as *AAS*). Translation taken from Bouscaren, *The Canon Law Digest* (2 vols., Milwaukee: The Bruce Publishing Company, 1934–143) I, 465 (hereafter cited as Bouscaren).

[79] Cf. canon 987, 2°.

[80] Cf. canon 258.

be enumerated. However a general dispensation will remove any simple impediment, even though it has in good faith been left unmentioned. If through bad faith the existence of a simple impediment has not been expressed in the application, even a general dispensation will not remove the impediment.[81] For the validity of a granted dispensation it is not necessary that in the application there be expressed the number of causes which gave rise to the impediment, if the causes are of the same species, since the multiplication of the same cause does not multiply the impediment.[82]

The absence of a just and reasonable cause would invalidate the dispensation, unless the Roman Pontiff granted the dispensation.[83] A general dispensation is applicable for the reception of all Orders, minor and major; and the one who has been dispensed can obtain any non-consistorial benefice, even if the care of souls is attached to it.[84] A dispensation when granted by the ordinary in virtue of canon 81 can apply to the reception or the exercise of an Order only if the delay of its reception or exercise until a dispensation had been obtained from the Holy See would give rise to grave harm.

When a dispensation is granted, it is to be granted in writing. However, if the matter has been handled in the internal non-sacramental forum, the written grant of the dispensation should be entered in a secret book of the curia,[85] or in a secret book of the Sacred Penitentiary, if the latter method more effectively forestalls all danger of infamy.[86] An application for a dispensation may express the real name of the party who is impeded, provided that the impediment is a public one. If an occult case is involved, a fictitious name should be used.[87] The recommendation of the ordinary will serve to facilitate the granting of the dispensation.

---

[81] Canon 991, § 1.
[82] Canon 989.
[83] Canon 84, § 1.
[84] Canon 991, § 3.
[85] Canon 991, § 4.
[86] Cappello, *De Sacra Ordinatione,* n. 517.
[87] Hickey, p. 88.

When the application for the dispensation has been made in the external forum, the execution of the rescript which grants the dispensation must be made in writing.[88] The executor of the rescript must observe all the conditions specified in the grant of the dispensation. He must proceed in accordance with the instruction received in the mandate, and unless he complies with the essential conditions specified in the rescript, and follows in substance the required manner of procedure, the execution will be invalid.[89]

---

[88] Canon 56.
[89] Canon 55.

PART II

IMPEDIMENTS BASED ON PERSONAL OBLIGATIONS

CHAPTER II

ON OBLIGATIONS TOWARD PHYSICAL PERSONS

Article I. Husband to Wife

A. Historical Synopsis

Although in the beginning it was with special predilection that Christ chose men from the ranks of the unmarried to become His apostles, still it appears that a number of His apostles may have been married men. The relatively small number of unmarried men as then living in Palestine made it necessary to select apostles from the ranks of the married to carry on the work of Christ.[1] In the rule of St. Paul only a man who had been married twice was excluded from the reception of Orders. "A bishop, then, must be blameless, married but once . . ."[2] The Apostles by word, example and administration, showed their preference for an unmarried and celibate clergy in the hierarchical Orders—the diaconate, the priesthood and the episcopacy.[3] Although no specific mention of it is contained in the *Decretum* of Gratian, the Council of Elvira (ca. 305) Spain offers the oldest positive legislation dealing with the celibacy of the clergy. It required that all in Sacred Orders—bishops, priests and deacons—even if they were married, were to lead a celibate life under

[1] Wernz-Vidal, IV, pars I, n. 257.

[2] I Tim., III, 2.

[3] Cf. c. 3, D. LXXXII; c. 3, D. LXXXIV; *Glossa Ordinaria* ad c. 1, D. XXXI, s.v. *Ante triennium;* Borgasio, *Tractatus de Irregularitatibus et Impedimentis Ordinum, Officiorum et Beneficiorum Ecclesiasticorum* (Venetiis, 1574), pars VI, *Qui clerici, vel voventes matrimonium contrahere possint,* n. 6.

pain of deposition.[4] In the East, the Council of Ancyra (314) forbade deacons to marry, unless prior to their ordination to deaconship they had either manifested their desire to marry, or declared their inability to lead a celibate life. If they failed to comply with this demand, and then married, they were to cease exercising the ministry,[5] and if priests married, they were to be deposed in view of the penal legislation enacted in the Council of Neocaesarea (314–325).[6]

Pope Siricius (384–399) in the year 385 wrote to Himerius, Bishop of Tarragona, demanding that celibacy be observed by those who were in hierarchical Orders.[7] St. Jerome in writing against Jovinian in the latter part of the fourth century gave voice to the same legislation.[8] The early Councils of Carthage, representative of the Western Church, legislated for a celibate clergy in the hierarchical Orders,[9] and in the subdiaconate.[10] It was permissible for those who were in minor Orders to marry.[11]

Pope Innocent I in the year 404 in a letter to Victricius, Bishop of Rouen, ruled that priests were not to continue their marital relations with their wives.[12] Pope Leo I (440–461) in a letter

---

[4] Can. 33—Mansi, *Sacrorum Conciliorum Nova et Amplissima Collectio* (53 vols. in 60, Paris-Leipzig-Arnhem, 1901–1927), II, 11 (hereafter cited as Mansi).

[5] Can. 1—C. 8, D. XXVIII; Mansi, II, 525.

[6] Can. 1—C. 9, D. XXVIII; Mansi, II, 540.

[7] C. 3, D. LXXXII; Jaffé, *Regesta Pontificum Romanorum ab condita Ecclesia ad annum post Christum natum MCXCVIII* (2. ed., 2 vols. in 1, correctam et auctam auspiciis Gulielmi Wattenbach curaverunt S. Loewenfeld, F. Kaltenbrunner, P. Ewald, Lipsiae, 1885–1888), n. 255 (hereafter the letters L, K, and E will be joined with the letter J to designate the editors of the documents cited from Jaffé's work in its second edition. The letter of Siricius is designated thus: JK, n. 255.

[8] C. 2, D. XXXI.

[9] II Council of Carthage (390), can. 2—Mansi, III, 692; c. 3, D. XXXI; III Council of Carthage (397), can. 2—Mansi, III, 869; c. 8, D. XXXII.

[10] V Council of Carthage (401), can. 3: "Placuit episcopos, presbyteros, diaconos, subdeaconos secundum priora institua etiam abstinere ab uxoribus: quod nisi fecerunt, ab ecclesiastico removeantur officio, ceteros vero clericos ad hoc non cogi, sed uniuscuiusque ecclesiasiae consuetudinem observari debere."—Mansi, III, 967; cf. also c. 13, D. XXXII.

[11] *Loc. cit.*

[12] C. 4, D. XXXI; JK, n. 298.

to Anastasius of Thessalonica renewed this legislation, adding that subdeacons were to lead a celibate life and that those who had no wife were to remain without one.[13] Bishop Aurelius (419) supposedly restated the legislation of the II Council of Carthage (390) relative to a married clergy. It was ruled that it was not permissible for subdeacons, deacons, priests or bishops to take a wife,[14] and that bishops, priests and deacons were to abstain from marital relationships with those whom they had taken to wife prior to their reception of Sacred Orders.[15] Huguccio (+1210), mindful of the practice in the East, was of the opinion that cc. 3–4, D. LXXXII, referred simply to the taking of a wife,[16] but Bartholomaeus of Brescia (+1258) upheld the observance of celibacy as a requisite to be followed in the West, irrespective of the practice in the East.[17]

In the Council of Agde (506) legislation on the ordination of deacons gives an insight into the meaning of the celibacy which was held obligatory for those who were ordained to one of the hierarchical Orders.

> Sane si coniugati iuvenes consenserint ordinari, etiam uxorum voluntas ita requirenda est, ut sequestrato mansionis cubiculo, religione praemissa, posteaquam pariter conversi fuerint, ordinentur.[18]

Pope Gregory I (590–604) wrote to Peter, a subdeacon in Sicily, in the year 591, and explained the obligation then in force, namely, that subdeacons be celibate even though the wife had been taken by them while they were in minor Orders.[19] Gregory

---

13 C. 1, D. XXXII; JK, n. 411.

14 II Council of Carthage (390), can. 2—Mansi, III, 692; c. 3, D. LXXXIV.

15 C. 4, D. LXXXIV.

16 *Glossa Ordinaria* ad c. 3, D. LXXXIV, s.v. *Cum in praeterito.*

17 *Glossa Ordinaria* ad c. 4, D. LXXXIV, s.v. *Cum de quorundam.* "Sed ego Bartholomaeus Brixiensis satis credo quod haec duo capita (III & IV) intelligi possunt in ecclesia occidentali, et de matrimonio iam contracto quo uti non debent clerici in sacris ordinibus constituti."

18 Can. 16—Mansi, VIII, 327; c. 6, D. LXXVII.

19 "Eos autem, qui post prohibitionem factam a suis se uxoribus continere noluerint, ad sacrum ordinem nolumus promoveri, quia nullus debet

again referred to the necessity of celibacy in a letter to Boniface, Bishop of Reggio in Aemelia, in the year 593,[20] while in his letter to St. Augustine of England (602) he permitted clerics in minor Orders to take a wife.[21]

In the latter part of the seventh and in the beginning of the eighth century Venerable Bede (673–735), a representative of the Church in the Isles, wrote in his commentary on St. Luke that all priests were to forego marriage.[22]

The Synod in Trullo (692) which legislated for the Eastern Church did not demand absolute continency of its married clergy,[23] but it did not change the legislation of the Council of Ancyra (314), which forbade marriage to those who were in Sacred Orders—deacons, priests and bishops.[24] Bishop Stephen III (768–772), according to Gratian, commented on this and gave a picture of the legislation for the first seven centuries.

> Aliter se habet orientalium ecclesiarum traditio, aliter huius sanctae Romanae ecclesiae. Nam eorum sacerdotes, diaconi atque subdiaconi matrimonio copulantur; istius autem ecclesiae vel occidentalium nullus sacerdotum a subdiacono usque ad episcopum licentiam habet coniugium sortiendi.[25]

Pope Nicholas I (858–867) renewed the legislation prevalent in the Church.[26]

The next four centuries witnessed the legislation of penal measures for violations of the already existing law. Pope Nicholas

---

ad altaris ministerium accedere, nisi cuius castitas ante susceptum ministerium fuerit approbata."—c. 1, D. XXXI; JE, n. 1112.

[20] C. 9, D. XXXII; JE, n. 1276.

[21] C. 3, D. XXXII; JE, n. 1843.

[22] C. 2, D. XXXI.

[23] Can. 13—Mansi, XII, 51; c. 13, D. XXXI.

[24] *Glossa Ordinaria* ad c. 7, D. XXXII, s.v. *diaconi*.

[25] C. 14, D. XXXI. This text is attributed to Pope Stephen III in the Lateran Council of 769, but it belongs to the eleventh century, to Stephen IX (1057–1058), perhaps in the Council of Rome (1058). Cf. JL, n. 4375.

[26] C. 4, D. XXXII. A letter written to the Archbishop of Vienna in the year 864. Cf. JE, n. 2755.

II (1059–1061)[27] and Pope Alexander II (1061–1073)[28] forbade the hearing of a mass celebrated by a priest who had attempted marriage and was living in concubinage. Alexander II also attached severe penal sanctions to the law which demanded absolute continency of subdeacons, deacons and priests. Gregory VII (1073–1085) early in his pontificate (1074) put violators of the vow of continency under interdict—*interdictum ab ingressu ecclesiae.*[29]

By way of summary covering the first twelve centuries one can state that a married man was not impeded from the reception of either major or minor Orders. Clerics in minor Orders could marry unless a particular law to the contrary forbade it.[30] Those in major Orders could not marry, and if they had married prior to the reception of the subdiaconate they were obliged to promise absolute continence or total abstinence from marital relations.[31] Violation of this promise was punishable by their removal from the exercise of all Sacred Orders, and their deprivation of whatever office and benefice they previously held.[32] Before making the promise of absolute continency a cleric had to consult the will of his wife.[33]

In the Decretal legislation the development of this impediment became more pronounced. A married cleric was not to be admitted to any ecclesiastical benefice or to Sacred Orders unless he had made a vow of perpetual chastity, and had been married but once to a woman who previously had not been married.[34] This ruling of Pope Alexander III (1159–1181) was made more specific relative to the wife of the aspirant to Sacred Orders or

[27] C. 5, D. XXXII; JL, n. 4399.

[28] C. 6, D. XXXII; JL, n. 4501.

[29] C. 15, D. LXXI; JL, n. 4827.

[30] C. 14, D. XXXII; Pope Leo IX (1049–1054) against the doctrine prepared in a letter of Abbot Nicetas Stethatas of Constantinople in the year 1054; JL, n. 4308.

[31] C. 12, D. XXXII; Pope Urban II (1088–1099) in the Synod of Melfi (1089)—Mansi, XX, 723.

[32] C. 10, D. XXXII.

[33] C. 11, D. XXXII.

[34] C. 2, X, *de clericis coniugatis,* III, 3; Alexander III to the Bishop of Hereford; JL, n. 13946.

to an ecclesiastical benefice. The pope ruled that the permission of the wife was not sufficient for the taking of the vow of continency on the part of the cleric as a prerequisite for higher ordination. The wife also had to make a promise—either to enter religion or to observe perpetual chastity in the world.[35]

Pope Innocent III (1198–1216) forbade clerics in major Orders to marry, and if they transgressed this prohibition they were to be punished. This punishment consisted in their deprivation of whatever benefice they had.[36] This prohibition did not affect the discipline of the Eastern Church. In it clerics were not obliged to be unmarried.[37] But if in the Western Church a cleric in minor Orders married he had to leave his benefice and go to his wife, whereas a subdeacon or one in higher Orders had to give up his wife and do penance. If he refused, he was to be suspended and excommunicated.[38]

Pope Boniface VIII (1294–1303) prohibited the conferral of tonsure on a married man unless he intended to enter religion or to be promoted to Sacred Orders.[39]

The Council of Trent (1545–1563), as an extraordinary measure to restore to use the functions of the four minor Orders, did countenance the services of married minor clerics of approved life.[40] This was permitted only in those localities in which there was an insufficient number of celibate clerics to carry on the functions proper to their particular minor Order.

The commentators on the legislation of Alexander III [41] were

[35] C. 1, X, *de conversione coniugatorum,* III, 32; Alexander III to the Bishop of Hereford; JL, n. 13946.

[36] C. 5, X, *de clericis coniugatis,* III, 3; Pope Innocent III to the Bishop of Norwich; Potthast, *Regesta Pontificum Romanorum inde ab anno post Christum natum 1198 ad annum 1304* (2 vols. in 1, Berolini, 1874–1875), n. 1944 (hereafter cited as Potthast).

[37] C. 6, X, *de clericis coniugatis,* III, 3; Innocent III to the Archbishop of Acerenza; Potthast, n. 1991.

[38] C. 1, X, *de clericis coniugatis,* III, 3; JL, n. 13813.

[39] C. 4, *de tempore ordinationum et qualitate ordinandorum,* I, 9, in VI°.

[40] Conc. Trident., sess. XXIII, *de ref.,* c. 17—"Quod si ministeriis quatuor minorum ordinum exercendis clerici caelibes praesto non erunt, suffici possint etiam coniugati vitae probatae, dummodo non bigami, ad ea munia obeundi idonei, et qui tonsuram et habitum clericalem in ecclesia gestent."

[41] C. 2, X, *de clericis coniugatis,* III, 3.

in agreement that, whether the marriage which was involved was simply *ratum* or also *consummatum,* the exclusion of the married from the reception of Orders referred to the reception of minor Orders and tonsure.[42] This is also attested by a decree of the Sacred Congregation of the Council.[43]

Under the legislation of the Council of Trent the condition under which a married man could be admitted to the clerical state remained the same. The wife had to give her consent.[44] Mere silence could never mean consent.[45] By adultery the sinning wife forfeited her conjugal rights, so that her consent then no longer was necessary,[46] unless her sin had been condoned by the use of the marriage rights after the sin, or unless the other consort had also been guilty of the same offense.[47] Apostasy or heresy on the part of the wife, which had been officially judged so by the ecclesiastical court, was sufficient to warrant a separation. If this separation was ordered by the court, the consent of the wife was no longer needed, even if she later returned to the Church.[48] If the husband of a marriage between two infidels became a convert and the wife was unwilling to live with him, or, if willing, became the occasion of a probable danger of perversion or of contempt for religion, then she was not entitled

---

[42] Cf. Pirhing, *Ius Canonicum Novo Methodo Explicatum* (5 vols. in 4, Diliginae, 1674–1678), lib. IV, tit. 15, n. 20: "Uxoratus, cui ne prima quidem tonsura conferri potest . . ." (hereafter cited as Pirhing); Schmalzgrueber, lib. III, tit. 3, n. 20.

[43] S. C. C., *Tricaricen.,* 23 ian. 1610 ad 2—*Codicis Iuris Canonici Fontes cura Em̃i Petri Card. Gasparri editi* (9 vols., Romae [postea Civitate Vaticana]: Typis Polyglottis Vaticanis, 1923–1939, Vols. VII–IX ed. cura et studio Em̃i Iustiniani Card. Serédi), n. 2384 (hereafter cited as *Fontes*).

[44] Pirhing, lib. III, tit. 32, n. 61.

[45] Sanchez, *De Sancto Matrimonii Sacramento Disputationum Tomi Tres* (Lugduni, 1669), lib. VII, disp. 38, n. 15 (hereafter cited as Sanchez). Cf. Schmalzgrueber, lib. III, tit. 32, n. 23.

[46] Pirhing, lib. III, tit. 32, nn. 34–35.

[47] Reiffenstuel, lib. III, tit. 32, nn. 28–29; Boenninghausen, Fasc. III, p. 175; Gasparri, *De Sacra Ordinatione,* n. 527; Wernz, *Ius Decretalium* (6 vols., Romae et Prati, 1898–1905), II, n. 127 (hereafter cited as Wernz).

[48] Pirhing, lib. III, tit. 32, n. 41; Reiffenstuel, lib. III, tit. 32, n. 35.

to be asked for her consent to the future ordination of her husband.[49]

In accompaniment with the consent of the wife there was required her entrance into a religious community whose members professed solemn vows, or her promise to observe perpetual chastity in the world.[50] This was required to take place at the same time as the reception of tonsure by the husband.[51] For the wife to remain in the world was not a matter of her own simple choice. She could determine to make her promise to observe perpetual chastity in the world only when she was advanced in years or when there was no danger of incontinence in her life.[52]

The force of these conditions can be well appreciated from a decision given by the Holy Office.[53] It was decided that a married man who together with his wife had made the simple vow of chastity, although he was well qualified for and desirous of becoming a priest in consequence of his wife's consent, was forbidden to be ordained because there was no monastery within the territory into which the wife could go. Neither of the parties was well advanced in years. Nevertheless the opinions of the authors on the availability to the wife of the alternatives of entering a monastery or of taking the vow of chastity in the world were varied.[54]

Some maintained that, regardless of the age of the wife, the simple vow of chastity in the world sufficed.[55] Others held that the simple vow of chastity did not suffice in itself, although more could not be demanded if the wife was well advanced in years, or was beyond any suspicion of incontinence.[56] Then there were

---

[49] *Loc. cit.*

[50] Pirhing, lib. III, tit. 32, n. 58.

[51] S. C. Ep. et Reg., *Mutien.*, 12 aug. 1611—*Fontes*, n. 1650.

[52] Benedictus XIV, *De Synodo Diocesana*, lib. XIII, cap. 13, n. 4 et sq.; Verano, *Iuris Canonici Universi Commentarius* (5 vols., Monachii, 1703–1708), lib. III, tit. 5, n. 9 (hereafter cited as Verano).

[53] S. C. S. Off. (*Coreae*), 12 febr. 1851, ad 4—*Fontes*, n. 915.

[54] Cf. Boenninghausen, Fasc. III, p. 178, footnotes.

[55] E.g., Maioli, *De Irregularitatibus* (Romae, 1575), lib. I, cap, 34, n. 3 (hereafter cited as Maioli).

[56] E.g., Navarrus, *Consiliorum seu Responsorum in Quinque Libros iuxta*

those who contended that if the wife was well advanced in years a simple vow of chastity did suffice; but if there was danger of incontinence she had to enter the cloistered religious life.[57] Finally there was an opinion which maintained that regardess of the factor of age or the question-of continence, the least requirement was that of a solemn vow of chastity for the wife in the world.[58] The last expressed opinion seemed more in harmany with a decision of the Sacred Congregation of the Council[59] and a decision of the Sacred Congregation of the Holy Office.[60] An indult from the Holy See was held to be necessary before the taking of the vow of chastity in the world by the wife sufficed, if the wife refused or was unable to enter a monastery, even though she was well advanced in years and in no way suspected of or endangered by incontinence.[61]

Celibacy of the clergy, a postulate for the non-existence of this impediment, has been the constant concern of the Latin Church. The numerous laws, general and particular, which have been promulgated to bring about the observance of celibacy among the clergy bear testimony to this great concern.[62]

Numerum et Titulos Decretalium Distributorum Tomi Duo (Venetiis, 1621), I, cons. in lib. III, *de conversione coniugatorum*, cons. XIII, n. 4.

[57] Sanchez, lib. VII, disp. 39, n. 6; Pirhing, *ibid.*, n. 59; Gasparri, *ibid.*, n. 535; Wernz, *ibid.*, n. 127.

[58] Boenninghausen, Fasc. III, p. 177.

[59] S. C. C., *Parisien.*, 6 maii 1645: "Si Sanctissimo placuerit, dispensationem petitam suscipiendi sacros ordines de consensu uxoris concedendam esse Ioanni de Morheron, in forma tamen commissoria, verificatis aetate ipsius 62 annorum et aetate uxoris 58 annorum, quodque ipsa emiserit votum solemne castitatis in manu Archiepiscopi Parisiensis, et quod ex attestatione eiusdem in dicta uxore cesset omnis incontinentiae suspicio et ipse bene meritus sit Sedis Apostolicae ob servitium praestitum S. Congregationi de Propaganda Fide." This is contained in the *Thesaurus Resolutionum Sacrae Congregationis Concilii* (167 vols., 1718–1908), under *Veronen.*, 18 dec. 1728, IV, 249 (hereafter cited as *Thesaurus Resolutionum*).

[60] S. C. S. Off. (*Coreae*), 12 febr. 1851, ad 4—*Fontes*, n. 915.

[61] S. C. C., *Veronen.*, 18 dec. 1728—*Thesaurus Resolutionum*, IV, 249.

[62] Cf. Roskovány, *De Coelibatu et Breviario* (13 vols., Pestini, 1861–1888), Vols. I–IV.

B. CANONICAL COMMENTARY—"VIRI UXOREM HABENTES"

1. *Preliminary Consideration—The Law of Celibacy*

From the foregoing historical synopsis the ever present solicitude of the Holy See concerning a celibate clergy is evident. This solicitude is given a full expression in the enactments of the present Code of Canon Law. Clerics in major Orders are forbidden to marry, and likewise are under obligation to observe virginal chastity. If they violate it they are guilty of a sacrilege.[63] Clerics in minor Orders may indeed contract marriage, but by the very fact of doing so they lose their clerical status, unless their contract of marriage was null and void as a result of force or fear inflicted upon them.[64] "The law of clerical celibacy cannot be permitted to be in any way brought into question, as the Holy See regards it as the peculiar ornament of the Latin Church, and one of the principal sources of its active vigor."[65] "The Holy See will never in any way mitigate, much less abolish, this most sacred and most salutary law."[66]

One in major Orders who, in violation of this law of celibacy, presumes to contract marriage incurs a *latae sententiae* excommunication which is reserved *simpliciter* to the Holy See for its absolution.[67] The absolution from this censure, when the violator is a priest, is reserved to the Sacred Penitentiary in such a way that no one, except in the case of danger of death, can ever absolve from it, regardless of whatever faculties are granted by canon 2254, § 1, or by privilege, or by any other law or right.[68] The violation of this law of celibacy is also a violation of the

---

[63] Canon 132, § 1.

[64] Canon 132, § 2.

[65] Benedictus XV, ep. "*Dilecte fili Noster,*" 12 mart. 1919—*AAS,* XI (1919), 122-123. Translation taken from Bouscaren, I, 121.

[66] Benedictus XV, allocut. "*Cum multa,*" 16 dec. 1920—*AAS,* XII (1920), 587. Translation taken from Bouscaren, I, 121.

[67] Canon 2388, § 1.

[68] S. Poenit., decr. "*Lex sacri coelibatus,*" 18 apr. 1936—*AAS,* XXVIII (1936), 242-243; S. Poenit., declar., 4 maii, 1937—*AAS,* XXIX (1937), 283-284.

oath which is taken by all clerics prior to the reception of major Orders.[69]

As in the legislation prior to 1918, so also in the present Code of Canon Law, in order to insure celibacy among the clergy, those men who have a wife are impeded from the reception of Orders.[70] In order to understand the nature of this impediment it is necessary to determine when and under what conditions it can be said a man has a wife.

2. *Meaning of the Term "Uxor"*

In legislating on the status, rights and duties of the parties of a marriage, the present Code of Canon Law refers to them as *coniuges* when there exists no necessity for a distinction between the man and the woman.[71] When there is question of an invalid marriage, the Code refers to the individuals as *partes.*[72] The woman of a matrimonial union is called *uxor.* Is the term "*uxor*" in designation of the woman employed only when her matrimonial union is valid, or is the term used also in designation of a woman in an invalid union?

According to its usage in the past the term "*uxor*" could be referred to a woman who was united to a man in a matrimonial union irrespective of its validity.[73] In order to obviate any misunderstanding the word "*legitima*" was at times placed before the term "*uxor.*"[74]

From the use of the term "*uxor*" in the Code,[75] the presumption is in favor of the interpretation that "*uxor*" exclusively refers to a woman who is united to a man in lawful wedlock. In canon 93, the Code deals with an *uxor* who is not lawfully separated from her husband. The question of the lawfulness or the unlawfulness of a separation could not be contemplated

[69] S. C. de Sacramentis, instr. 27 dec., 1930, Appendix, Mod. I—*AAS,* XXIII (1930), 127.

[70] Canon 987, 2o.

[71] Cf., e.g., canons 542, 1o; 1110; 1971.

[72] Cf., e.g., canons 1015, § 4, and 1990.

[73] Cf. Forcellini-Furlanetti, *Lexicon Totius Latinitatis* (4 vols. in 8, Patavii, 1864–1887), VII, s.v. *uxor.*

[74] Cf. Docum. VII, in fine Codicis.

[75] Canons 93; 987, 2o; 1112; 1456.

in the canon if the marriage was invalid, since in such a case a separation would be obligatory. In canon 1112, an *uxor* is according to the common law made a participant in the canonical status of her husband. This participation the law does not intend to effect when the union of the man and the woman is invalid. In virtue of the law expressed in canon 18, the term "*uxor*" is to be considered as referring to a woman lawfully united to a man by the bond of marriage which by its nature is perpetual and exclusive.[76]

3. "Habens Uxorem" and "Habens Mulierem"

There exists no doubt concerning the status of a man who is joined with a woman in a valid marriage. He has a wife—*uxorem*—and he will continue to have a wife until the matrimonial bond is broken. If, however, the marriage is an invalid one, then the status of the man can be that of one having a wife—*habens uxorem*—or of one having a woman—*habens mulierem*. The specifically acknowledged status will depend on the conscious knowledge of the one who must decide on the validity or the invalidity of the marriage.

In the internal forum the status is that of one *habens mulierem* if the man of the marriage knows of the invalidity of his attempted union. In the external forum the determination of the status of a man who is in an invalid union presents some difficulty.

When the invalidity of the attempted union is certain before the Church inasmuch as it has been proved with certitude, and is known to both of the parties of the invalid union, the status of the man is not that of one *habens uxorem*. If the invalidity of the attempted union is doubtful in the eyes of the Church inasmuch as it has not been proved with certitude, then in virtue of the rule of canon 1014,[77] the marriage is to be considered as valid. The favor of the law insists that such a union be regarded as valid until the contrary is proved. This is a presumption of

[76] Cf. canon 1110.

[77] "Matrimonium gaudet favore iuris; quare in dubio standum est pro valore matrimonii, donec contrarium probetur, salvo praescripto can. 1127."

law.[78] Thus a union which is invalid before God must, in such a particular case, still be considered as valid by the operation of the law of the Code. Does this juridical consequence of the law effect a status for the man so that he is as one *habens uxorem* and is consequently impeded from the reception of Orders?

Whenever there is a presumption of law, the legislator has accepted and acts upon the probable result of an event after the fashion in which the results of similar events usually turn out, in order to forestall what otherwise could, and in all likelihood would, become a general danger for the welfare of the community. The presumption enacted by and accepted in the law still retains its juridical force, even though in a particular event it does not harmonize with fact and reality, as long only as that fact or reality is not established by certain proof. An exception to the rule as set up by the legal presumption obtains as soon as the exception is demonstrated. If it is demonstrated only doubtfully but not conclusively, then the law of the presumption will remain in force in the particular event under investigation.[79]

The candidate for Orders, if he wants effectively to certify his freedom from the impediment here in question, must prove either that the alleged matrimonial contract was devoid of the very appearance and character of marriage, and therefore never had existence as a contract for the contraction of marriage, or that because of some invalidating law the contract when made remained null and void of juridical effect from the beginning.[80] Unless he can prove the invalidity of the marriage, he will be obliged in the external forum to consider himself as one *habens uxorem.* Yet this specific operation of the law of presumption will not justify the guilty parties, who are involved in the invalid union, in living as husband and wife in marital relations, if in the forum of conscience these parties have a certain knowledge

---

[78] Manning, ***Presumption of Law in Matrimonial Procedure,*** The Catholic University of America Canon Law Studies, n. 94 (Washington, D. C.: The Catholic University of America, 1935), p. 53 (hereafter cited as Manning).

[79] Cf. Manning, p. 15.

[80] *Ibid.*, p. 53.

which militates against the presumption adopted in the external forum.

The same conclusion can be applied to a putative marriage. Contrary to Petrovits, who states that, as long as the good faith of at least one of the persons concerned perseveres, the putative marriage according to a long established rule has all the effects of lawful wedlock,[81] a putative marriage can not effect a matrimonial bond which by its nature is perpetual and exclusive.[82] The Code itself implies that there is no actual bond when it employs the words "matrimonium invalidum" in the definition of a putative marriage.[83]

In the external forum a putative marriage will have the same effect as a valid union in relation to the impediment until a declaration of nullity has been granted. This is based on the fact that the impediment is the result of the enactment of an ecclesiastical law, which has been directly and immediately made for the external forum, that is, in order to promote reverence for the sacred ministry.[84]

The conclusion which presents itself from the above consideration is the following: A man who is bound by a matrimonial bond, whether in both the internal and the external forum, or in either the internal or the external forum alone—the latter arising simply from the operation of the law of presumption—is bound by the impediment to which are subject *viri uxorem habentes*. His subjection to this impediment continues until the objectively valid bond has been severed or dissolved, or also until the presumptively valid bond has been authoritatively declared as non-existent for him.

---

[81] Petrovits, *The New Church Law on Matrimony*, The Catholic University of America Canon Law Studies, n. 6 (Washington, D. C.: The Catholic University of America, 1919), n. 54 (hereafter cited as Petrovits). McDevitt states: "It may be remarked incidentally that the author [Petrovits] is not altogether accurate when he attributes all the effects of lawful wedlock to putative marriage."—*Legitimacy and Legitimation*, The Catholic University of America Canon Law Studies, n. 138 (Washington, D. C.: The Catholic University of America Press, 1941), p. 75, footnote n. 57.

[82] Cf. canon 1110.

[83] Cf. canon 1015, § 4.

[84] Cappello, *De Sacra Ordinatione*, n. 435.

C. CESSATION OF THE MARRIAGE BOND—VARIOUS POSSIBILITIES

1. *General Norms*

The basis for this impediment is constituted by the *vinculum matrimonii* which exists between the married parties.[85] This matrimonial bond is by its very nature perpetual and exclusive, and arises from a valid marriage.[86] In the law prior to the present Code of Canon Law the reason for the impediment, other than the promotion of the honor and the dignity of the clerical state, was based on the right of the wife, which was exclusive of others, over her husband. If she was willing to forego the use of this exclusive right, and if the danger of incontinency was securely obviated, the impediment was removed. This discipline has been changed in the present law.[87] The consent of the wife to relinquish the use of her exclusive right has no bearing on the existence of the impediment as such, but only on the possibility of the granting of a dispensation from the impediment. Under the present law, the impediment exists as long as the marriage bond, which by its nature is perpetual, remains.[88]

The perpetual nature of the matrimonial bond in an individual case depends on the continued existence in life of the married couple, so that if the wife were to die, the bond would no longer exist. Death, then, is the more common way through which cessation of the matrimonial bond is effected. However, under certain circumstances the matrimonial bond can cease in other ways, as mentioned in the law itself.

---

[85] "Coniugatus arcetur a statu clericali quamdiu durat vinculum matrimoniale."—Wernz-Vidal, IV, pars I, n. 257.

[86] Canon 1110.

[87] Cf. Blat, III, pars I, n. 356: "Sic melius est provisum quam in praec. iure, quando ex uxoris consensu vir promoveri poterat, sub conditione pro diversitáte casuum ex praxi S. Congr. Conc. interpretante cap 5 de conversione coniugatorum (tit. 32, Lib. III) in quo statuit Alex. III. 'Nullus coniugatorum est ad ss. ordines promovendus, nisi ab uxore continentiam profitente fuerit absolutus'"; Cappello, *De Sacra Ordinatione,* n. 520; Wernz-Vidal, IV, pars I, n. 257.

[88] Ayrinhac, *Legislation on the Sacraments,* p. 372.

2. *Particular Application*

a. Putative Bond—Invalid Union

When the invalidity of an attempted union is certainly known to be such not only by the parties but also by those in the Church who are empowered to judge on the invalidity of the union, the marital status has no existence either factually or even presumptively. When an invalid union, e.g., a putative marriage, cannot be proved to be invalid in the eyes of the Church, then the marriage must be considered as valid to the extent at least that it effects an impediment to the reception of Orders.

Even though the nullity of the marriage has been declared by the Church, a civil separation or divorce, if the parties are bound by a civil bond, should be obtained. Such a procedure will obviate any future litigations in the civil courts. Unless the man can substantiate with civil documents his right to be freed from any claims of his wife, the latter can bring him to court. This will not only embarrass the cleric, but also bring harm to the Church and to the clerical state. Even when the parties of a valid union agree to follow a higher calling, and both request permission of the Holy See to enter the religious life, the Holy See demands that a civil divorce or separation precede the execution of the rescript which contains a dispensation from the impediment.[89]

b. Actual Bond—Valid Union

1° Legitimate Marriage

A marriage which has been validly contracted between two non-baptized persons is called a legitimate marriage.[90] If the conditions as set in the law are present when the conversion and baptism of one of the parties has taken place, the Pauline Privilege can be used. In virtue of the Pauline Privilege a convert may contract another marriage, and in virtue of the second marriage the first union, even though consummated, becomes *ipso*

[89] Cf. Cappello, *De Sacra Ordinatione*, n. 520.

[90] Canon 1015, § 3.

facto dissolved.[91] The first union remains with all of its effects until the infidel party has become guilty of physical or moral desertion and furthermore the converted partner, having observed all the conditions as prescribed by law, has contracted another marriage.[92] It is therefore the second marriage, the Christian union which dissolves the first marriage, which was contracted in infidelity. Unless there has been granted a dissolution of the bond "*in favorem fidei,*" or "*super matrimonio rato et non consummato,*" even apart from the prospect of a second union, it is the second marriage whereby the dissolution of the bond takes place. The law states: "Vinculum prioris coniugii, in infidelitate contracti, tunc *tantum solvitur,* cum pars fidelis novas nuptias valide iniverit." [93]

As stated before,[94] the basis for the impediment is the marriage bond itself. Contrary to some authors, such as Cappello [95] and Hickey,[96] the availability of the use of the Pauline Privilege does not of itself permit the entering of religion [97] or the receiving of Orders in lieu of the contraction of a second marriage.[98] Vermeersch-Creusen,[99] Payen [100] and Gregory [101] also maintain

---

[91] Canon 1126; Petrovits, n. 553.

[92] Petrovits, *loc. cit.;* Blat, III, pars I, n. 537.

[93] Canon 1126. Italics are the writer's.

[94] Cf., *supra,* p. 32.

[95] Cappello says in his book *De Matrimonio,* n. 772: "Fidelis autem, qui discedat, potest qualemcumque vitae statum eligere, v. g. coelibatum in saeculo profiteri aut ingredi religionem, aut si agatur de viro, ordines suscipere . . ."

[96] Hickey states on page 75: "A man converted, is not at liberty by virtue of the Pauline Privilege to be advanced to orders, if the other infidel party should consent to cohabit peaceably and should be willing to subscribe to all the conditions required by law, but be unwilling to be converted. If the infidel wife is unwilling to conform to this, the converted husband may be advanced to orders."

[97] Cf. canon 542, 1o: "Invalide ad novitiatum admittitur coniux, durante matrimonio."

[98] Cf. canon 987, 2o.

[99] *Epitome,* II, n. 433.

[100] *De Matrimonio in Missionibus et Potissimum in Sinus Tractatus Practicus et casus* (2. ed., 3 vols., Zi-ka-wei: In typographia T'ou-sè-wè, 1935–1936), II, n. 2221 (hereafter cited as Payen).

[101] *The Pauline Privilege,* The Catholic University of America Canon

that the mere fact of the availability of the use of the Pauline Privilege does not of itself permit the receiving of Orders. A dispensation from the impediment which results from the existing bond of the marriage must be obtained.

Cappello in justification of his opinion appeals to the old law and to the prescriptions of canon 6, 3°, 4°, and canon 23. In the law prior to the Code it was not necessary to appeal to the Holy See when in the presence of circumstances which permitted the use of the Pauline Privilege a candidate wished to receive Orders. However, as Cappello admits,[102] there has been a change from the earlier law. Now, unless this change is other than that the perpetual bond of marriage is the basis for the exclusion from the reception of Orders, it does not seem correct in this instance to appeal to canon 6, 3°, 4° and canon 23. In the pre-Code law the basis for the impediment was the woman's exclusive right which flows from the marriage bond. Thus, if she was willing to forego her right and to enter religion, or had lost her right, there was no need of a dispensation.

However, in the present law the basis for the impediment is not simply the woman's exclusive right which flows from the marriage bond. In virtue of the fact that the Pauline Privilege has become available for use the converted husband does not change in his status from one who has a wife to one who does not have a wife. Rather he is simply given a lawful option of a second marriage through which the bond between him and the wife of the first union will be dissolved. Therefore a dispensation from the impediment arising from his continued marital status would be necessary before the converted husband, who could lawfully invoke the use of the Pauline Privilege, could likewise lawfully receive Orders.[103]

Law Studies, n. 68 (Washington, D. C.: The Catholic University of America, 1931), p. 106 (hereafter cited as Gregory).

[102] "Quare mutata est disciplina antiqua permittens ut vir ordines reciperet, si uxor libere in monasterium ingrederetur. Proinde maritus nequit ordines suscipere sine venia S. Sedis, licet uxor licentiam concedat et castitatem voveat."—*De Sacra Ordinatione*, n. 520.

[103] Cf. Vermeersch-Creusen, II, n. 433.

2° Marriage Ratified but not Consummated

A marriage between two baptized persons which has been validly contracted but never consummated is called a *matrimonium ratum.*[104] A marriage between a baptized person and a non-baptized person which has been validly contracted but never consummated may be called a *matrimonium non-ratum et non-consummatum.* A non-consummated marriage which has been contracted between two baptized persons or between a baptized person and a non-baptized person is dissolved *ipso iure* by the solemn religious profession of either one of the parties of the marriage,[105] and also by a dispensation granted by the Holy See. The granting of this dispensation depends upon the lawful request of at least one of the parties, even though the other party is unwilling that such a dispensation be granted.[106]

The dissolution of the marriage bond by means of solemn profession has little bearing on the impediment to Orders which derives from a man's continued marital status, since it is to be assumed that a dispensation has been obtained for the valid admission into the novitiate,[107] and for the licit admission into a religious institute whose members are destined for the priesthood.[108] However, if the non-consummated marriage was dissolved by the solemn profession of the woman of the marriage, then a dispensation will not be necessary for the valid admission of the man into the novitiate, or for the licit reception of Orders. Once the marriage bond has been dissolved the same bond cannot return.

When a dispensation[109] "*super matrimonio rato et non-consummato*" is granted, the Roman Pontiff in virtue of his vicarious power directly dissolves the bond of matrimony,[110] and the parties of the marriage are free from the juridical effects of this former

---

104 Canon 1015, § 1.

105 Cf. Conc. Trident., *de Sac. matrim.,* can. 6.

106 Canon 1119; S. C. de Sacramentis, decr. "*Catholica doctrina,*" 7 maii, 1923—*AAS,* XV (1923), 389.

107 Canon 542, 1o.

108 Canon 542, 2o.

109 The term "dispensation" is used in a wide sense.

110 Cappello, *De Matrimonio,* n. 762.

valid union.[111] Thus the man of this former union is no longer bound by the impediment to Holy Orders which arises from an extant bond of marriage, and unless there be in the rescript a clause which forbids the reception of Orders, the man is free to enter the ranks of the clergy.

3º Marriage Ratified and Consummated

A sacramental marriage which has been consummated cannot be dissolved by any human power or by any other cause than death.[112] Therefore, unless death takes the wife, the husband will always be bound by the impediment of his marital status until a dispensation from the same has been obtained from the Holy See.

D. DISPENSATION FROM THE IMPEDIMENT

1. *General Norms*

It is possible to obtain a relaxation of the law wherein is enacted the particular impediment to Orders which derives from an existing bond of marriage.[113] However, such a relaxation is very rarely granted,[114] and never without the expressed or tacit consent of the wife.[115]

It is advisable, though by law not strictly necessary, to seek approval for a married man to enter the seminary. Such approval, when granted, would come from the Sacred Congregation for Seminaries and Universities, the competent Congregation in such matters.[116] But the practice of this Sacred Congregation is such that it rarely grants such approval. It does so only under certain specified conditions.[117] This approval seems not of itself

---

111 Cappello, *ibid.*, n. 766.

112 Canon 1118.

113 Cf. canon 80.

114 Cappello, *De Sacra Ordinatione*, n. 520.

115 Vermeersch-Creusen, II, n. 259; Hickey, p. 76.

116 Cf. canon 256.

117 "Venia ingrediendi Seminarium rarissime conceditur, uxore adhuc vivente. Aliquando tamen conceditur, si mulier consentiat libere et sponte omnino, absit causa gravis (v. g. morbus perpetuus impediens matrimonii usum) et nullum sit periculum proximum incontinentiae."—Cappello, *De Sacra Ordinatione*, n. 520.

to remove the impediment to Orders, unless there be a statement to that effect in the rescript which grants the permission.

According to Cappello, however, the approval to enter the seminary, when granted by the Sacred Congregation for Seminaries and Universities, implies also a dispensation from the impediment to Orders which in the case is based on the still extant bond of marriage.[118]

The competent Congregation to which a request for a dispensation from this impediment is to be sent is the Congregation for Religious when the candidate is a member of a clerical religious institute. A dispensation which has been granted in order that one who is bound by the bond of marriage can nevertheless be validly admitted to the novitiate [119] does not remove the obligation of further obtaining a dispensation from the impediment to Orders, unless the rescript which granted the former dispensation included the added grant of the latter also. All grants of dispensations are to be interpreted strictly.[120]

2. *Conditions for the Granting of a Dispensation*

Since the rights and duties of the wife are involved in a dispensation from this impediment, the Holy See demands proof that such rights are not being violated. If a man is legitimately separated from his wife, even though the separation from her is acknowledged in law as permanent for any of the reasons legally sanctioned,[121] he is not at liberty to receive Orders, although of course in such a case the Holy See would be favorably inclined to grant a dispensation.[122] The sinful actions of the wife which in such a case have furnished cause for the permanent separation forfeit for her whatever claim to the use of marital rights she had, and constitute an equivalent of the

[118] That Cappello considers this to be the practice of this Congregation is concluded from his words: "Si vir ingressus sit Seminarium ex venia S. C. de Seminariis et Universitatibus studiorum, non indiget deinceps licentia S. C. de Sacramentis ubi agitur de ordinibus suscipiendis."—*De Sacra Ordinatione*, n. 520.

[119] Cf. canon 542, 1o.

[120] Canon 85.

[121] Cf. canon 1129.

[122] Cappello, *De Sacra Ordinatione*, n. 520.

tacit consent on her part which is necessary before a dispensation from this impediment will be granted to her husband. When an ordinary applies for a dispensation in such a case, he should mention the reason which underlies the separation and should also indicate the basis on which certitude is had of the existence of that reason. A civil separation or divorce, if the parties are bound by the civil bond, should likewise precede the application for the desired dispensation.

In the case of a legitimate separation, granted according to the norms of canon 1131, and effected either judically or administratively according to the individual circumstances, an explanation of the reasons for the granting of the separation, and a statement regarding the absence of any founded hope for the resumption of marital life, must accompany the application for a dispensation. Through legitimate separation the wife has lost, at least for the present, all right and claim to conjugal life, so that her consent is not required, inasmuch as the law regards it as already tacitly given.[123] If the wife be in a state of perpetual insanity, then the obtaining of her consent becomes impossible, and is therefore not required.

When conjugal life is constituted as an existing obligation for the parties of the marriage, then the consent of the wife is necessary before a dispensation will be granted. This is all that is directly required. The entrance of the wife into a religious institute, or her taking of the vow of chastity, either for life or for as long as her husband lives, is required only indirectly, that is, whenever without the use of such means there would exist some danger of incontinency. However, it is advisable to consult the Holy See in advance, so that the requirements in each individual case may be properly determined. By following such a procedure the danger of raising any false hopes will be avoided, although Cappello maintains that the Holy See will not impose on the wife the obligation to enter a religious institute, or to take a perpetual vow of chastity, whenever there is no danger of incontinency present in her life. But if the wife on her own accord and without intervention from others

[123] Cappello, *loc. cit.*

declares that she is about to enter a religious institute or to take a perpetual vow of chastity, the permission for her husband to receive Orders will be more readily granted.[124]

The rights of the children to parental love and guidance must be respected. If the children are still in need of parental care, which could be supplied in no other way than by the father's continued life in the world, the Holy See will not grant a dispensation from the impediment created by his marital status. The possible future reactions of the community in which the ordained person will be called upon to serve must likewise be considered by the ordinary before he applies for a dispensation. The Holy See will do nothing which would endanger or compromise the esteem which it wants to see accorded to the law which calls for a celibate clergy in the Latin Church.

The furnished consent of the wife, when it is required, should be provable from an authentic document.[125] In order to obviate any future civil litigations in the event that a wife should revoke her consent, a civil separation should be obtained. The reception of sacred Orders gives rise to a status in which the ordained person is forbidden to return to his previous marital relations.[126] If it should happen that a married man, even in good faith, received Orders without an apostolic indult, he would be prohibited from the exercise of the Orders thus received.[127]

Cappello presents a list of circumstances under which the Holy See occasionally grants the faculty to a married man to permit him to embrace the clerical state.[128] Thus the Holy See may reply favorably to the petition which asks that a married man be dispensed to make lawful his adoption of the clerical state: (1) When a man leaves his wife because of her sin of adultery, and

---

[124] Cappello, *loc. cit.*

[125] Cappello, *loc. cit.*

[126] Cf. canon 1114.

[127] Canon 132, § 3; 986, § 2.

[128] Cappello states: "Praecipua adiuncta peculiaria in quibus *interdum* facultas a S. Sede datur viro amplectendi statum ecclesiasticum, sunt ista: . . ." From this it appears that the merits of each case are so variable that it is not possible to state absolutely that each case will be decided in the same manner. (The italics inserted in Cappello's statement are the writer's.)

she has obtained a civil divorce and also has contracted a civil marriage with another man; (2) when it is at least probable that one of the spouses has become affected with impotence which arose only after the marriage was validly contracted; (3) when the wife has lost her mind, and the mental illness on her part has been declared permanent by qualified doctors; (4) when the wife has been given a life-term prison sentence because of a very grave crime; (5) when the wife has obtained a civil divorce from her innocent husband and now lives in an adulterous union with another man; (6) when both spouses, by their mutual and free consent, wish to live a more holy life in a higher state of perfection. To this list may be added also the case in which it would be permissible for the man to make use of the Pauline Privilege.

3. A Casuistic Report

Although there is a change in the law which relates to the enactment of the impediment, yet there seems to be retained the practice of the earlier law in the granting of a dispensation from the impediment which derives from a man's continued marital status. The method employed in the solution of an individual case does not necessarily establish a uniform rule of action. However, it may serve a useful purpose here to record, in general, a case concerning which there has come to the present writer a knowledge of the things which were required of the involved parties. This case occurred since the promulgation of the present Code of Canon Law.

A married couple expressed to each other their mutual desire to dedicate themselves more completely to the service of God. There were no children of their union. Both parties were well advanced in years. An application for a dispensation from the impediment to Orders was sent to the Holy See. In the rescript a dispensation was granted on the condition that a civil separation had been previously obtained, and that the wife had made her final profession of vows. Thus, it was required that, before the husband could receive Orders, his wife had first to make her final profession, even though she was well advanced in years and in her mode of life furnished full evidence that the danger of incontinence was in no way predicable in the case.

The facts of this case are here presented for the sake of indicating what the Holy See may in all likelihood demand in any similar case. It will be a matter of prudent foresight to try to discover beforehand how much time must elapse before the wife can be admitted to her final religious profession. Whether that profession be made with solemn vows, or with perpetual simple vows, will not alter the considerations which underlie the ultimate settlement of the case.

Article II. Slave to Master

A. Historical Synopsis

It is not the purpose of this study to outline the historical development of slavery and the various forms of liberation. This is left to others who treat that matter *ex professo*.[1] Posited the existence of slavery and the varied form of liberation, it is asked: Was it permissible to ordain a slave?

As early as 443 Pope Leo I wrote to all the bishops that they were not to presume to promote one to the clerical state unless he had been freed from slavery.[2] Pope Gelasius I (492–496) contributed most of the legislation on this impediment. In dealing with a case presented by Bishops Martin of Tarragona in Spain and Iustus of Acerenza in Lucania, in which there was question of the right procedure to follow when a slave had been ordained without the knowledge of his master, he ruled that the slave was free if he received the order of priesthood. If he received the order of diaconate, then a substitute had to be supplied by the deacon, and if he was unable to do so, he himself had to return to the service of his master. If he was ordained to any other order, then the cleric had to return to his original

[1] Cf. Leage-Ziegler, *Roman Private Law* (2. ed., New York: Macmillan and Co., Ltd., 1937), pp. 54–74.

[2] C. 1, D. LIV, "Nullus episcoporum servum alterius ad clericatus officium promovere presumat, nisi forte eorum petitio aut voluntas accesserit, qui aliquid sibi in eo vindicant potestatis. Debet enim esse immunis ab aliis, qui divinae militae est aggregandus, ut a castris dominicis, quibus nomen eius adscribitur, nullius necessitatis vinculis abstrahatur."—JK, n. 402.

status under his master.[3] The master of a slave could, if he so wished, have the one who was freed by his ordination to the priesthood located at his church, not of course in the status of a slave, but for the celebration of the priestly functions.[4]

Pope Gelasius also gave a ruling on a case involving a deacon who had been ordained to that order against the will of his master. Such a one was to be removed from his office.[5] Consent of the master was necessary before a slave could be admitted to the ranks of the clerics.[6] In the event that a slave through stealth obtained ordination to the priesthood he was to be punished by the loss of whatever money he ever obtained.[7]

St. Raymond of Peñafort (+1275)[8] and Henry of Segusia, Cardinal of Ostia (+1271),[9] evolved particular conclusions relative to the opposition or agreement of the master, and relative also to the knowledge which was had of the master's attitude on the part of the one who ordained the slave or of the one who presented him for ordination. The main conclusion was that slaves were not to be ordained.

In the IV Provincial Council of Toledo (655) reference was made to a slave of the Church. Such a slave was not to be ordained unless the bishop had previously given him his freedom. When a slave of the Church was ordained to minor orders he thereupon had to be acknowledged as free. If then he led a good life, he could be raised to higher orders. If his life was not blameless, he was obliged to return to the servitude of the Church.[10] St.

---

[3] C. 9, D. LIV; JK, n. 653.

[4] C. 10, D. LIV; Pope Gelasius I to Bishops Herculentius, Stephen and Iustus in the year 494; JK, n. 653.

[5] C. 11, D. LIV; the letter was sent to Bishops Rufinus and Aprilis in the year 494; JK, n. 658.

[6] C. 12, D. LIV; Pope Gelasius I to all the bishops in the year 494; JK, n. 658.

[7] Palea, C. 8, D. LIV and Gratian's comment *Caeterum* on c. 8.

[8] *Summa* (ed. nova, Veronae, 1744), lib. III, tit. 17, *De servis non ordinandis et de manumissionibus eorumdem*, p. 270 (hereafter cited as *Summa* of St. Raymond).

[9] *Commentaria in Quinque Decretalium Libros* (5 vols. in 3, Venetiis, 1581), lib. I, cap. 4, p. 119 (hereafter cited as Hostiensis).

[10] Can. 11—Mansi, XI, 29; cf. c. 4, D. LIV.

Raymond distinguished slaves into *servi privati* and *servi ecclesiae.*[11]

The Council of Tribur (895) made it obligatory prior to ordination that a formal document denoting the slave's freedom be shown, and that the information regarding the action of liberation be made public.[12]

In the decretal collections some of the earlier legislation of the early Councils of Toledo was restated.[13] To this was added the legislation of the Council of Altheim (916), in which it was permitted, with the consent of the bishop, for a master to offer one of his slaves for ordination with the provision that the newly ordained recite the canonical hours for his former master. Failure to return to his master an ordained slave who was not fulfilling this obligation could bring excommunication.[14]

The uncertainty surrounding the status of a slave ordained to the subdiaconate was cleared away by the legislation of Innocent III (1198–1216) in his letter to the Bishop of Vacz in Hungary. He was to be treated according to the legislation enacted with regard to deacons.[15] The only other addition to the decretal collections was offered by Gregory IX (1227–1241). In a decretal to the Archbishop of Naples he made clear that the status of a person relative to his ordination was to be determined by the

---

[11] *Summa, loc. cit.*

[12] Can. 29: "Nulli de servili conditione ad sacros ordines promoveantur, nisi prius a propriis dominis legitimam libertatem consequantur; cuius libertatis charta ante ordinationem in ambone publice legatur, et si nullus contradixerit, rite consecrabuntur. Porro, servus non canonice consecratus, postquam de gradu deciderit, eius conditionis sit, cuius fuerat ante gradum."—Mansi, XVIIa-XVIIIa, 146–147. C. 2, D. LIV.

[13] C. 1, 2, 3, X, *de servis non ordinandis et eorum manumissione,* I, 18.

[14] Cans. 27–28: ". . . Quisquis vero talem secum habuerit, et postquam rem illius praedictam [defectum recitationis horarum canonicarum] audierit, et domino suo non reddiderit, vel a se non proiecerit, sive episcopus, sive comes, sive clericus, sive laicus, anathematis illius societate innodatus poenam excommunicationis ducet."—Mansi, XVIIIa-XVIIIa, 329. Cf. c. 4, X, *de servis non ordinandis et eorum manumissione,* I, 18, which reproduces this text.

[15] C. 6, X, *de servis non ordinandis et eorum manumissione,* I, 18 (a. 1207); Potthast, n. 3117.

status of the mother if she was a free person the while the father was a slave.[16]

Relative to the exclusion of slaves from the dignity of the clerical state commentators of the period from the Council of Trent to the present Code of Canon Law confined their remarks to what has been stated before.[17] For the most part this particular impediment was treated in a very brief manner throughout this entire period.[18]

It was held that a slave was not to be ordained unless he had been freed or unless he had received the permission of his master.[19] A dispensation from this impediment could come only from the Pope, and it was granted only rarely.[20] Men who hired themselves to an employer for a yearly salary were not considered slaves in the sense used by the legislator and understood by the commentators.[21] There were some who raised a doubt about such a kind of employment, and were at least partly inclined to the idea of considering persons in such employment subject to the impediment arising from slavery, at least insofar as they were to be classed as irregular in consequence of the defect of liberty.[22]

Justinian (527–565) permitted a bondsman fixed to the soil (*adscriptitius*) to be ordained as long as he fulfilled the work imposed by the landowner.[23] Such a slave was considered to be attached to the land, and not directly subjected to the will of the owner of the land.[24] At times the name *adscriptitii* was applied not only to those who were fixed to the soil, but also to those who were personally obligated to the will of a master by

---

16 C. 8, X, *de servis non ordinandis et eorum manumissione,* I, 18; Potthast, n. 9552.

17 Schmalzgrueber, lib. I, tit. 18, nn. 1–7; Reiffenstuel, lib. I, tit. 18, nn. 1–21; Devoti, *Ius Canonicum Universum Publicum et Privatum* (3 tom., ed. nova, Romae, 1837), Tom. II, lib. I, tit. 13 (hereafter cited as Devoti); Gasparri, *De Sacra Ordinatione,* n. 549; Wernz, II, n. 124.

18 Boenninghausen, Fasc. III, p. 167.

19 Reiffenstuel, lib. I, tit. 18, n. 17.

20 Schmalzgrueber, lib. I, tit. 18, n. 3.

21 Schmalzgrueber, *loc. cit.*

22 Boenninghausen, Fasc. III, p. 167.

23 N. (123. 17).

24 Schmalzgrueber, lib. I, tit. 18, n. 6.

reason of some allegiance other than absolute servitude. In certain localities, particularly in Germany, these were called *Leibeigene.*[25]

Authors who made a distinction between the *adscriptitii* properly so called and the *Leibeigne* were in agreement that the latter were not to be ordained, but the former could be ordained under the condition set by Justinian.[26] There was also an opinion which, in not positing any distinction, maintained absolutely that an *adscriptitius* was not to be ordained.[27] This disagreement in interpretation among the authors made the impediment doubtful relative to slaves of the soil, nevertheless there was an opinion which, irrespective of the existence of any impediment, regarded the condition of such slaves as repugnant to the clerical state.[28]

Children, although under the power of their father, were held not to need the consent of their parent in order to receive Sacred Orders lawfully, in spite of what the civil laws may have demanded to the contrary.[29]

The institute of slavery with each succeeding generation was becoming more and more nearly extinct, and correspondingly the legislation remained unmodified.[30]

B. CANONICAL COMMENTARY—"SERVI, SERVITUTE PROPRIE DICTA ANTE ACCEPTAM LIBERTATEM"

1. *Duties of Clerics—In General*

The present Code has restated many of the duties of the clerics. Through ordination an individual is singled out for that service which is necessary in the governing of the faithful and in the ministry of divine worship.[31] A cleric is bound by a special obligation to show reverence and obedience to his ordinary.[32] A

---

[25] Pirhing, lib. I, tit. 18, n. 8.

[26] Cf. Pirhing, *loc. cit.;* Schmalzgrueber, *ibid.,* nn. 2 & 6.

[27] Reiffenstuel, lib. I, tit. 18, n. 15; Boenninghausen, Fasc. III, p. 167, footnote.

[28] Gasparri, *De Sacra Ordinatione,* n. 549.

[29] Schmalzgrueber, lib. I, tit. 18, n. 5; Boenninghausen, Fasc. III, p. 168.

[30] Devoti, Tom. II, lib. I, tit. 13, n. 4; Wernz, II, n. 124.

[31] Canon 948.

[32] Canon 127.

man who has received Orders is obliged to fulfill faithfully whatever duties have been committed to him by his ordinary.[33] Every cleric is forbidden to occupy himself with lucrative trading, whether this is done for his own personal gain or for the gain of others.[34]

Such duties and prohibitions necessarily presuppose a freedom in one's action which is incompatible with a condition of servitude or slavery. A slave suffers a defect in his liberty;[35] it is because of this that he is impeded in the reception of Orders, and not because of his lowly state in life.[36] As St. Thomas says: "In susceptione ordinis mancipatur homo divinis officiis. Et quia nullus potest alteri dare quod suum non est; ideo servus, qui non habet potestatem sui, non potest ad ordines promoveri."[37]

2. *Slavery*

a. Definition

Slavery, in general, may be defined as that state of existence in which a person is subjected in the exercise of his bodily faculties to the commands of others. Slavery, as an institute, has taken its origin from man, and was supposedly justified on the eventualities of war.[38]

Among the Romans it was argued that since a prisoner of war could be put to death, he could also be deprived of his personal liberty and therefore be subjected to complete slavery. Such argumentation was an attempt to justify the conflict between the law of the people (*ius gentium*) and the natural law (*ius naturae.*)[39] The personality of a slave was at times denied, so that he was regarded as a mere chattel with no rights or duties.

[33] Canon 128.

[34] Canon 142.

[35] Cappello, *De Sacra Ordinatione,* n. 522.

[36] C. 4, 5, 7, D. LIV.

[37] *Summa Theologica* (5 vols., Taurini: Marietti, 1938), V, *Supplementum Tertiae Partis,* q. XXXIX, art. 3.

[38] I. (1. 5); D. (1. 1) 4; (1. 5) 4.

[39] I. (1. 3) 2:—"Servitus est constitutio iuris gentium qua quis domino alieno contra naturam subiicitur."

He could be bought, sold, injured or destroyed, as if he were a dumb animal. This is slavery in its extremes.[40]

A slave in the exercise of his bodily faculties is subject to a command which is foreign to his own will. The execution of his own desires can in no way interfere with the desires and the needs of his master. The will of the slave indeed can defy all direct control by man, but it cannot escape its indirect curtailment when the faculties of the body are needed in and for the fruition of its acts.

b. Division

Slavery, as it has been defined above, can be considered according to a twofold general division. One part of this general division is " slavery properly so called," and the other part is " slavery improperly so called." Slavery in its strict sense may be defined as that state in which a person is completely and directly subjected in the exercise of his bodily faculties to the will of his owner.[41] This subjugation does not necessarily demand that the slave be considered, either in law or in fact, as a mere chattel, as a piece of property without any rights or duties. It is not necessary for the verification of slavery properly so called that the slave can be bought and sold as one would buy and sell a horse.[42]

Such a condition of slavery is servitude in its vilest form, as it was prevalent among the Romans of very early times. If the ownership of the bodily faculties of a slave and of the fruits of his labor belongs to another, then there is present slavery properly so called. If, by reason of ownership, a slave can be told to go and he must go, to come and he must come, to do this and he must do it, regardless of the nature of the command, then he is a slave properly so called as opposed to a free person.[43]

---

[40] Buckland, *Roman Law of Slavery* (Cambridge: University Press, 1908), p. 2.

[41] Augustine, *A Commentary on the New Code of Canon Law* (8 vols. [Vol. IV, 1. ed., Vol. V, 2. ed.], St. Louis: Herder, 1919–1924), IV, 499; V, 234 (hereafter cited as Augustine).

[42] Cappello, *De Sacra Ordinatione,* n. 522.

[43] Cf. Blat, III, pars I, n. 359.

Slavery improperly so called may be defined as that state in which a person is indirectly subjected in the exercise of his bodily faculties to the commands of another, without however having lost his status as a free person. Such a subjugation may be predicated of various groups.

There were the *adscriptitii* or *glebae addicti.*[44] These were persons who were attached to a certain piece of property, or to an estate, in such a manner that they could be sold only with the property itself. They were only indirectly subjected to the land-owner. They tilled the soil, took care of the estate, but were in no way obligated to assume other obligations or duties. In the law which admitted of such an institute the *adscriptitii* were considered as free men.[45]

Children who were born of *adscriptitii* were called *originarii.* The term "*originarii*" referred only to one's origin, and not to one's free state. The children of parents who were *adscriptitii* were in law like their parents.[46]

The *servi poenae* constituted another group which belonged to the institute of slavery improperly so called. They were those persons who, because of some crime which they had committed, were placed in a prison. According to some authors they were impeded from the reception of Orders.[47] Among the slaves improperly so called some authors also included those persons who had lent themselves out for hire for a certain period of time, and they maintained that they were impeded from the reception of Orders. These were called *famuli conductitii.*[48]

The institute of *servi ecclesiae* has disappeared from the Church. Children who have not been emancipated can in only a very wide and loose use of the term be compared to slaves improperly so called, namely, inasmuch as they are subject to the reasonable commands of their parents.[49]

[44] Cf. Schmalzgrueber, lib. I, tit. 18, nn. 1, 2; Gasparri, *De Sacra Ordinatione,* n. 549; Vermeersch-Creusen, II, n. 259.

[45] Gasparri, *De Sacra Ordinatione,* n. 549.

[46] Gasparri, *loc. cit.*

[47] E.g., Boenninghausen, Fasc. III, p. 167.

[48] Cf. Boenninghausen, *loc. cit.,* Gasparri, *De Sacra Ordinatione,* n. 545; Blat, III, pars I, n. 359.

[49] Boenninghausen, Fasc. III, p. 168; Wernz-Vidal, IV, pars I, n. 260.

c. Application

The institute of slavery has for the most part disappeared, although it may still be found in some remote localities. Although a person may through force, fear, etc., be under the domination of another, and thus be treated as a slave, slavery does not exist as an impediment to Orders, unless such a condition can be substantiated by an appeal to the civil laws which admit the existence of slavery in the locality in which the appeal must be made. For such a person, when he was given the opportunity to assert his freedom, could maintain his assertion through the judgment of the civil courts.

Is it necessary that the term "slave" or "slavery" be found in the laws of the state before an impediment to Orders could exist in that state? If the phrase "*proprie dicta*," as it is given in the canon, were used not only to specify the kind of slavery as it is understood by common usage, but also to signify an element of the impediment needing recognition by the civil law, then the absence of the term "slavery" in the civil law could imply also the absence of the impediment to Orders. But the phrase "*proprie dicta*" does not depend for its interpretation on the actual use of the term "slave" or "slavery" in the civil law. If the effects of the status on an individual are the same as the effects of "slavery properly so called," as it has been defined above, and these effects are justified in civil law, then the impediment which is based on slavery properly so called exists in the individual who is subjected to such effects.

Prior to the present Code the general law implied in effect that slaves were not to be ordained. The specification of this prohibition was to a great extent left to the commentators, who, as history shows, were not in agreement. The present Code specifies the impediment to Orders which derives from slavery by means of the phrase "*servi servitute proprie dicta.*" Therefore the servile status of an individual makes it necessary that he be considered as bound by the impediment only when he is a slave properly so called. From this it can be concluded that servitude improperly so called does not bring a person within the sphere of the impediment as mentioned in canon 987, 4°.

Although in an individual case a candidate could be rejected from the reception of Orders if he were a slave improperly so called, his rejection would not be occasioned by the impediment of slavery, but by the judgment of the ordinary who decided that the candidate lacked the qualifications necessary to perform the functions of the sacred ministry.

Adscriptitii, originarii, servi poenae, famuli conductitii and *filii* do not come under the extension of the impediment enacted in canon 987, 4°. *Adscriptitii* and *originarii* as classes of slaves have completely disappeared.[50] *Servi poenae* under the laws of civilized countries are not slaves properly so called, although it is not beyond the realm of possibility that some nations or peoples may treat them as such. If civil laws were of such a nature that they reduced one who is imprisoned for some crime, or one who has been captured as an enemy in the prosecution of a war, to the state of slavery, such a one would be impeded from the reception of Orders.

It is not the professed purpose of this work to argue against the supposed justice of such an enslavement. The Church has constantly noted and consistently opposed the injustice of all forms of slavery, but there were times when She could not openly condemn all unjustifiable distinction of classes without enkindling a social and economic revolution.[51] Under such circumstances no one could ever plead the non-existence of the impediment simply on the grounds that the slavery was unjust. However, incarnation, and generally also the infamy which is connected with the status of a *servus poenae*, is sufficient in itself to exclude one from the reception of Orders.[52]

Those whose labor has been hired for a certain period of time are bound by the virtue of justice to fulfill the condition of a just contract into which they have freely entered. Although such an obligation does not place the obligated person under the impediment which is here under consideration, a request for

---

[50] Gasparri, *De Sacra Ordinatione*, n. 549.

[51] McKenna, "The Mystical Body in the Social and Political Sphere"—*The American Ecclesiastical Review* (formerly *The Ecclesiastical Review*), (Philadelphia, 1889–1943; Baltimore, 1944–), CIII (1940), 210.

[52] Gasparri, *De Sacra Ordinatione*, n. 545.

ordination could not be granted until the just contract had been fulfilled. Prior to the Code Boenninghausen (1825–1867), in appealing to the demands of justice, considered as impeded from the reception of Orders those who had hired their labors to another.[53] His conclusion can be admitted today, but not in the sense that a simple impediment is present.

Children can be admitted to the reception of Orders without the consent of their parents. This has been the constant teaching of the Church. The choice of a state of life does not depend on the parental consent.[54] The civil law is not competent to demand the consent of the parents when a child wishes to enter the clerical life. If the civil law does demand such consent, there is no obligation to follow the law. It is, however, prudent to consult the parents and to try to obtain their consent, in order that the possibility of any future civil litigations may be forestalled.[55]

C. CESSATION OF THE IMPEDIMENT—"POST ACCEPTAM LIBERTATEM"

Since slavery properly so called depends for its existence on the written and unwritten law of the land, it is necessary to consult the scope of these laws for determining the various forms of liberation (*manumissio*) which will have the legal effect of freeing the person from the state of slavery. The condition of slavery properly so called will make the slave subject to the juridical effect of the impediment as enacted in canon 987, 4°, and this subjection will continue until the slave has obtained his freedom.

The nature of this freedom is not specifically determined in the canon. However, a consideration of the entire legislation on this impediment substantiates the statement that absolute and full

---

[53] *De Irregularitatibus,* Fasc. III, p. 167.

[54] C. 12, X, *de regularibus et transeuntibus ad religionem,* III, 31: "Tunc enim, quia liberum habet arbitrium, in electione propositi sequi parentum non cogitur voluntatem." Cf. Schmalzgrueber, lib. I, tit. 18, n. 4; Schmier, *Iurisprudentia Canonicocivilis* (2 vols., Venetiis, 1754), I, lib. I, tract. 4, cap. 6, n. 579 (hereafter cited as Schmier); Boenninghausen, Fasc. III, p. 168.

[55] Wernz-Vidal, IV, pars I, n. 260.

liberty or freedom is not necessary. A person of course cannot be a slave properly so called and at the same time be a free person. But if a person is considered by the law to be free, then any servile condition under which he may simultaneously exist can only effect a condition of slavery improperly so called. Therefore when freedom is granted a slave upon certain licit and honorable conditions as placed by the master, the freed slave is no longer bound by the impediment. This was the accepted doctrine and practice in the former law.[56] But for the present such a practice should not be invoked without a previous consultation of the Holy See, since a mitigated form of slavery which correspondingly points to but a partial possession of freedom will hardly leave it possible for an ordained person to enlist his activities unreservedly under the authority of his ordinary.

Ordination, even to the priesthood, does not necessarily effect full freedom for the slave. The effect of ordination on a slave, relative to his servile condition, must be determined by the civil law, since it is civil law which permits the institute of slavery, and not the ecclesiastical or the divine law. In the pre-Code law freedom from slavery could be effected by ordination inasmuch as the civil law permitted this form of liberation. An appeal to this earlier law in virtue of canon 6, 3°, would not be justified in order to obtain such a liberation, unless the basis for this form of liberation, namely the civil law, has continued unchanged. Until the status of an ordained slave has been changed from the status of a slave properly so called to at least that of a slave only improperly so called, he cannot licitly receive further Orders or even exercise the Orders which he has already received.[57]

A slave who flees to a country which offers him protection from the injustice of slavery, and grants him citizenship, so that his deportation may no longer be effected, can be ordained. It is beyond the power of the unjust law of slavery to bind him in this case. Slaves who have been freed from servitude through an abrogation of the law which previously permitted the existence

---

[56] C. 10, D. LIV.

[57] Canon 968.

of the institute of slavery may likewise be ordained. Such a case could have been verified with the abolition of slavery as it was effected in the United States upon the close of its war between the States.

D. DISPENSATION FROM THE IMPEDIMENT

A dispensation from this impediment will rarely, if ever, be granted. A petition for such a dispensation will necessarily come from a locality in which the institute of slavery exists. Before the Holy See will grant such a dispensation, a complete explanation of the law of the land should be given. If the law of the land permitted the attainment of freedom by one who was ordained, the Church would not be averse to granting a dispensation in the presence of a still existing state of slavery. If ordination to the priesthood, diaconate or subdiaconate effected freedom, then the Church, in her well-founded expectation of this liberation, would under such favorable conditions grant a dispensation for the reception of minor Orders. The law of the country must be thoroughly consulted in each and every case, for in this matter the Church will not grant a dispensation when as a result of it there can readily arise an occasion which would involve either a person in ecclesiastical authority, or also the beneficiary of her granted dispensation, within the toils of the civil law.

CHAPTER III

ON CIVIC AND CONTRACTUAL OBLIGATIONS

Article I. Military Service

A. Historical Synopsis

In the present day legislation those who are bound by civil law to ordinary military service cannot be ordained licitly until they have completed this service.[1] Civil law governing such service, even for seminarians, is of rather modern origin. Because of this no mention of this impediment can be found in the earlier ecclesiastical legislation.[2]

Although the reason for the present day legislation regarding those who are obligated to ordinary military service is different from the reason which prompted the ancient impediment which forbade the ordination of soldiers, as a historical background a consideration of the latter may be of some help. Soldiers actually engaged in war were not to be promoted to the clerical state. In the I Provincial Council of Toledo (400) a law was passed which forbade any one who had been a soldier to receive the dignity of the diaconate.[3] Unless a dispensation had been granted[4] a soldier was not to be raised to the clerical state.[5]

Legislative enactments on the impediments of slavery and on the impediment arising from the obligation of rendering an account in secular affairs can be regarded as laws enacted "*in similibus*," and accordingly help to illustrate the historical background in the perspective of which the future laws on the present matter were enacted.[6]

[1] Canon 987, 5°.

[2] Wernz-Vidal, IV, n. 261.

[3] Can. 8—Mansi, III, 1013; c. 4, D. LI.

[4] *Glossa Ordinaria* ad c. 4, D. LI, s. v. *si ad clericum admissus fuerit.*

[5] C. 1, D. LI (Pope Innocent I to the bishops gathered in a Synod at Toledo, a. 404); JK, n. 292.

[6] Cf. c. L, D. LIII, ". . . Qui militiae vel rationibus sunt publicis obligati

During the last half of the nineteenth century compulsory military training made its appearance in the civil legislation of Italy. It was binding on all regardless of their clerical or religious standing or aspiration. Pius IX (1846–1878)[7] deplored this encroachment on the immunity of clerics by the secular powers.[8] Realizing the dire consequences of trying to circumvent the civil authorities, and mindful of the dignity of the priestly and the religious life, the Pope instructed the bishops of Italy to postpone the conferral of Sacred Orders until the completion of the compulsory military training.[9]

Doubts arose concerning the obligatory force of this instruction. When asked the Sacred Congregation of the Holy Office replied that it was preceptive and not merely directive.[10] This instruction was considered to oblige only the bishops of Italy, as it was sent only to them, and promulgated only in Italy. For the bishops of other countries it remained directive.[11]

In territories where it was permissible to defer the fulfillment of this military service until one had reached the age of twenty-six, the bishop could licitly ordain a young man to the priesthood, but it was advised even in this case not to ordain him until the service had been completed.[12] One who was rejected from military service could be ordained, all other things being considered, provided that there was no danger of his rejection being revoked.[13]

The Superiors General of the various communities of Regu-

. . . qui seculis actionibus implicati sunt, in clero ecclesiae prepropere suscipiendi non sunt . . ." (Pope Gregory the Great, a. 598); JE, n. 1497. Cf. also c. 1, 2, 3, C. XXI, q. 3; c. 5, 6, C. XXIII, q. 8.

[7] *Allocutio Pii IX,* 15 mart. 1875—*Acta Sanctae Sedis* (41 vols., Romae, 1865–1908), VIII (1874), 301 (hereafter cited as *ASS*).

[8] On the immunity of clerics cf. Schmalzgrueber, lib. III, tit. 49, n. 9 sq.; Cavagnis, *Institutiones Iuris Publici Ecclesiastici* (2. ed., 2 vols., Romae, 1888), II, 63 sq.; Wernz, II, n. 167.

[9] S. C. S. Off., instr. 16 sept. 1875—*ASS,* XXIII (1890), 44–48; *Fontes,* n. 1045.

[10] S. C. S. Off., 1 sept. 1904—*ASS,* XXXVII (1904), 238–239; *Fontes,* n. 1274.

[11] Gasparri, *De Sacra Ordinatione,* n. 542.

[12] S. C. S. Off., instr. 16 sept. 1875—*ASS,* XXIII (1890), 44–48; *Fontes,* n. 1045.

[13] *Loc. cit.*

lars in Italy were also instructed to postpone solemn profession and admission to Sacred Orders until the imposed military service had been completed.[14] Candidates were required to take simple vows for only six months at the end of their novitiate. This six month period was to be repeated until the danger of summons for military service had passed, or the candidate had been called into service.[15] A later decree changed this, so that the candidate took simple vows which extended up to the time of his call into service.[16] When the religious received his call for service the vows immediately ceased. On his return to the religious life the candidate was to take simple vows for a three year period preceding solemn profession.[17] In congregations, where only simple vows were taken, perpetual profession was forbidden until the imposed military service had been completed.[18]

Definite rules were enacted for the Superiors in their watching over the candidates who were called to military service.[19] Every bishop was obliged to make prudent and diligent inquiries into the life of the candidate for Orders, but more especially if he had been a soldier, even though there existed no irregularity arising from homicide.[20]

When an individual had finished his *ordinary* military service of one, three or five years, the civil authorities placed him on the reserved list. Such a one was bound to take part in the yearly military exhibition which lasted for a short time. Such services did not impede one from the reception of Sacred Orders.[21]

To ordain an individual prior to his call to military service, and then to send him to a missionary country where such services were not demanded by the civil authorities was decided not to

---

[14] S. C. de Religiosis, decr. 1 ian. 1911—*Fontes,* 4407.

[15] *AAS,* II (1910), 60–62.

[16] S. C. de Religiosis, decr. 1 ian. 1911—*Fontes,* 4407.

[17] *ASS,* II (1910), 60–62.

[18] S. C. de Religiosis, decr. 1 ian. 1911—*Fontes,* n. 4407.

[19] *Loc. cit.*

[20] Gasparri, *De Sacra Ordinatione,* n. 541.

[21] Vermeersch, "Annotationes," n. 2—*Periodica de Re Canonica et Morali utili praesertim Religiosis et Missionariis* (Brugis, 1905–; ab anno 1927; *Periodica de Re Canonica, Morali, Liturgica*) V (1913), 284.

be illicit, but it was counselled that it should not (*non expedit*) be done.[22]

Throughout the official instructions on the subject of military service reference is made only to the reception of Sacred Orders, so that the conferral of tonsure and minor Orders was not prohibited in view of the mandatory future military service.[23]

Civil laws demanding ordinary military service were the product of European countries. Particular ecclesiastical laws relative to ordination were enacted for coping with the newly occasioned situation. Individuals bound by such laws were not to be raised to Sacred Orders. Under the present Code of Canon Law the prohibition is universal. It extends to the reception of tonsure and the minor Orders as well as the reception of major Orders.[24]

B. CANONCAL COMMENTARY—QUI AD ORDINARIUM MILITARE SERVITIUM CIVILI LEGE ADSTRINGUNTUR, ANTEQUAM ILLUD EXPLEVERINT

1. *Preliminary Consideration—Clerical Immunity*

The present Code of Canon Law enacts positive legislation on the immunity of the cleric:

Clerici omnes a servitio militari . . . immunes sunt.[25]

History shows that the Church has always opposed any legislation that would disregard clerical immunity, and particularly any legislation that would endanger clerical freedom from compulsory military training.[26]

In some countries, particularly in Europe, this right of the cleric has not always been respected. In order to offset some of this disrespect and disregard for the immunity of the cleric, positive law forbids the cleric voluntarily to take up military

[22] S. C. super Statu Regularium, 22 iul. 1901—*ASS*, XXXV (1902), 253.

[23] Wernz, II, n. 126.

[24] Canon 987, 3o.

[25] Canon 121.

[26] For a further study of clerical immunity, cf. Downs, *The Concept of Clerical Immunity*, The Catholic University of America Canon Law Studies, n. 126 (Washington, D. C.: The Catholic University of America Press, 1941) (hereafter cited as Downs).

service at any time without the permission of his own ordinary, even if he wishes to do so for the purpose of freeing himself more quickly from the obligation of compulsory military service.[27] If a cleric violates this law, he by that very fact renounces whatever office he may have.[28] A cleric in minor Orders loses his clerical status by the very fact that he violates the law which prohibits his enlistment in the military service.[29] Added to the above legislation, the Church has also enacted a law which prohibits from the reception of Orders all those who are bound by civil law to undergo a period of ordinary military service. This law is expressed in canon 987, 5°.

2. *Military Service*

a. Definition

Military service signifies that state of life in which as a soldier one is subordinated to the mandates of the military authorities of a country for the purpose of achieving a preparedness in the eventuality of war, or a trained fitness in the time of war. A soldier is bound out of his devotion to duty to obey the licit commands of his superior officer. Such obedience curtails the freedom of action which is generally connected with civilian life. History shows that the life of a soldier occasions many spiritual dangers. These dangers are not absent even in time of peace. A soldier is taught the modern methods of waging war and of violently counteracting all hostile attacks, all of which tends to dull his appreciation for the commands and the counsels of the Eternal Priest in whose service a cleric aspires to consecrate has activity.

b. Species

1° Ordinary Military Service

There are various kinds of military service. One is *ordinary* military service.[30] Ordinary military service may be defined as

[27] Canon 141, § 1.

[28] Canon 188, 6°.

[29] Canon 141, § 1.

[30] Canon 987, 5°: "ordinarium militare servitium."

that military training which must be taken by one who, through the preceptive force of law, has been called, generally for the first time, to such a service for a definite period of time. The obligation of undergoing such military training may arise either from a direct law which makes it compulsory, or from a voluntary enlistment which, once one has entered upon it, demands a service for a certain period of time.[31]

This ordinary military service, according to the practice of those nations which demand this service, generally is to be rendered once, whereupon the obligation ceases. However, it is not beyond the realm of possibility that a nation may demand this service the first time for the period of a year, and later again for another year after a period of civilian life has intervened. In such a situation both terms of military service would be included under the phrase "ordinary military service." The laws of each state or nation must be consulted if one is to know what must be included under this phrase.[32]

An attempt has been made by some legislators and authors to determine from the laws of the various states the period of time specified for the ordinary military service. It is said to extend from one to three years.[33] However, it is impossible to determine the specific amount of time by way of a general norm, for the duration of the time will be determined by each state in accord with its particular law.

The purpose underlying such military service generally is this: to offer a basic training in military technique, so that in the event of war the state will not be entirely unprepared. This service is a peace-time measure. Its execution may however coincide also with the time of war.

When the law of a state or of a nation demands such ordinary military service, then the one who is subject to the fulfillment of the law is automatically also subject to the contraction of a simple impediment which bars him from the reception of Orders. Since one who enlists becomes bound to ordinary mili-

[31] Wernz-Vidal, IV, pars I, n. 261.

[32] Cappello, *De Sacra Ordinatione,* n. 523.

[33] Cf. S. C. de Religiosis, decr. 1 ian. 1911—*Fontes,* n. 4407; Cappello, *De Sacra Ordinatione,* n. 523.

tary service, such a pact, if enforceable by law, makes the ordinary military service to be at least indirectly obligatory by law, and therefore places the enlisted person under the impediment. Ordinary military service has also been referred to as *active* service.[34]

A civil law which demands ordinary military service of all men irrespective of their clerical status or religious vocation is unjust.[35] If the law exempts, as it should, seminarians, religious and clerics, then they are not bound by the impediment. When the law permits the postponement of the service of *bona fide* candidates or students for the ministry, as it does in Canada during this present war,[36] it is necessary to determine from the law whether or not the postponement is the equivalent of an exemption, as long as the student is studying for the ministry. If this postponement is an exemption which attains its complete force when and if the student becomes an ordained minister or priest, then the impediment does not exist. In the United States the students of the ministry enjoy immunity from military service, even in time of war. The guaranty of this immunity is not contained in the Constitution; rather it is based on the grant of Congress, which is acting in accordance with a traditional American policy of deference to one's holy calling.[37]

Prior to the Code the prohibition from the reception of Orders as deriving from the obligation of ordinary military service extended only to the reception of Sacred Orders, and not to tonsure and the minor Orders. Furthermore, the prohibition as a law was not of universal obligation. Under the present Code, however, the impediment extends as a law to the Universal Church and prohibits the reception of tonsure as well as the minor Orders. The simple impediments to Orders affect the licitness of any and every sacred ordination.[38] But in the law "sacred ordination" refers to tonsure and the minor Orders as well as to the major

[34] Cf. S. C. de Religiosis, decr. 1 ian, 1911—*Fontes*, n. 4407.

[35] S. C. Const. decr. "*Redeuntibus*," 25 oct. 1918: "lex iniusta"; "grave vulnus ecclesiasticae disciplinae" *AAS*, X (1918), 481.

[36] *The Jurist* (Washington, D. C., 1941–) IV (1944), 175.

[37] *The Jurist*, III (1943), 633.

[38] Canon 968, § 1.

Orders.[39] Ayrinhac nevertheless states that *regularly* men who are bound by the civil law to military service may not receive any Orders, *particularly* Sacred Orders, till they have served their regular time, unless they have been dispensed, or until they have been discharged unconditionally.[40] The use of the terms " regularly " and " particularly " could occasion some doubt as to the extension of the impediment. In virtue of the definitions and statements contained in canon 945, 950, and 968, § 1, the Code leaves no room at all for any doubt.

Although one may be obligated by the law to undergo a period of ordinary military service, if the provisions of the law state that the seminarians, religious and clerics are called only for the care of the sick, either in hospital duty or in ambulance work, then the ones who are subject exclusively to the rendering of this kind of service would not be bound by the impediment.[41]

Military service in its strict sense refers to the occupation of a soldier in his capacity of a soldier, which is directly ordered to actual combat, and not to the care of those who have been wounded.[42] The same conclusion can be made relative to those who are called exclusively for the care of the spiritual needs, such as the chaplains, or the chaplains' aides, whose exclusive work is that of preparing the chapel, the altar, the articles for Mass, etc. At least there is a probable doubt whether the impediment which derives from the ordinary military service extends to them, so that in virtue of canon 15, the impediment would not affect them.[43]

If the law which demands ordinary military service is promulgated after one has received Orders, then the one bound by such a law cannot licitly exercise the Orders which he has received.[44] A civil law of this nature which in its implied consequences occasions for an ordained cleric the prohibition to exercise his

---

[39] Canon 949–950.

[40] *Legislation on the Sacraments*, p. 373.

[41] Cappello, *De Sacra Ordinatione*, n. 523; Ayrinhac, *Legislation on the Sacraments*, pp. 373–374.

[42] Claeys Bouuaert-Simenon, *Manuale Iuris Canonici* (3 vols. [Vol. I, 3. ed., 1930, Vol. II, 2. ed., 1935], Gandae et Leodii: Seminarium Gandavense et Leodiense), I, nn. 279; 301 (hereafter cited as Claeys Bouuaert-Simenon).

[43] Cf. Cappello, *De Sacra Ordinatione*, n. 523; Downs, p. 44.

[44] Canon 968, § 2.

Orders would necessarily bring about a serious hardship. If there were present a danger of grave harm through any delay in the granting of the needed dispensation and at the same time the Holy See could be approached only with difficulty, then the ordinary could use the dispensatory faculties which canon 81 accords to him under these limited conditions, for it is the usual practice of the Holy See to grant a dispensation under such circumstances.

It is not necessary that one be actually called into service before one becomes subject to the juridical effect of this impediment; it suffices that one be subject to the law which authorizes the call to service. Even if one could finish his theological studies and be ordained to the priesthood before the call to service would actually be put into effect, still one could not receive tonsure or any Orders if one perhaps will be called to the service.[45]

2° Extraordinary Military Service

The term "extraordinary" is used to designate another kind of military service. This service may be defined as that which is necesary for the preservation of the state in the time of war. Thus, in the present World War II, if the authorities of a belligerent country passed a law which obliged even seminarians, religious and clerics to subject themselves to military service, they would be bound by *extraordinary* military service. This kind of military service does not give rise to the impediment of canon 987, 5°. The ordinary, *as far as the impediment of military service is concerned,* could continue to ordain his subjects even though the one ordained would be called the next day. However, the Ordinary in all probability would refrain from ordaining such individuals because of the many dangers both spiritual and corporal which are lurking on all sides at a time of war, especially for the combatants.

3° Periodical Military Service

The third type of military service is known as *periodical* serv-

[45] Cf. Pontificia Commissio ad Codicis Iuris Canonici Canones authentice Intepretandos, 2-3 iun. 1918 (hereafter cited as P. C. I.)—*AAS*, X (1918), 344.

ice. It may be defined as that service which, after the ordinary military service has been completed, is demanded on several days or weeks out of each year for the purpose of keeping the nation prepared for war, or of making a public manifestation of the military strength and discipline of the armed forces.[46] This may be called a program of action which is undertaken for the purpose of refreshing the members in military technique. As a general rule, this type of service does not continue more than a few weeks. Periodical service is not included under the scope of the impediment listed in canon 987, 5°.[47] Nevertheless, any law which demands such a service of clerics is a violation of the immunity of the clergy.

4° The National Guard

In the United States of America a unique organization exists. It is the union of many sovereign states. Each state can make its own laws except in those matters which have been delegated to the national legislature; or forbidden by the Federal Constitution of the United States.[48] The power of a state to enact a law which would demand ordinary military service of all the men of a particular group is among the powers prohibited by the Federal Constitution. The individual states are forbidden to keep troops of war in time of peace.[49]

However, during the time of peace each state has the authority to maintain a state police force which forms part of the National Guard.[50] If one enlists in this organization he is bound to render periodical service according to the laws of each individual state.

This periodical training can be called military only in a wide sense of the term. Under the present organization of the United

---

[46] Cf. Cappello, *De Sacra Ordinatione*, n. 523.

[47] Cappello, *De Sacra Ordinatione*, n. 523; Ayrinhac, *Legislation on the Sacraments*, p. 373.

[48] Article X, Bill of Rights, Federal Constitution. Cf. Robinson, *Elementary Law* (New Edition, Boston: Little, Brown and Company, 1910), nn. 413–414 (hereafter cited as Robinson).

[49] *The Constitution of the United States of America*, Art. I, sect. 8, §§ 11, 12, 14, 15, 16, 18; sect. 10, § 3.

[50] *The Encyclopedia Americana* (30 vols., ed. 1943, New York: Americana Corporation), XIX, s. v. *National Guard.*

States there is a distinction between membership in the army and membership in the National Guard, as there exists a distinction between policeman and soldier. A member of the National Guard may be called a soldier, but according to the strict sense of the word a soldier is a man of war, and the individual state cannot keep troops of war during peace time, although they can keep members in the National Guard.

The primary purpose of the state police force or of the National Guard is to keep peace among individuals and imperfect societies, so that the tranquility of the perfect society may be maintained. The primary purpose of the army, however, is the maintenance or the procurement of that peace which should exist among perfect societies, between states. Even in the organization of the army there is a specific group whose purpose is to keep order among the soldiers. The members are referred to as the military police.

In the United States the National Guard in each state can be called to defend the corporate states of the union, but the mere fact of membership in the National Guard does not make the members a part of the regular army. This call to service in defense of the corporate states is not automatic, but depends on the command of the authority of the United States.[51]

The periodical training which is demanded in the National Guard would not subject one to the impediment which arises from compulsory ordinary military training. In the event that compulsory ordinary military service becomes effective in the United States, the suggestion has been made that this service might be fulfilled by periodical service in the National Guard.[52] If this suggestion were incorporated into the law which would demand compulsory ordinary military service, then the periodical service in the National Guard would become ordinary military service and would give rise to the impediment. The purpose of the National Guard would thus become directly twofold, the maintenance of peace in the individual states, and the preparedness to

[51] *The Constitution of the United States of America*, Art. I, sect. 8, §§ 15–16; Art. II, sect. 2, § 1.

[52] Cf. Reilly, *Compulsory Military Training* (Washington, D. C.: Civilian Military Education Fund, 1940), p. 20 (this is a pamphlet).

maintain peace for the United States. Under the present law the former is the direct purpose, while the latter is only an indirect purpose, depending on the command of the authority of the United States.

The danger to a religious vocation may of course be considerably lessened in view of the demand of the specific periodical fulfillment of the law by way of service in the National Guard, but it would not be entirely removed, and hence the impediment would still exist in such a situation. A dispensation would be necesary for one who was still bound to undergo this service, even if the periodical fulfillment was confined to the summer months when the regular course of seminary studies is interrupted.

C. CESSATION OF THE IMPEDIMENT

The cessation of the obligation which demands ordinary military service can be accomplished in various ways. The more common way is indicated in canon 987, 5°, with the words "*antequam illud expleverint.*" Primarily these words express the duration of the impediment as it affects the individual. However, the idea conveyed by these words can also be expressed in another way. Once an individual has complied with the law which demands ordinary military training, he is no longer under the effects of the impediment.

The law of each state which makes ordinary military service compulsory must be specifically considered. If the law demands a service of but one year, then, after the year's service has been completed according to the norms of the civil law, the impediment ceases. If two, three or five years are demanded, then, after two, three or five years of service have been finished, the individual who has served the necessary time is by that very fact freed from the impediment.

The official declaration of the civil authorities, namely, to the effect that a person is not bound by the law, is another means whereby it can be established that the effects of the impediment no longer are present. This declaration may be prompted in view of the inability of the person either to begin or to continue the military service as imposed by the law. This discharge or rejection must be permanent, otherwise the individual will continue to be bound by the impediment. If the rejection or the discharge is given under the condition that the individual must submit to another examination within a certain period of time, then the impediment will continue to bind him.[53] Since it is the civil authority which has imposed the obligation, it is its exclusive right to declare the cessation of the obligation.

Deferment because of nonage does not remove the impediment, for as long as one is *liable* to military service the impediment continues.[54] If the law is applicable only within a certain age limit, then the attainment of the maximum age will free one from the military service, and consequently also from the impediment. One's liability to military service must be based on an existing law, and not on the mere possibility of the enactment of a law which would demand ordinary military service, or even on the assured prospect of the enactment of a law which might perhaps make such a demand. When there is no law, there is no liability which in any way can be related to the impediment. The impediment, to be such, can arise only from an actual liability to ordinary military service as implemented by law.

The impediment can also cease of itself by the forthright exemption granted to seminarians, religious and clerics in the law itself, or by the repeal of the entire law which previously imposed the obligation of military service. When states contemplate the passing of a law which will demand ordinary military service during peace time, then it is the duty of all ordinaries to protect the immunity of the clergy, and to bring to the civil authorities a correct appreciation and understanding of this clerical right of exemption. There will be states which will turn a deaf ear to all the pleas for clerical immunity, and which will demand ordinary military service even of clerics. The Church realized this. In consequence it has enacted the impediment now under consideration. In states which demand this military training of all, irrespective of their religious vocation, the ordinary must demand an authentic document which will attest the freedom of the candidate for Orders from the impediment.

---

[53] P. C. I., 3 iun. 1918—*AAS*, X (1918), 344.

[54] *Loc. cit.*

When the impediment has been removed by the fulllment of the required service, a record of the time and the place of the fulfillment should be carefully kept, and then submitted to the ordinary by the candidate for Orders. There has been no definite instruction on the manner in which the ordinary should inquire into the life of the seminarian, or of the cleric who has returned from fulfilling his *ordinary* military training. However, the ordinary should be guided in his inquiries by the decree of the Sacred Congregation for Religious, "*Inter Reliquas*," of January 1, 1911,[55] which is still obligatory for religious superiors,[56] and by the decree of the Sacred Consistorial Congregation, "*Redeuntibus*" of October 25, 1918.[57] The first of these two decrees was occasioned by those laws which demanded ordinary military service of the religious, and the second was occasioned by the return of clerics from the battlefields of the first World War in 1918, after they had been forced to bear arms.

A seminarian or cleric who has been called for ordinary military service should inform his ordinary of his location in the army, so that the ordinary in turn may notify the ordinary of the place in which the seminarian or cleric is now stationed. The ordinary of the place is to inquire into the life of those clerics and seminarians who have served for at least three months as soldiers in his territory. The proper ordinary is then to be informed of these findings.[58]

The most expeditious manner of fulfilling this obligation is to employ the services of the chaplain or of the pastor of the church which is located near the camp. The cleric or seminarian could be put under obligation to report each month to the chaplain or to the local pastor. The report could then be forwarded to the ordinary of the place, who in turn would send it to the proper ordinary of the cleric or seminarian. This information must be

[55] *Fontes*, n. 4407. The full text of this decree may be consulted in *AAS*, III (1911), 37–39. A summary of the decree is contained in Bouscaren, I, 106–109.

[56] S. C. de Religiosis, declar. 15 iul. 1919—*AAS*, XI (1919), 321–323.

[57] *AAS*, X (1918), 481–486. Translation in Bouscaren, I, 99–104.

[58] Cf. canons 993, 4o; 994.

supplemented by a personal examination conducted by the proper ordinary.[59]

According to the prescriptions of the decree "*Redeuntibus,*" which, as was noted before, was issued at a time when clerics were returning from *extraordinary* military service, clerics in major Orders must present themselves to their ordinary within ten days after their return from military service. Those who fail to do so are to be punished. Priests who return from bearing arms in time of war are bound to the same obligation. Failure on their part to fulfill it entails for them *ipso facto* a suspension *a divinis,* from which they will not be freed unless they have fulfilled the demand which the law has placed upon them.[60] When and if ordinary military training becomes compulsory for seminarians and clerics, the ordinary should enact statutes which will govern the course of action to be followed by the returning men. These statutes should be in conformity with the two decrees which have here been referred to.

D. DISPENSATION FROM THE IMPEDIMENT

As long as the impediment which derives from compulsory ordinary military training exists, one thus bound cannot be ordained, nor can he exercise the already received Orders. The competent Sacred Congregation for the granting of a dispensation from this impediment can be determined from the previous considerations given to dispensations in general.[61]

The cause of religion will be the determining factor in the grant of such a dispensation. If the conditions were such that the postponement of the reception of Orders, or of the exercise of Orders already licitly received, would seriously affect the care of souls, then the Holy See would dispense. This would be the case, for instance, if some enacted law obligated all men from the age of 18 to 30 to undergo a certain period of ordinary military training. Unless a dispensation were granted, the services of a considerably large number of young priests would not be available.

---

[59] Cf. S. C. Const. decr. "*Redeuntibus,*" 25 oct. 1918, n. 10, b—*AAS*, X (1918), 484.

[60] *Ibid.*, n. 1—*AAS*, X (1918), 482-483.

[61] Cf. *supra*, pp. 14-17.

Article II. Secular Affairs Involving the Rendering of an Account

A. Historical Synopsis

St. Paul said: " No one serving as God's soldier entangles himself in worldly affairs." [1] One's freedom in exercising the ministry could be seriously curtailed by the obligations arising from secular pursuits, especially when such offices necessitated the rendering of an account.[2]

Realizing the incompatibility of ecclesiastical and secular offices Pope Innocent I (402–417) enacted definite rules. In a letter to the bishops of Toledo he prohibited those who were actually engaged in a court trial from being enrolled in the ranks of the clergy.[3] This prohibition he also extended to those who were obligated to work in the imperial curia,[4] and to those who were occupied in public functions subject to the scrutiny of the emperor. The reason for the prohibition rested on the ruler's power to call the ones so employed to render an account.[5] While they were subject to such an accounting they were not acknowledged as fit candidates for the reception of Orders.[6] There was, moreover, the frequent probability that the candidate's desire to be ordained rested on his wish to evade his duties.[7]

In the Council of Chalcedon (451) an insight is given into the occupations unbecoming to clerics with particular reference to secular negotiations involving the rendering of an account. It decreed that bishops, clerics and monks could not be involved in secular administrations, unless by law it became necessary to take care of minors, or unless the bishop of the city commanded

[1] II Tim., II, 4.

[2] Wernz-Vidal, IV, pars I, n. 258.

[3] C. 1, D. LI; JK, n. 292.

[4] C. 2, D. LI (written to Bishop Nucerianus); JK, n. 314; cf. *Summa* of St. Raymond, lib. III, tit. 16. *De curialibus et obligatis ad ratiocinia an sint ordinandi vel non.*

[5] C. 3, D. LI (Pope Innocent to the Bishop of Rouen, in 407); JK, n. 286.

[6] IV Provincial Council of Toledo (633), can. 31—Mansi, X, 628; c. 5, D. LIV.

[7] C. 1, D. LIII (Pope Gregory the Great to all the bishops, in 598); JE, n, 1497.

them to look after the orphans and widows. Violation of this law subjected the offender to ecclesiastical correction.[8] Taking care of their own financial affairs was not unbecoming to clerics, but rather was to be preferred to the employment of another for the purpose of taking care of such financial matters.[9]

In the decretal collections there is but one *caput* under the title, *de obligationis ad ratiocinia ordinandis vel non.* If procurators,[10] agents, executors,[11] and guardians were to have been ordained[12] before they would have been freed from the duties of their secular office or negotiations, such a practice would have brought disgrace to the Church.[13]

Pope Eugene III (1145–1153) ruled that clerics were to avoid the administration of secular affairs.[14] In the III General Council

[8] Can. 3: ". . . Decrevit igitur sancta et magna sinodus neminem horum deinceps, hoc est episcopum, sive clericum, aut monachum, conducere possessiones aut misceri secularibus procurationibus posse, nisi forte, qui legibus ad minorum aetatum tutelas sive curationes inexcusabiles attrahuntur, aut cui ipsius civitatis episcopus ecclesiasticarum rerum commiserit gubernacula, et orphanorum atque viduarum, quae indefensae sunt, aut earum personarum, quae maxime ecclesiastico indigent amminiculo propter timorem Dei. Si quis vero transgressus fuerit haec praecepta, ecclesiasticae correctioni subiaceat."—Mansi, VII, 374; c. 26, D. LXXXVI.

[9] C. 5, D. LXXXIX (Gregory the Great, in 599); JE, n. 1731.

[10] C. (2, 12), *de procuratoribus.*

[11] C. (12, 60), *de executoribus.*

[12] I. (1, 23), *de curatoribus.*

[13] C. un., X, *de obligatis ad ratiocinia ordinandis vel non,* I, 19: "Magnus Episcopus Augustensis dixit: Quid dilectioni vestrae videtur, procuratores, actores, executores seu curatores pupillorum si debeant ordinari? Gratus episcopus dixit: Si post deposita onera et reddita ratiocinia, actus vitae ipsorum fuerint comprobati in omnibus, debent cum laude Dei (si postulati fuerint) honore munerari. Si enim ante libertatem negotiorum vel officiorum fuerint ordinati, ecclesia infamatur. Universi dixerunt: Recte statuit Sanctitas vestra, ideoque ita est nostra sententia." Taken from I Council of Carthage (348), can. 8—Mansi, III, 143.

[14] C. 2, X, *ne clerici vel monachi saecularibus negotiis se immisceant,* III, 50: "Sacerdotibus autem et clericis tuis denuncies publice, ne ministri laicorum fiant, nec in rebus eorum procuratores existant. Quod si postmodum facere praesumperserint, et occasione ipsius administrationis propter pecuniariam causam deprehendantur in fraude, indignum est eis ab ecclesia subveniri, per quos constat in ecclesia scandalum generari."

of the Lateran (1179) it was forbidden for clerics to take part in offices which entailed secular jurisdiction.

> Sed nec procurationes villarum aut iurisdictiones etiam saeculares sub aliquibus principibus et saecularibus viris, ut iustitiarius eorum fiat, clericum quisquam exercere praesumat.[15]

It was also forbidden under penalty of excommunication for clerics to exercise the office of civil notary—*exercentes officium tabellionatus.*[16]

Thus those who were obliged to render an account to secular persons were not to be promoted to Orders.[17] If the obligation had to be rendered to an ecclesiastical person, or to a person in need of mercy, e.g., to orphans or widows, then the person so obligated could be promoted to Orders.[18]

The nature and import of the simple impediment found in the present Code of Canon Law was well defined at the time of the decretal legislation. Thus the historical development of this impediment from the Council of Trent to the present Code revolved around fine points in the application of the law.

Two elements must be borne in mind: the *first* is the office or the position which involves the administration of others' goods, whether money or real property; the *second* is the obligation regarding the fulfillment of which an account must be rendered.[19] Obligations arising from contracts, i.e., sales, rentals and the like, are not in themselves included as foundations for

---

[15] Can. 12—Mansi, XXII, 226; c. 4, X, *ne clerici vel monachi saecularibus negotiis se immisceant,* III, 50.

[16] C. 8, X, *ne clericis vel monachi saecularibus negotiis se immisecant,* III, 50 (Pope Innocent III to the Bishop of Ascoli, in 1211); Potthast, n. 4337.

[17] *Glossa Ordinaria* ad c. un., X, *de obligatis ad ratiocinia ordinandis vel non,* I, 19, s. v. *ratiocinia.*

[18] *Loc. cit.*

[19] Barbosa, *Collectanea Doctorum tam Veterum quam Recentiorum in Ius Pontificum Universum* (6 vols. in 3, Lugduni, 1656), lib. I, tit. 19 (hereafter cited as Barbosa, *Collectanea*); Fagnanus, *Commentaria in Quinque Libros Decretalium* (4 vols., Venetiis, 1697), lib. I, tit. 19 (hereafter cited as Fagnanus); Pirhing, lib. I, tit. 19, n. 4; Boenninghausen, Fasc. III, p. 169; Gasparri, *De Sacra Ordinatione,* n. 550; Wernz, II, n. 125.

this impediment, for they do not involve the administration of others' goods.[20]

For the cases wherein one had finished the duties of his office or of his administrative position, but in which there still remained the obligation of rendering an account, authors expressed diverse opinions. If the administration was one which related to private goods, some authors maintained that the obligation of rendering an account did not impede the reception of Orders on the part of one who had completed the administration.[21] Some authors thus made a distinction between the administration of public goods and the administration of private goods,[22] while others disclaimed any foundation in law for such a distinction.[23] The latter, in refusing to admit any distinction, demanded that both the administration and the rendering of the account be completed before admission to the clerical state.[24]

Litigation based on fraud or deceit in the administration of goods, whether private or public, always impeded one from the clerical state until the case had been solved and the obligations fulfilled.[25] In general it can be said that any occupation involving trade or public business was characterized as unbecoming, and was therefore prohibited to clerics. As long as it was

---

[20] Barbosa, *Collectanea,* loc. cit.; Schmalzgrueber, lib. I, tit. 19, n. 6; Gasparri, *De Sacra Ordinatione,* n. 554.

[21] Fagnanus, lib. I, tit. 19, n. 24; Schmalzgrueber, *loc. cit.*

[22] Fagnanus, *loc. cit;* Schmalzgrueber, *loc. cit.*

[23] Pirhing, lib. I, tit. 19, n. 4; Boenninghausen, Fasc. III, p. 171. The latter wrote: "Si quis igitur in bonis alienis administrandis versatus ss. ordinibus initiari in optatis habeat, non sufficit, ut idem administrationem bonorum sese abdicaverit, sed omnino necesse est, ut rationem administrationis peractae reddiderit. Neque audiendi sunt, qui provocantes ad can. 1, dist. 53, et can. 1, dist. 55, inter administratores rerum publicarum et administratores rerum quae ad personam privatam spectat ita distinguunt, ut *illos quidem rationibus necdum redditis ab ordinibus arceri velint, non hos* . . . Neque enim illa distinctio in iure ullum fundamentum habet . . ." Cf. also Gasparri, *De Sacra Ordinatione,* n. 550, to the same effect.

[24] Suarez, *De Censuris,* disp. LI, sect. 3, n. 21; Pirhing, lib I, tit. 19, n. 4; Boenninghausen, Fasc. III, p. 172; Gasparri, *De Sacra Ordinatione,* n. 550.

[25] Fagnanus, lib. I, tit. 19, n. 25.

not relinquished, any such occupation was regarded as impeding the reception of tonsure.[26]

Obligations arising from the position of procurator or guardian of widows, of orphans and of others destitute of help, were not considered as incompatible with the clerical life.[27] The administration of church goods, or of the goods of other pious organizations, was also permitted.[28] When a cleric was prohibited from entering a particular transaction personally, he could do it through someone else.[29] Based either on the acquiescence of the Pope or on long custom,[30] the position of head of the Chancellery and of the Council, and even of judge in civil cases, was not considered incompatible with the clerical state.[31] Nonlucrative negotiations were not forbidden to clerics.[32]

In dealing with the problem of bankruptcy (*cessio bonorum*) and its effect on one who was obligated to render an account authors differed. Many maintained that one who had rendered an account of this administration, but who was still obligated in view of unpaid debts, became capable of receiving Orders, if he went into bankruptcy. This was based on the supposition that bankruptcy took the place of the liquidation of the debts inasmuch as the bankrupt individual could not be molested until he succeeded in becoming solvent.[33] Other authors maintained that when an individual went into bankruptcy and was unable to meet the debts he owed he could not receive Orders.[34] The latter opinion appeared to be more in harmony with a decision of the Sacred Congregation of the Council.[35]

---

[26] Boenninghausen, Fasc. III, p. 170; Wernz, II, n. 125.

[27] Schmalzgrueber, lib. I, tit. 19, n. 3; Galganettus, *De Tutela et Cura* (Venetiis, 1617), ljb I, tit. 4, n. 26.

[28] Schmalzgrueber, *loc. cit.*

[29] Gibalinus, *De Universa Rerum Humanarum Negotiatione* (Lugduni, 1663), lib. I, c. 3, a. 2 (hereafter cited as Gibalinus).

[30] Pirhing, lib. I, I, tit. 19, n. 3.

[31] Schmalzgrueber, lib. I, tit. 19, n. 3.

[32] Gibalinus, *loc. cit.*

[33] Schmalzgrueber, lib. I, tit. 19, n. 5; Pirhing, lib. I, tit. 19, n. 5.

[34] Boenninghausen, Fasc. III, footnotes on p. 172; Gasparri, *De Sacra Ordinatione*, n. 550.

[35] S. S. C., *Atrien.*, 23. iun. 1725: "An cessio bonorum obstet Michaeli,

A dispensation from the irregularity or impediment deriving from the existing obligation of rendering an account (*ratiocinia*) was held to be reserved to the Pope, and to be rarely granted by him.[36]

B. CANONICAL COMMENTARY—" QUI OFFICIUM VEL ADMINISTRATIONEM GERUNT CLERICIS VETITAM CUIUS RATIONES REDDERE DEBEANT " . . .

The present Code of Canon Law evinces the ever present solicitude of the Church for the disengagement of all clerics from secular affairs. In canon 987, 3°, certain positions are considered as incompatible with the clerical life, and as such form the basis for the impediment expressed in the same canon.

1. *Officium vel Administratio*

The phrase "*officium vel administratio*," which is used in this canon, is not to be interpreted according to the ecclesiastical or the canonical use of the term "*officium*" or of the term "*administratio*." The office or administrative position to which canon 987, 3°, refers is a secular one in contradistinction to an ecclesiastical office or administrative position. In the government of the Church the powers of jurisdiction and administration are usually united in one and the same person, but in civil law they are given to distinct persons.[37] The inclusion of both powers is achieved in this canon through the use of the phrase "*officium vel administratio*." For a definition which would include the entire signification of the phrase "*officium vel administratio*," an analagous appeal can be made to the wide definition of an office as contained in canon 145, § 1. A comprehensive definition of "*officium vel administratio*" is: Any employment which is secular in its origin and is ordained to a secular end. The appointment to such an office or administrative position comes from

---

quin ad sacros ordines promoveri possit?" The Sacred Congregation replied that he was not to be promoted.—*Thesaurus Resolutionum,* III, 180.

[36] Schmalzgrueber, lib. I, tit. 19, n. 7; Reiffenstuel, lib. I, tit. 19, n. 11.

[37] Brunini, *The Clerical Obligations of Canon 139 and 142,* The Catholic University of America Canon Law Studies, n. 103 (Washington, D. C.: The Catholic University of America, 1937), p. 23 (hereafter cited as Brunini).

an authority which is different from the authority of the Church. The purpose of such an office or administrative position is secular in nature, and not spiritual.

No distinction is made in canon 987, 3°, between a public or a private office or administrative position. Since the law makes no distinction, no distinction should be made by others. If a person has a position which was accepted from an authority other than the Church, such a position is included in the phrase "*officium vel administratio.*" Regarding the inclusion of both private and public offices or administrative positions under the *defectus libertatis* which impedes the reception of Orders, the difference of opinions which existed prior to the Code [38] is no longer justified under the present law of the Code.

2. *Clericis Vetita*

The mere holding of an office or of an administrative position, as explained above, is not in itself sufficient to establish an impediment to Orders. The law regarding the impediment under consideration qualifies the office or administrative position with the addition of the words "forbidden to clerics" (*clericis vetitam*). The office or administrative position must be one that has been forbidden to clerics. It is in the same nature that the position will also be forbidden to a candidate for the clerical state. The characterization of the offices and administrative positions as functions which are forbidden to clerics is postulated for the emergence of the impediment.

For its source this prohibition can look not only to the natural and positive divine law, but also to the positive ecclesiastical law. Authors are not in agreement when they attempt to determine all the offices and administrative positions which are forbidden to the cleric. In their explanation of the "*vetita*" of canon 987, 3°, Cappello [39] and Augustine [40] refer to canon 139 in its entirety; Beste refers to canon 139, § 1 and § 2; [41] Blat refers to canon

---

[38] Cf. Gasparri, *De Sacra Ordinatione*, n. 553.
[39] *De Sacra Ordinatione*, n. 521.
[40] *Commentary*, IV, 499.
[41] *Introductio in Codicem*, p. 535.

139, § 2 and § 3;[42] Vermeersch-Creusen refer to canon 139, § 3;[43] and Woywod[44] and Brunini[45] refer to both canon 139 and canon 142 in their entirety.

Both of these canons are concerned with occupations which are forbidden to clerics.[46]

It is impossible to give a complete list of the occupations or positions which are forbidden to clerics in virtue of the laws enacted in these two canons. Canon 139, § 1, contains a general prohibition. Many occupations can be envisioned under this portion of canon 139, which are not included by way of express mention either in the remaining part of canon 139 or in canon 142. The last three paragraphs of canon 139 do not enumerate all the occupations which are foreign to the clerical life. If such an enumeration had been intended by the legislator, it seems that paragraphs 2, 3 and 4 would have been arranged as subdivisions of paragraph 1.[47]

It must be granted that the list is not fully comprehensive, and

---

[42] *Commentarium Textus Codicis,* III, pars I, n. 358.

[43] *Epitome,* II, n. 259.

[44] *A Practical Commentary on the Code of Canon Law* (2 vols., 4. ed., New York: Wagner, 1932), I, 539 (hereafter cited as Woywod).

[45] *The Clerical Obligations of Canon 139 and 142,* p. 4.

[46] Canon 139, § 1—Ea etiam quae, licet non indecora, a clericali tamen statu aliena sunt, vitent [clerici].

§ 2—Sine apostolico indulto medicinam vel chirugiam ne exerceant; tabelliones seu publicos notarios, nisi in Curia ecclesiastica, ne agant; officiia publica, quae exercitium laicalis iurisdictionis vel administrationis secumferunt, ne assumant.

§ 3—Sine licentia sui Ordinarii ne ineant gestiones bonorum ad laicos pertinentium aut offica saecularia quae secumferunt onus reddendarum rationum; procuratoris aut advocati munus ne exerceant, nisi in tribunali ecclesiastico, aut in civili quando agitur de causa propria aut suae ecclesiae; in laicali iudicio criminali, gravem personalem poenam prosequente, nullam partem habeant, ne testimonium quidem sine necessitate ferentes.

§ 4—Senatorum aut oratorum legibus ferendis, quod *deputatos* vocant, munus ne sollicitent neve acceptent sine licentia Sanctae Sedis in locis ubi pontificia prohibitio intercesserit; idem ne attentent aliis in locis sine licentia tum sui Ordinarii, tum Ordinarii loci in quo electrio facienda est.

Canon 142—Prohibentur clerici per se vel per alios negotiationem aut mercaturam exercere sive in propriam sive in aliorum utilitatem.

[47] Brunini, p. 2.

that the ordinary would have the power to list other occupations under the general prohibition of paragraph 1.[48] These occupations, when so listed, would be forbidden to clerics, and would come under the term "*vetita*" of canon 987, 3°. This supposition would not attribute to the ordinary the power of establishing an impediment, any more than the permission granted by the ordinary to engage in the occupations which are forbidden by canon 139, § 3, would be attributing to him the power to dispense from an impediment, although it is true, of course, that his permission obviates the prohibition inherent in the term "*vetita,*" and consequently precludes the possibility of the emergence of an impediment.

In virtue of canon 139, § 2, unless an apostolic indult permits otherwise, clerics are forbidden to practice medicine or surgery. This prohibition does not in itself include the ordinary care or nursing of the sick.[49] In virtue of canon 139, § 2, unless contrary to the extant prohibition of the Holy See an apostolic indult has been obtained, a cleric is forbidden to assume a public office which involves the exercise of lay jurisdiction or administration. Clerics have not only the right of exemption from such duties,[50] but also the obligation not to seek them and not to canvass votes for assuming them.

Brunini presents a list of offices as contemplated under canon 139, § 2. This list includes the offices of mayors, commissioners, governors, judges, sheriffs, attorney-generals, prosecuting attorneys, tax-commissioners, state superintendents of schools, heads of municipal and state departments.[51] Merely consultative offices are not in themselves forbidden, although by reason of the ordinary's prohibition such offices may become *clericis vetita.* The office of president, treasurer, secretary, etc. of public institu-

---

[48] Maroto, *Institutiones Iuris Canonici ad Normam Novi Codicis* (2 vols., Vol. I, 3. ed., Romae, 1921), I, n. 566 (hereafter cited as Maroto); Brunini, p. 2.

[49] Brunini, p. 14.

[50] Canon 121.

[51] Brunini, p. 23.

tions or organizations for charitable purposes are prohibited to clerics.[52]

Without an apostolic indult which would permit otherwise, it is forbidden for clerics to hold the office of a public notary outside of an ecclesiastical curia.[53] For a cleric to hold the office of a public notary, if he employs this office only for the expediting of secular matters which are connected with the work of a chancery, does not seem to go contrary to the Code.[54]

Unless there is had the ordinary's permission to the contrary, a cleric is forbidden to accept the administration of property which belongs to a lay person; and he is also forbidden to accept any secular office that imposes the obligation of rendering an account.[55] The prohibition thus implied in the law can be removed indirectly by the ordinary. If the permission of the ordinary has preceded the acceptance of an office as countenanced in canon 139, § 3, then the office is no longer *vetitum clericis* in the particular case. The power to render inoperative the prohibition which is here under consideration was in pre-Code legislation reserved to the Holy See. The Code however has abrogated the requirement of obtaining from the Holy See the permission to accept such an office.[56] Cappello states that the term " secular offices " as used in canon 139, § 3, includes in general all municipal duties,[57] which, as Brunini observes, refers to those offices which are not already excluded in virtue of canon 139, § 2.[58]

The pre-Code law did not forbid clerics to assume the guardianship of minors who were related to the cleric through legitimate birth, and of orphans and widows who were unable to care for themselves; nor did it forbid the care, in general, of such persons who were in need of ecclesiastical charity. Under the present law such offices are forbidden in virtue of canon 139, § 3, unless

[52] Maroto, I, n. 567; Cocchi, *Commentarium in Codicem Iuris Canonici ad usum scholarum* (5 vols. in 8, Vol. I, 4. ed., 1931, Taurinorum Augustae: Marietti), I, 134 (hereafter cited as Cocchi).

[53] Canon 139, § 2.

[54] Brunini, p. 26.

[55] Canon 139, § 3.

[56] Cf. P. C. I., 3 iun. 1918—*AAS,* X (1918), 344.

[57] *Summa Iuris Canonici,* I, n. 245.

[58] *The Clerical Obligations of Canons 139 and 142,* p. 31.

the permission of the ordinary has preceded the acceptance of such offices or positions.[59]

The II Plenary Council of Baltimore (1866) required the consent of the bishop except in the care and the guardianship of relatives.[60] The III Plenary Council of Baltimore (1884) re-enacted the same law.[61] The office of a trustee or of an executor of a will is likewise forbidden to clerics in virtue of canon 139, § 3.[62] The II Plenary Council of Baltimore also condemned the custom of depositing sums of money in the hands of priests with the understanding that the money was to be returned at a certain time without interest.[63]

Without the permission of the ordinary a cleric is likewise forbidden to exercise the office of a procurator or of an advocate, except in ecclesiastical courts, or in civil courts when their own welfare or that of the Church to which they pertain is involved. Authors disputed among themselves whether a cleric can act as a procurator or as an advocate for his relatives and for persons in distress.[64] Most of the authors are on the affirmative side. Their doctrine can safely be followed when there is question simply of the consideration which regards the emergence or the existence of a consequent impediment to the reception of Orders, or to the exercise of Orders already received.

The permission of the ordinary must precede a cleric's participation in a criminal trial in the civil courts when this trial involves grave personal punishment, even if his participation consists only in the giving of testimony, unless he is forced to testify by the civil law.[65].

---

[59] *Ibid.*, p. 32.

[60] *Concilii Plenarii Baltimorensis II, in Ecclesia Metropolitana Baltimorensi, a die VII ad diam XXI Octobris, A. D. MDCCCLXVI, habiti, et a Sede Apostolica Recogniti, Acta et Decreta* (Baltimorae, John Murphy, 1868), n. 157 (hereafter cited as *II Plenary Council of Baltimore*).

[61] *Acta et Decreta Concilii Plenarii Baltimorensis Tertii, A. D. MDCCCLXXXIV* (Baltimorae, John Murphy, 1886), n. 82 (hereafter cited as *III Plenary Council of Baltimore*).

[62] Brunini, p. 32.

[63] N. 159.

[64] Cf. Brunini, p. 39.

[65] Canon 139, § 3.

In those places where a pontifical prohibition is in force against a cleric's soliciting or accepting legislative offices, permission of the Holy See and of the cleric's own ordinary and of the ordinary of the place in which the election is to occur is necessary before the prohibition enacted in canon 139, § 4, will be made inoperative. If the legislative office, e.g., a senatorship in the United States Government, is gained by appointment, then a cleric would be obliged to obtain the permission of his ordinary.[66]

Canon 142 forbids clerics to engage, either personally or through an agent, in commercial business or trading, whether for their own utility or for the utility of others. Lucrative commercial trading[67] and artificial trading[68] are the types of businesses which are forbidden by this canon.[69]

In order to determine the extent to which these two canons, namely 139 and 142, apply to the legislation of canon 987, 3°, a consideration of the impediment in its entirety, and not merely in reference to the prohibition which is contained in the phrase "*clericis vetitam,*" is necessary. The word "*vetita*" in canon 987, 3°, refers to both offices and administrative positions, and not merely to the latter. Once the holding of an office or an administrative position which is here and now forbidden to a cleric is verified, and only then is it possible to proceed with a further consideration of the full import of the impediment.

3. *Removal of the Prohibitive Qualification*

Strictly considered, the positions referred to in canons 139 and 142 are forbidden to clerics and not to laymen. Through the operation of the law which is expressed in canon 987, 3°, this prohibition extends to a layman when he presents himself as

66 P. C. I., 25 apr. 1922—*AAS*, XIV (1922), 313. Cf. *III Plenary Council of Baltimore*, n. 83.

67 Brunini (*The Clerical Obligations of Canons 139 and 142*, p. 77) defines this as: "The buying of things with the intention of selling them unchanged at a higher price."

68 Brunini (*op. cit., loc. cit.*) defines this as: "The buying of material with the intention of changing it by means of hired labor and of selling the articles at a profit."

69 For a complete study of the positions forbidden to clerics the reader is referred to the dissertation of Brunini here cited.

a candidate for tonsure. In virtue of his aspiring to the clerical life he is brought under the scope of the law enacted in canons 139 and 142, so that what was formerly permitted to him now becomes forbidden. The permission of the ordinary, or of the Holy See, granted after the reception of Orders for the continued engaging in such occupations as are forbidden to clerics would not be sufficient to remove the occupations or positions from the classification referred to in canon 987, 3°. The permission of the Holy See, or of the ordinary, as mentioned in canon 139, must precede the acceptance of an office or an administrative position if it is to stand qualified as no longer prohibited. To maintain that the permission of the ordinary, or of the Holy See, would be sufficient to displace the office or position, when it has already been accepted by a layman or a cleric, from the contemplated classification of canon 987, 3°, would be to attribute to the ordinary and the Holy See the power of removing the impediment when it existed. The ordinary does not have such power except in the cases contemplated by canons 15 and 81.

Although the Holy See could rule that the permission of the Holy See to continue in an office already accepted would also imply a dispensation from the impediment which has been contracted, it is not likely that such a procedure would be followed. The Holy See would demand that a dispensation be granted directly. Thus, if a cleric had without permission of the competent authority accepted a forbidden administrative position of which he had to render an account, he would be bound by the impediment. If the same cleric, prior to his acceptance of the position, had obtained the permission of the competent authority he would have avoided the inclusion of himself under the prohibitive force of canon 987, 3°. The prior permission of the competent authority removes the prohibitive qualification from the position in question. However, since the cleric accepted the position without the necessary permission, any permission consequent to his acceptance of a forbidden office will not remove the impediment. The ordinary's permission will be of no avail, since the emergence of the impediment removes the entire case from the hands of the ordinary and places it in the hands of the Holy See.

4. *Cuius rationes reddere debeant*

Granted that the position in question is one which is forbidden to a cleric, before the impediment exists in the case the position must be one in which the holder of the same would be obliged to render an account. As the word "*vetitam*" in canon 987, 3°, refers to both *officium* and *administratio,* so too the phrase "*cuius rationes reddere debeant*" refers to both *officium* and *administratio.*[70]

The phrase "*cuius rationes reddere debeant*" is a restrictive clause, and not merely an explanatory one. Therefore an office which is forbidden to a cleric, but with regard to which he has no obligation to render an account, would not be such as to make the holder of such an office subject to the impediment, although for other reasons he should not be ordained. The importance of this conclusion becomes evident when there arises the question of the exercise of Orders already received. If every office which is forbidden to a cleric gave rise to an impediment, then the cleric who came under the scope of the impediment by reason of the forbidden office he holds could not licitly exercise the Orders he has already received.[71]

In virtue of canon 19 a strict interpretation is to be given to canon 987, which helps to substantiate the conclusion that the phrase "*cuius rationes reddere debeant*" is to be considered as restricting in scope the meaning of both *officium* and *administratio.* The previously used phrase "*vetitam clerics*" restricts both in meaning; and logic dictates that the legislator proceed from the less specific to the more specific.[72]

In the pre-Code law emphasis was placed on the obligation of

---

[70] Blat, III, pars I, n. 358.

[71] Canon 968, § 2.

[72] Wernz-Vidal (*Ius Canonicum,* IV, pars I, n. 258) seem to hold a wider interpretation:—". . . officium clericis vetitum ac proinde deponendum, vel administratio pariter clericis vetita, a qua quis plane liber non est donec administrationis rationes redditae fuerint."

rendering an account (*ratiocinia*). Title 19 of Book I in the Decretal collections is worded: "*de obligatis ad ratiocinia ordinandis vel non.*" Pirhing, in his commentary on this title, joins the notion of "*officium*" and "*administratio*" with the words "*nisi desposito munere*" and furthermore adds "*redditis rationibus.*"[73] He also uses the expression "*administratio seu officium.*"[74] The celebrated text of the I Council of Carthage (348) employs the expression "*post deposita onera et reddita ratiocinia.*"[75]

In summary, it may be said that if a candidate for the clerical life or a cleric himself has a position, irrespective of its classification, which is forbidden to a cleric, and this position likewise entails the rendering of an account, he is under the impediment of canon 987, 3°. Thus the extent to which the prohibited offices mentioned in canon 139 and 142 form a basis for the impediment listed in canon 987, 3°, will depend on the added obligation of the rendering of an account which is connected with the forbidden office or administrative position.

The phrase "rendering of an account" applies not only to a reckoning regarding goods or money involved, but applies also to an account of the justice shown by the cleric or the candidate for the clerical life in exercising the office or administrative position.[76] The rendering of an account may be required by the civil authorities, or it may also be necessary in order to vindicate one's good name in the eyes of one's employer, or in the eyes of the people who were served by the holder of the office in question. As Brunini states, the vindication of one's name in the eyes of the people is likely to be of greater importance in a democratic country than the necessity of complying with the requirements of the civil authorities.[77]

---

[73] Lib. I, tit. 19, n. 2.

[74] *Ibid.*, n. 4.

[75] Cf. *supra*, footnote on page 71.

[76] De Meester, *Iuris Canonici et Iuris Canonico-Civilis Compendium* (3 vols. in 4, nova editio, Brugis, 1921–1928), I, n. 381 (hereafter cited as De Meester).

[77] *The Clerical Obligations of Canons 139 and 142*, p. 30.

C. CESSATION OF THE IMPEDIMENT—". . . DONEC DEPOSITO OFFICIO ET ADMINISTRATIONE ATQUE RATIONIBUS, REDDITIS, LIBERI FACTI SINT"

Canon 987, 3°, legislates the manner in which it is possible for this impediment, once it exists, to cease. Freedom from the impediment will be achieved after the office or the administrative position has been relinquished and the account necessarily connected with the position has been rendered. Both the relinquishing of the position and the rendering of the account must have taken place. If only the one has been achieved then the impediment does not cease.

The relinquishing of the office or of the administrative position must have occurred according to the norms acknowledged by the civil authorities or by the employer from whom the position was received. If the employment is the result of a contract, the contract must be terminated in such a way as to obviate any litigation whatsoever. When the proper authority unjustly refuses to accept the relinquishing of the position, the injustice is to be proved by a decree of the court, if there is danger that the unjust employer will appeal to the courts to secure the continuance in office of the one who has resigned.

The rendering of the account which is to be given implies in general a satisfactory explanation of the activities engaged in during the resigner's incumbency. This explanation is accomplished through the submission of a sufficiently itemized report which will obviate any litigations. Each individual case will offer a different mode for the rendering of the account; however, the general purpose is to demonstrate that there was no fraud, deceit or injustice practiced, and that all debts of money, property, justice, etc., have been liquidated. In a word, the account rendered must be so given that the debits balance with the credits, and, when that balance is lacking, that there is no cause for litigation. An account will not be sufficiently rendered until the possibility of future litigation has been made an improbability. A statement of the authorities from whom the position was received will be sufficient to establish one's freedom from any obligation, if this statement proclaims that every account has been satisfactorily given.

If the position is one in which the candidate for the clerical state, or also the cleric, is his own employer, e.g., a business of his own which is forbidden to clerics, then the rendering of his account will be in relation to his creditors, if he has any. When the pleas of his creditors have been satisfied, he is free of any further necessity of rendering an account. If the debtor is unable to satisfy his creditors, and an appeal to the operation of bankruptcy has been lodged, then, when the assignee, who has been appointed either by the court or the bankrupt according to the exigencies of the case, has rendered his final account, so that its acceptance by the court releases the assignee from further duties, the debtor may thereupon apply for his discharge. He is entitled to this discharge if he has complied with all the requirements of the civil law.[78]

If the creditors expressly agreed that the debtor is entirely free, or if the disposition of the law extinguishes all further obligation of making good the remaining debt, then the debtor has fulfilled the obligation of rendering an account. This freedom of further obligation presupposes that there has been no blame or fraud in the actions which made the bankruptcy necessary.[79]

Therefore, until the forbidden office or administrative position has been forsaken, and the necessary account has been rendered, the candidate for Orders is impeded in the reception of Orders, and the cleric is forbidden to exercise the Orders he has already received. Prior to the Code it was considered permissible for a cleric to exercise his Orders even though he had an office of which he had to render an account.[80] Under the law of the Code such permission is not granted.[81]

---

[78] Robinson, n. 406.

[79] Merkelbach, *Summa Theologiae Moralis* (ed. altera, 3 vols., Parisiis: Typis Desclée De Brouwer, 1935–1936), II, n. 341 (hereafter cited as Merkelbach).

[80] Cf. Gasparri, *De Sacra Ordinatione*, n. 555.

[81] Canon 968, § 2.

D. DISPENSATION FROM THE IMPEDIMENT

A listing of the reasons for the establishing of the impediment will show sufficiently why the Holy See will rarely, if ever, grant a dispensation from this impediment. Brunini presents a list of reasons for the prohibition of certain offices. These reasons are likewise apropos with reference to the impediment.

The following are the reasons listed by Brunini: (1) Rarely can a man be found who can fulfill one office perfectly, much less two or more offices well; (2) It is easier to follow the tendency of fulfilling temporal duties than those of a spiritual nature; (3) The holding of civil offices can readily endanger the liberty and discipline of the Church, making clerics dependent on civil powers and temporal masters with a resultant lack of prompt obedience to ecclesiastical superiors; (4) There is danger that such men may receive sacred Orders, not for the love of God, but to avoid the rendering of an account of their deeds; (5) This latter contingency would lead to grave inconvenience for creditors and for those to whom the account must be rendered; and (6) The good name of the Church would be endangered.[82]

The Holy See would be inclined to dispense from the impediment if the Church would otherwise suffer greatly from the privation of the services on the part of some cleric. This could occur in the case of a cleric in major Orders who had accepted an office and then found difficulty in rendering an account when he wanted to resign from it. The same difficulty could arise as a result of unjust demands on the part of an employer or a creditor, if the cleric were unable to have the civil courts justify his claims.[83]

---

[82] *The Clerical Obligations of Canons 139 and 142*, p. 5.

[83] Regarding the competent Congregation for the granting of the dispensation the reader is referred to pages 14–17.

PART III

IMPEDIMENTS BASED ON THE DEFECT IN FAITH

CHAPTER IV

IN THE INDIVIDUAL

A. Historical Synopsis

St. Paul in writing to Timothy ruled that a neophyte should not be admitted to the ranks of the episcopate.[1] As with the other impediments listed by St. Paul, so too this one was related primarily to candidates for the episcopal office.[2] With the growth of the Church this legislation was made more explicit. It was extended directly to candidates for the priesthood and the diaconate,[3] and then also to candidates for minor Orders.[4] That this impediment extended to candidates for minor Orders was disputed among authors, but St. Raymond of Peñafort favored the position that a neophyte was impeded from the reception of even minor Orders.[5]

The reason for this prohibition was expressed in the words of St. Paul: " Lest he be puffed up with pride and incur the condemnation passed on the devil." [6]

According to the etymology of the word, the term " neophyte " signifies a new convert who is young in his faith and has been

[1] I Tim., III, 6.

[2] I Tim., III, 2.

[3] I General Council of Nicaea (325), can. 2—Mansi, II, 667; c. 1, D. XLVIII; Council of Sardica (343), can. 10; c. 10, D. LI; IV Provincial Council of Toledo (633), can. 19—Mansi, X, 624; c. 5, D. LI.

[4] C. 6, C. XIX, q. III (Pope Gregory I to Bishop Fortunatus of Naples, in 600); JE, n. 1776.

[5] *Summa* of St. Raymond, lib. III, tit. 14, *De neophytis non ordinandis*, p. 266.

[6] I Tim., III, 6.

recently baptized.[7] This term was extended in later legislation to mean also those who had recently been admitted into the ranks of the religious,[8] and as such were not fit subjects for the full power enjoyed by that particular group into which he had only recently been admitted. The neophyte's advance should be gradual. Pope Gregory the Great noted the two kinds of neophytes when he said:

> Sicut neophytus tunc dicebatur, qui in initio sanctae fidei erat eruditione plantatus, sic modo neophytus habendus est, qui repente in religionis habitu plantatus ad ambiendos sacras ordines irrepserit . . .[9]

Gratian made the same observation for the twelfth century when he said:

> Neophyti vero hodie appellantur ad propositum sacrae religionis noviter accedentes.[10]

The Nicene Council renewed the legislation of St. Paul. It ruled that neophytes were not to be ordained. The Council admitted exceptions to the general rule, exceptions based on the absence of the reasons prompting this particular legislation.[11] But the proper understanding concerning the exceptions became a disputed question. St. Ambrose (+397), a neophyte, defended his ordination on the grounds that with the cessation of the cause the effect also ceased, although he realized the necessity of the general legislation.[12] St. Raymond held that it was not because of the absence of the reason for not ordaining a neophyte, but because of divine inspiration that St. Ambrose and others were ordained. Under ordinary circumstances the neophyte was under the necessity of furnishing proof to the proper authorities that he was ready to assume the responsibilities of the clerical life.[13]

---

[7] *Glossa Ordinaria* ad c. 2, D. XLVIII, s. v. *sicut neophytus.*

[8] Gratian on c. 1, D. XLVIII.

[9] C. 2, D. XLVIII (written to all the bishops, in 599); JE, n. 1747.

[10] *Loc. cit.*

[11] Can. 2—Mansi, II, 667; c. 2, D. XLVIII.

[12] *Glossa Ordinaria* ad c. 9, D. LI, s. v. *neophytus.*

[13] *Summa* of St. Raymond, lib. III, tit. 14, *De neophytis non ordinandis,* p. 266.

Pope Innocent I (402–407) in his letter to Aurelius, bishop of Carthage, gave voice to the extant legislation concerning neophytes when he said:

> Miserum est, eum fieri magistrum, qui nunquam fuit discipulus; eumque summum fieri sacerdotem, qui in nullo gradu umquam obsecutus fuerat sacerdoti.[14]

In the decretal legislation there is no explicit mention made of neophytes. The failure to treat them does not argue the abandonment of this impediment to Orders, but only the fact that it was deemed unnecessary to repeat such an obvious legislation.

Henry Cardinal of Ostia in his commentary on the decretals of Gregory IX confined his consideration of the neophyte to the fifth book of the decretals on the subject *De Magistris.* He stated that no matter how ingenious a neophyte might be, he ought not to be selected for a ruling position in the Church. "*Neophytus quamvis ingeniosus non est assumendus.*"[15] In the decretal collections of Boniface VIII (1294–1303) and of Clement V (1305–1314) it was not found necessary to reiterate the legislation governing the ordination of neophytes. The law governing other requisite qualities on the part of a candidate for Orders argued the continued force of the rule initially enacted by St. Paul.[16]

The Council of Trent dealt directly with neophytes in the clerical and religious life,[17] but only indirectly with neophytes in the life of faith.[18] The neophyte in the faith constitutes the particular interest and consideration of this study. He was an adult who had been recently converted and made a member of the Church through the sacrament of baptism.[19] But baptism

---

[14] C. 4, D. LXI.

[15] Hostiensis, lib. III, c. 1, n. 7.

[16] C. 14, *de electione et electi potestate,* I, 6, in VI°; c. 1, *de aetate et qualitate et ordine praeficiendorum,* I, 6, in VI°.

[17] Conc. Trident., sess. XXIII, *de ref.,* c. 11.

[18] *Ibid.,* c. 4.

[19] S. C. C., *Milevitana,* 13 aug. 1718—*Fontes,* 3173; Fargna, *Commentaria in Canones de Iurepatronatus* (3 vols., Romae, 1717–1719), Pars VI, c. 22, cas. 6 (hereafter cited as Fargna). Gasparri, *De Sacra Ordinatione,* n. 267; Wernz, II, n. 118.

conferred in infancy did not lend itself as occasioning this impediment or irregularity.[20]

An adult convert recently baptized was the subject of a canonical irregularity,[21] and this irregularity barred not only the reception of Sacred Orders, but, according to the common teaching of the canonists and the constant practice of the Church, also the reception of minor Orders and even of tonsure.[22]

Clinici was the term used in reference to those who, although they were instructed in the truths of the Catholic Church and had been born of Catholic parents, had deferred the reception of baptism until they were overtaken by serious sickness or became consciously subject to the fear of death.[23] Since *clinici* occasioned special legislation,[24] it seems that they were not comprehended under the meaning of the term "neophyte." Their status seems to imply a new irregularity. Practice and the common teaching of the authors was to the effect that *clinici* labored under a total irregularity. Gasparri was of the opinion that not all *clinici* were irregular, but only those who had deferred the reception of baptism until fear of death or grave infirmity had overtaken them. If the deferral of the reception of baptism was interrupted for any other reason, then the *clinicus* was not under the irregularity.[25]

---

20 Fargna, *loc. cit.*

21 Caponi, *Institutiones Canonicae* (2 vols., Coloniae Allobrogum, 1734), lib. I, tit. 25, n. 161 (hereafter cited as Caponi); Bonacina, *De Morali Theologia* (3 vols., Venetiis, 1687), I, 464, nn. 4, 5 (hereafter cited as Bonacina); Boenninghausen, Fasc. III, p. 141.

22 Geraldi, *Expositio Iuris Pontificii iuxta Recentiorem Ecclesiae Disciplinam* (2 vols., Romae, 1829), II, sec. 96, n. 6 (hereafter cited as Giraldi); Boenninghausen, Fasc. III, p. 141; Wernz, II, n. 118.

23 ". . . ille [clinicus], qui licet ex parentibus christianis ortus, ac in fidei veritatibus instructus, tamen baptismum differt, illumque non suscipit nisi in gravi infirmitate constitutus, mortis metu," Gasparri, *De Sacra Ordinatione,* n. 267. Cf. also Wernz, II, n. 118.

24 Council of Neocaesarea (314–325), can. 12; c. I, D. LVII; cf. also Benedictus XIV, *De Synodo Dioecesana,* lib. XII, c. 6, n. 7.

25 "Dubitari autem potest num sit irregularis et ille qui baptismum recepit, nonquidem in lecto decumbens propter gravem infirmitatem, sed constitutus in alia necessitate, e.g., ad grave damnum temporale evitandum. Plerique affirmant . . . Sed his non obstantibus, putamus veram irregularitatem in

In attempting to decide when a neophyte ceased to be such, authors came to varied conclusions. All were agreed that there had to be some time of probation after the conferral of baptism, regardless of the particular qualities of the neophyte.[26] The length of time was variously determined by the authors, such as one, two and ten years.[27] The majority of the authors maintained that this determination of the time in a particular instance was to be left to the prudent judgment of the bishop.[28] If the bishop was unable because of the lack of priests to permit the lapse of time involved for the full probation of the neophyte, a dispensation, granted by the Holy See, had to be obtained.[29]

Not all the authors were agreed on the temporal nature of this impediment. Some maintained that it was perpetual in its duration, and that no amount of time employed for a probation obviated the impediment for the neophyte, even though his baptism could no longer be called recent.[30] Most of the authors, however, maintained that the passage of time which removed the newness of one's conversion or the newness of one's baptism would also remove the individual from the irregularity affecting the neophyte. Gasparri summed up this doctrine with the words:

> Porro doctores passim tradunt hanc irregularitatem per se cessare quando quis non est amplius neophytus, idest *recenter* baptizatus, aut quando, experimento probatus,

---

casu non adesse, quia fatendum est hunc casum non esse in iure expressum. Equidem in ipso ratio legis pro alio casu latae verificatur, sed id non sufficit ad irregularitatem adstruendam. Caeterum, ipso fatente Suarez, sententia pro irregularitate est tantum probabilis: unde irregularitas est dubia. Sed prudentia suadet taliter baptizatos ex necessitate non esse promovendos nisi cum magna cautela." Gasparri, *De Sacra Ordinatione,* n. 272.

[26] Suarez, *De Censuris,* disp. 43, sect. 3, n. 7; Benedictus XIV, *De Synodo Dioecesana,* lib. XII, c. 6, n. 7; Caponi, lib. I, tit. 25, n. 161; Boenninghausen, Fasc. III, p. 142.

[27] Cf. Suarez, *ibid.,* n. 5; Benedictus XIV, *ibid.,* n. 6; Gasparri, *De Sacra Ordinatione,* p. 269.

[28] S. C. C., *Milevitana,* 13 aug. 1718—*Fontes,* n. 3173; Benedictus XIV, *loc. cit.;* Suarez, *ibid.,* n. 7; Bonacina, I, 464, n. 4; Fargna, Pars VI, c. 22, cas. 6; Caponi, lib. I, tit. 25, n. 161; Boenninghausen, Fasc. III, p. 141.

[29] Suarez, *loc. cit.;* Boenninghausen, *loc. cit.*

[30] Cf. Giraldi, II, sec. 96, n. 6.

> est firmus et instructus in fide, ac simul humilitate, prudentia aliisque virtutibus necessariis praeditus, licet deinde minime conveniant quandonam quis non sit amplius neophytus, aut quantum temporis neophyti probationi sit praemittendum, nonnullis requirentibus unum annum, alii biennium, alii decennium, aliis tandem putantibus id remitti arbitrio et prudentiae episcopi.[31]

Among the authors who admitted that the bishop had the right to determine the fitness of the neophyte after a time of probation, it was agreed that the bishop did not dispense from any irregularity, but rather issued an authentic declaration that the irregularity had ceased.[32]

The legislation of the Council of Trent relative to the nonconferral of Orders on an individual who had not been confirmed[33] lent weight to the consideration that a neophyte could not be ordained until he had been proved in his faith. Authors disagreed among themselves whether or not a new canonical irregularity was constituted by this legislation.[34]

B. Canonical Commentary—"Neophyti, donec, iudicio Ordinarii, sufficienter probati fuerint"

1. Meaning of the term "neophyte"

The term "neophyte" as first used by St. Paul referred to those adult converts who had been recently baptized and were not proved in their faith. The subsequent legislation evinces no change in this conception of a neophyte. Its meaning was never changed. When heretical groups broke away from the Church the meaning of the term "neophyte" was not enlarged to include converts from heretical sects. Among the pre-Code authors no mention of baptized heretics who had been recently converted

[31] *De Sacra Ordinatione,* n. 269.

[32] Caponi, lib. I, tit. 25, n. 161; Boenninghausen, *loc. cit.*

[33] Conc. Trident., sess. XXIII, *de ref.*, c. 4: "Prima tonsura non initientur qui sacramentum confirmationis non susceperint."

[34] Among those who held for the emergence of a new irregularity were: Giraldi (II, sec. 91, n. 1), Boenninghausen (Fasc. III, p. 156), Wernz-Vidal (IV, n. 263) and others. Holding the opposite opinion were: Suarez (*De Censuris,* disp. 42, sect. 3, n. 14) and Bonacina (I, 464, n. 8.)

to the Catholic faith as belonging to the group known as neophytes can be found. The irregularity arising from heresy, and the irregularity based on the heretical belief of an individual's parents or grandparents, were sufficient to cover the exigencies. Thus a neophyte can be defined as a new adult convert who has been recently incorporated into the Church through the valid reception of baptism.[35]

A convert may be defined as one who was born and reared in beliefs opposed to the Church's teaching, but now, moved by divine grace, embraces the Catholic Faith and seeks active membership in the Church.[36] This active membership will be effected either by the valid reception of baptism or by the removal of the obstacle which prevents active membership even though baptism has been received. Conversion is the change from the state of non-Catholic belief or from the state of infidelity to the state wherein one accepts the truths of the Catholic religion.[37] A convert, then, is one who has acquired by divine grace at least the habit of divine Catholic faith—*fides informis*—but not necessarily the theological virtue of faith—*fides formata.* After the convert has been baptized, or, if already baptized, has been absolved from sin and freed from whatever obstacle hinders his active membership, then his previously acquired *fides informis* is raised to a *fides formata.*[38]

The acquisition of this divine Catholic faith takes place in adult age. An adult is one who enjoys the use of reason.[39] The age at which one is presumed to have attained the use of reason is

---

[35] Cf. Ferraris, s. v. *neophyti; A Catholic Dictionary,* Donald Attwater, general editor (The Catholic Action Society of the College of St. Robert Bellarmine, Heythrop: New York: Macmillan Co., 1941), s. v. *neophyte;* Wernz-Vidal IV, pars I, n. 263; Hickey, p. 81.

[36] Goodwine, *The Reception of Converts,* The Catholic University of America Canon Law Studies, n. 198 (Washington, D. C.: The Catholic University of America Press, 1944), p. x (hereafter cited as Goodwine).

[37] *Kirchenlexikon,* Hergenröther-Kaulen (2. ed., 13 vols., Freiburg im Breisgau: Herder, 1882–1903), III, col. 1049, s. v. *Conversion.*

[38] For a discussion of *fides informis* and *fides formata,* cf. St. Thomas, *Summa,* II-II, q. IV, art. 4, 5, and esp. ad 3 and ad 4 of art. 5.

[39] Canon 745, 2°.

seven years.[40] The term "adult" includes minors and those who are still under the care of their parents or their guardians.[41]

A convert while he is preparing himself for the reception of baptism is called a catechumen.[42] As a general rule a catechumen must know and believe with divine Catholic faith all the essential truths which are contained in the Sacred Scriptures and in Tradition as proposed by the Church, either in solemn judgment or by the ordinary and universal magisterium, to be believed as divinely revealed.[43]

Through the valid reception of baptism [44] a new convert becomes a neophyte. The validity of the baptism administered to the convert is the only requirement.[45] For the status of a neophyte it is not necessary that the baptism have been administered solemnly,[46] nor that the form for adult baptism have been used.[47]

Through the valid reception of baptism a convert is constituted as a person in the Church of Christ with all the rights and duties of all Christians, unless, as regards the matter of rights, there exists some obstacle which separates him from the ecclesiastical communion, or unless there be present some ecclesiastical censure.[48] The status of a neophyte is such as to give rise to the curtailment of a right. A neophyte is impeded from the reception of Orders.[49]

---

[40] Cf. canon 12; Benedictus XIV, ep. *Postremo mense,* 28 febr. 1747—*Fontes,* n. 377; S. Congr. de Prop. Fide, 3 mart. 1703—*Fontes,* n. 4495; Gillmann, "Die *anni discretionis* im Kanon *Omnis utriusque sexus,*"—Archiv für katholisches Kirchenrecht (Innsbruck, 1857–1861; Mainz, 1862–), CVIII (1928), 556–617.

[41] Canon 88.

[42] Cf. Goodwine, pp. 89–93 for a discussion on the term "catechumen."

[43] Canon 1323, § 1.

[44] Canon 737, § 1.

[45] "Neophyti intelliguntur qui in adulta aetate, ad fidem conversi, baptismum *absolute* receperunt. Non ideo veniunt haeretici qui, erroribus reiectis, sub conditione rebaptizantur." Cappello, *De Sacra Ordinatione,* n. 524.

[46] Cf. canon 737, § 2.

[47] Cf. canon 744.

[48] Canon 87.

[49] Canon 987, 6o.

2. TWO ELEMENTS—RECENT ADULT CONVERSION AND RECENT ADULT BAPTISM

From the foregoing consideration it is to be concluded that two elements are necessary to effect the status of a neophyte. First, the individual must be a recent adult convert to the Catholic faith; secondly, as an adult he must have been *recently* baptized validly. The definition of a neophyte as given by most of the authors includes all the ideas contained in these two elements.[50]

Although in practice the *clinici* may be treated as neophytes, they are not barred from the reception of Orders in consequence of the law enacted in canon 987, 6°. The impediment does not extend to them. A true *clinicus* is not a convert to the Catholic faith. He is one who has been born of and instructed by Catholic parents in the true faith. If the *clinici* are included under the meaning of the term "neophyte," then conversion which is necessarily connected with the meaning of the term neophyte would seem to connote a transition from the *fides informis* to the *fides formata.* This is not the meaning of conversion as it is used in the definition of the term neophyte.

A true *clinicus* has always been of the true faith and is not a convert to it from infidelity or from a heretical belief. He may be weak in his faith, but weakness of faith is not the element which places one within the scope of the meaning of the term "neophyte." By the reception of baptism the faith of the *clinicus* becomes actuated by charity, it becomes under ordinary circumstances a *fides formata.* A strict interpretation of the term "neophyte"[51] will not permit the inclusion of the group whose members are referred to as *clinici* under the prohibitive force of canon 987, 6°.

In an individual case the prudent judgment of the ordinary will decide whether or not a so called *clinicus* has in reality cultivated through God's grace a firmness in the Catholic faith that is his. However, when one defers the reception of baptism for a long time, there arises a suspicion that his faith is weak, since

---

[50] Cf. Cappello, *De Sacra Ordinatione,* n. 524; Wernz-Vidal, IV, pars I, n. 263.

[51] Canon 19.

his actions go counter to the importance and the necessity of baptism. The ordinary should be guided by the words of the Council of Neocaesarea (314–325).

> Si quis, in aegritudine fuerit baptizatus, ad honorem presbyteri non potest promoveri; quia non ex proposito fides eius, sed ex necessitate descendit: nisi forte sequens studium eius et fidem, atque hominum raritatem, talis possit admitti.[52]

Although this law is no longer in force, it may serve as a guide for the ordinary when he wishes to determine whether or not to confer tonsure on a suspected *clinicus.*

The conversion to the faith, as the first element for the effecting of the status of a neophyte, does not imply solely a transition from a non-belief in any religion (infidelity) to a belief in the doctrines of the Catholic Church. The religious belief of a convert prior to his conversion may have been any belief which is opposed to the Catholic Faith, e.g., Judaism, Buddhism, Atheism, Pantheism or any other sect, regardless of how close it may approach the Catholic teaching. The latter generic group includes all heretical sects, nevertheless this group is made less generic when the second element for the effecting of the status of a neophyte is considered, namely that of recent baptism. Many of these heretical sects validly administer baptism. If the faith of the individual is different from divine Catholic faith, then he is a subject for conversion to the true faith. *Conversio interna,* it must be noted, does not effect a change in the person's relationship to one particular religion; a *conversio externa* is necessary.

The second element necessarily predicated of a neophyte is his recent baptism. The conferral of baptism must be absolute.[53] If the convert had been a member of a non-Catholic sect which administers baptism, then a diligent inquiry must be made in order to determine whether the baptism was conferred validly.[54]

---

[52] Can. 12—Kirch, *Enchiridion Fontium Historiae Ecclesiasticae* (4. ed., Friburgi Brisgoviae: Herder & Co., 1923), n. 388; c. I, D. LVII; cf. also Benedictus XIV, *De Synodo Dioecesana,* lib. XII, c. 6, n. 7.

[53] Cappello, *De Sacra Ordinatione,* n. 524.

[54] Cf. S. C. S. Off., litt. (ad Ep. Harlemen.), 6 apr. 1859—*Fontes,* n. 950.

The III Plenary Council of Baltimore (1884) decreed that the investigation both of the fact and of the validity of the previous baptism must be a diligent one.[55] If the investigation proves that the ceremony of baptism was conferred, but that its validity remains doubtful, then conditional baptism is to be conferred. This conditional conferral of baptism recognizes the possibility that the first baptism was valid. Since it cannot be determined absolutely which of the two ceremonies constitutes the valid baptism, the convert is to be given the benefit of the doubt. In determining whether or not the conditionally baptized individual is a neophyte his first baptism is to be considered valid.[56]

Such a convert may be barred from the reception of Orders, because in the prudent judgment of the ordinary he does not have the qualities necessary in a candidate for Orders. However, this judgment of the ordinary will be based on the desired end of the law which enacts the impediment, and not on the law itself as such. The individual does not fall under the comprehension of the impediment in consequence of any statement in the law, although he will in practice be subjected to a probation in the same manner as a neophyte is subjected to a probation before he is ordained.

C. Cessation of the Impediment

There is no definite duration of time beyond which the conversion of an adult can no longer be called recent. The relative newness of any conversion is to be determined by the external manifestation of grace and charity,[57] but most especially of faith, and not by the number of years which have elapsed since the individual has formally adopted the faith.

Both the baptism and the conversion must be recent if the strict status of a neophyte is to be predicated of an individual. When the conversion is recent and the baptism has been conferred many years earlier,[58] or when the baptism is recent and

---

[55] N. 122. For a complete discussion of the investigation consult Goodwine, pp. 24–54.

[56] Cf. Cappello, *De Sacra Ordinatione,* n. 524.

[57] Blat, III, pars I, n. 361.

[58] "Non ideo veniunt sub nomine neophyti haeretici qui, erroribus reiectis,

the conversion has taken place many years earlier, the individual is not a neophyte.[59]

According to the words of the canon, *donec, iudicio Ordinarii sufficienter probati fuerint,* the ordinary is given the faculty to judge when the neophyte has sufficiently proved himself to be firm in the faith. The stability of one's faith cannot be measured by one's baptism, although the latter factor may serve as adminicular proof. The judgment of the ordinary, then, must center about the active faith of the individual. His judgment must be made concerning the *recent* conversion. The recentness of a neophyte's conversion stands in inverse ratio to the vigor of his faith. The firmer his faith, the less recent also will be regarded the fact of his conversion.

The reason which prompts the enactment of the impediment that affects a neophyte is the uncertainty of the constancy of his faith. The neophyte must prove that his faith is firm. This proof can be given only by the neophyte's outward manifestation of his inner convictions, for example, in his conversation, in his writing, by his behaviour in Church, by his devout reception of the sacraments, and by any other external profession of his inner faith. If the neophyte is known to be wavering in the acceptance of certain truths of divine Catholic faith, his faith certainly is not firm.

The presence as well as the firmness of one's faith is not a fact which admits of direct observation, but must be deduced from the effects produced. From the outward manifestations, then, the ordinary will judge whether or not the neophyte has sufficiently proved that his faith is firm. The mere passage of time does not necessarily bring a change to the newness of one's conversion.

---

sub conditione rebaptizantur." Cappello, *De Sacra Ordinatione,* n. 524. *A fortiori,* those who have been *validly* baptized before their conversion do not come under the name of neophyte.

[59] Such a case would be rare, but it could happen that a convert of many years suddenly finds out that his baptism was absolutely invalid. For many years he has been living as a Catholic, but only now does he receive baptism. Certainly he would not be termed a neophyte. His conversion can no longer be called recent.

The judgment of the ordinary relative to the fitness of every candidate for Orders is demanded by law.[60] This power can be delegated. However, if the ordinary delegates this power to another in all matters except in the judgment required by canon 987, 6° and 7°, it will be necessary for the delegate to decide when he must appeal to the ordinary and when he can rely on his own judgment in this matter. The norm which will govern his actions must be measured in relation to the second element which is necessary for the existence of the status of a neophyte, namely recent baptism. Ordinarily it is an easy task to determine when the sacrament of baptism was conferred. The passage of time will remove the newness of the baptism, and once the baptism is no longer recent, then the individual is no longer a neophyte. Since he is no longer a neophyte, the delegate can then judge on the faith of the individual, and he need not refer the matter to the ordinary in the case as here envisioned.

The ordinary, according to his conscientious discretion, is given the complete faculty of judging on the sufficiency of the proof concerning the firmness of the neophyte's faith. However, those who are charged with assisting the ordinary in the preparation of candidates for Orders must be given some general norm whereby they can determine when they should appeal to the judgment of the ordinary on this specific point, if the ordinary in his act of delegation has reserved the judgment required by canon 987, 6°, to himself.[61]

The principle is very clear, namely, no candidate who is not sufficiently firm in his faith can be ordained licitly, whether he be a *clinicus,* a convert from a heretical sect, or a neophyte. However, the status of a neophyte is here under consideration, and not that of every convert or every recently baptized person. It must also be borne in mind that the Code by the use of the term *donec* prohibits the ordination of the neophyte until the ordinary has given his judgment. Present day authors make no attempt to decide how many years must elapse before a baptism can no longer be called recent. The case is very theoretical, but

---

60 Canon 968, § 1.

61 It may be remarked that such a case is admittedly a hypothetical one. But its presentation helps to illustrate the principle in question.

if the baptism is no longer recent, then the individual is no longer a neophyte, and if the ordinary wishes that only the cases of true neophytes be referred to him, then his delegate can judge on the firmness of the faith. It may take a lifetime for an individual to prove the firmness of his faith, but it will not take many years to remove the newness of one's baptism.[62]

In the absence of any positive legislation on this point, it is the opinion of the writer that after three years the conferral of baptism can no longer be called recent.[63] If three years have elapsed since the conferral of baptism, then the baptism is no longer recent, and the second element for the constitution of a neophyte is not present. Consequently the judgment of the

[62] Cappello, *De Sacra Ordinatione*, n. 527.

[63] The term "recent" is of a relative character. That which is considered recent by a person of 80 may be considered as happening long ago by a youth of 10. Thus any determination of the meaning of the term "recent" is open to much criticism.

If the present age of the convert and the age when he became an adult are considered as the two extremes, and the time when baptism was conferred is considered as the mean, a definite relationship can be established. It is through this relationship that the meaning of the phrase "recent baptism" can be determined.

Under ordinary circumstances a convert who seeks admission to the clerical state will be no younger than 20, and will be no older than 40 years of age. Considering events as they ordinarily happen, the writer thinks that the conferral of baptism which has taken place three years earlier would not be considered as recent for one who is 40 or younger in age.

In an extraordinary case the individual who seeks admission to the clerical state can be older than 40. In such a case it might be argued that the time should be more than three years. However, the writer has no intention to consider every possible case or to determine when every recently baptized adult ceases to be a neophyte. The concern of this work is to establish a general norm which can be employed in the consideration of a neophyte as a candidate for Orders under ordinary circumstances.

This period of three years seems to represent the average amount of time which was considered by authors in the pre-Code legislation. Some authors required one year, some required two, and still others required ten years before an individual ceased to be a neophyte.

The conferral of tonsure ordinarily occurs at the end of the first year of theology. Thus a period of three years would allow for two years of philosophical training and one year of theological training in an approved school.

ordinary as especially required in the case of a neophyte, which in the case contemplated the ordinary has reserved to himself, would no longer be demanded. If the baptism has been conferred within the past three years the ordinary's judgment is necessary in the premise. This is a consequent of the interpretation as here advocated. However, the ordinary is empowered with the faculty to determine for his own territory or for those under his jurisdiction the length of time which must elapse before a baptism will no longer be considered recent. This determination could be made by a diocesan law or statute.

The impediment continues to exist until (*donec*) the ordinary has judged the neophyte to be sufficiently proved in his faith. The judgment of the ordinary directly removes the foundation on which the impediment rests. His judgment has this for its equivalent: The conversion is no longer recent, and therefore the status of a neophyte is not here and now verified in this individual.

Although an individual may have ceased to be a neophyte inasmuch as his baptism can no longer be considered recent, the newness of his conversion, that is, the lack of firmness in his faith, will be sufficient to bar him from Orders. Thus a heretic, although not a neophyte when converted, may be held back from Orders by the ordinary.[64] But this refusal to ordain the convert cannot be based on the presence of the impediment of canon 987, 6°, which alone is here under consideration.

D. The Ordinary and his Judgment

In law the term "ordinary" is applied to the Roman Pontiff, the residential bishop for his own territory, abbots or prelates *nullius* and their vicars general, administrators, apostolic vicars, and also those who through the prescriptions of law or through approved constitutions succeed in power during the vacancies of the offices previously held by the aforementioned persons. The term "ordinary" is also applied in law to major superiors in clerical exempt religious institutes in relation to their subjects.[65] The aforementioned persons are competent to judge on the

[64] Whether or not an irregularity (canon 985, 1°) is present must be investigated by the ordinary.

[65] Canon 198, § 1.

status of a neophyte who wishes to be ordained. In forming his judgment the ordinary generally will depend on the judicious observations of others, since he is unable in most cases to conduct a personal observation. Although the observation may be conducted by others, the judgment is to be made by the ordinary, unless other arrangements have been made according to the law of the Code.

The jurisdictional power of the ordinary in this matter is *ipso iure* connected with his office, and as such is ordinary power.[66] There is nothing expressed in law which forbids the delegation of this power to another. Therefore the rector of the seminary could be delegated to judge in such cases for the ordinary.[67] This power to judge in such matters is not a judicial power according to the sense of canon 201, § 2. It can be exercised outside the confines of a judicial process, and is therefore a voluntary or non-judicial power.[68] Thus, the ordinary could delegate the rector of a seminary outside the ordinary's diocese to judge on his candidates who are attending the seminary.[69]

The judgment which is made by the ordinary concerning a neophyte must be authentically declared by him, but it should not be arrived at arbitrarily.[70] If the ordinary is unable to judge because of the lack of proof, then the impediment continues to exist. If he is in doubt, his doubt is not to be construed as admitting the application of canon 15. Canon 987, 6°, definitely states that the firmness of the neophyte's faith must be sufficiently proved. The presence of a doubt rather points to or connotes the insufficiency of the proof which may have been obtained. The particular legislation of canon 987, 6°, must be sustained. A dispensation would be required before the neophyte could be ordained licitly.

---

[66] Canon 197, § 1.

[67] Cf. canon 199, § 1.

[68] Cf Kearney, *The Principles of Delegation,* The Catholic University of America Canon Law studies, n. 55 (Washington, D. C.: The Catholic University of America, 1929), p. 102.

[69] Canon 201, § 3.

[70] Wernz-Vidal, IV, pars I, n. 263.

E. Dispensation from the Impediment

A dispensation[71] will rarely, if ever, be granted when the neophyte has been judged to be lacking in that firmness of faith which is so necessary in the guidance of others in the true faith. Instead of being a help in furthering the kingdom of Christ, a neophyte may become a stumbling block. Such a danger cannot be ignored by the Holy See, and therefore a dispensation will not be granted.

[71] Cf. pp. 14–17 for the discussion on the competent Congregation.

CHAPTER V

IN THE PARENTS

A. Historical Synopsis

In the *Decretum Gratiani* and in the Decretal Collections no *ex professo* presented treatment can be found of the impediment which involved the children of non-Catholics.[1] That such children were subject to some stigma can however be deduced from the consideration, as found in Gratian, which involved the question whether the children of heretics could be punished for the sin of their parents.[2] The question was solved in favor of the occasional punishment, either temporal or spiritual, never eternal, of the children.[3] Although the capacity to inflict punishment on the one hand, and the imposition of the actual punishment on the other, differ greatly, still it was reasonable to conclude that in the mind of the legislator the dignity and the sacredness of the priesthood would be safeguarded to a greater degree if the children of non-Catholic parents were impeded in the reception of Holy Orders.

Prescinding from present day legislation and from the modern interpretation of the term "non-Catholic," one can classify infidels, Jews, Mohammedans, heretics, schismatics and apostates as not belonging to the Catholic Faith.

There scarcely was occasion for the children of infidels to be considered in the legislation of the period represented by the Decree of Gratian. The children of infidels were sufficiently barred from the reception of Orders in virtue of the irregularity affecting neophytes. But the children of Jews were considered in a letter of Pope Gregory IX (1227–1241) to the bishop of Strasbourg. This consideration, however, involved the right of the convert father over the children whose mother had remained

1 Wernz-Vidal, IV, pars I, n. 256.

2 *Glossa Ordinaria* ad c. 1, C. XXIV, q. 3, ad c. *quod autem.*

3 *Loc. cit.*

in the Jewish religion.[4] Their canonical capacity for receiving Orders was not touched in this letter.

Innocent III (1198–1216) legislated that the sons and grandsons of heretical progenitors were not to be given any public ecclesiastical office or benefice.[5] This legislation was later adopted and reaffirmed by Alexander IV (1254–1261). The prohibition was a penalty inflicted for the crime of heresy, and, as noted, extended to the heretics' sons and grandsons. In itself the prohibition did not give rise to an impediment to the reception of Orders.

> Haeretici autem, credentes, receptatores, defensores et fautores eorum, *ipsorumque filii* usque ad secundum generationem, ad nullum ecclesiasticum beneficium seu officium publicum admittantur. Quod si secus actum fuerit decernimus irritum et inane.[6]

From the words of the law the appointment of the children of heretics to an ecclesiastical office was shown to be not only illicit, but also invalid.

Pope Boniface VIII (1294–1303) was more specific in his ruling which governed the extent of this prohibition. It extended to the second degree in the paternal line, and to the first degree in the maternal line.

> Primum et secundum gradum per paternam lineam comprehendere declaramus: per maternam vero ad primum dumtaxat volumus hoc extendi.[7]

In the event that the heretical parent or parents were not converted before their death the prohibition continued to affect their children.[8]

There was no general law in this matter regarding the children of schismatics and apostates. Boniface VIII (1294–1303), however, in a particular case barred the children from gaining the

---

[4] C. 2, X, *de conversione infidelium,* III, 33; Potthast, n. 8399.

[5] C. 10, X, *de haereticis,* V, 7; Potthast, n. 633.

[6] C. 2, *de haereticis,* V, 2, in VIo. The italics are inserted by the writer.

[7] C. 15, *de haereticis,* V, 2, in VIo.

[8] *Loc. cit.*

dignity of the cardinalate, and from acquiring any office, benefice and ministries, etc.

> Contra natos insuper et posteros dicti Ioannes spiritualiter et temporaliter duximus multipliciter procedendum, eorum bonis et iuribus publicatis et confiscatis, ipsisque posteris dicti Ioannis, per masculinam et femininam lineam descendentibus, indignis perpetuo redditis ad cardinalatus honorem et quaelibet officia, beneficia et ministeria in ecclesiae memorata vel eius curia, alibi vero ad quartum generationem.[9]

But this decree simply effected a punishment for a crime. It did not constitute an impediment to Orders. It was later revoked by Benedict XI (1303–1304) in his decretal "*Dudum bonae.*"[10]

The legislation of Innocent III and of Alexander IV with reference to the sons and grandsons of heretics, as later modified by Boniface VIII, formed the basis for the development of the irregularity which today is listed under the simple impediments to the reception of Orders.[11] The legislation itself was to the effect that the sons and grandsons of a heretical man, but the sons only of a heretical woman, could not under pain of nullity be admitted to any ecclesiastical benefice of public office.[12]

Since the legislation spoke of the impediment in relation to benefices and public offices, the question arose as to how and in what way the same legislation did refer to the reception of Orders. There were those who argued that it did not refer to the reception of Orders, since Orders were not public offices, and irregularities moreover could not affect the validity of the Orders conferred.[13] However, the common opinion which was held by almost all was to the effect that the sons and grandsons of a

---

[9] C. un., *de schismaticis,* V, 3, in VI°.

[10] C. un., *de schismaticis,* V, 4, in Extravag. com.; Potthast, n. 25324.

[11] Canon 987, 1°.

[12] C. 15, *de haereticis,* V, in VI°.

[13] Cf. Petra, *Commentaria in Constitutiones Apostolicas* (2 vols., Venetiis, 1729), *in Const. XV Innocentii Papae IV,* tom. III, n. 44 (hereafter cited as Petra).

heretical father, and the sons of a heretical mother, could not licitly receive Orders.[14]

The juridical basis upon which the authors rested their arguments for this opinion was not uniformly the same.[15] There were some who based the exclusion of the offspring of heretics from the reception of Orders on infamy as its foundation.[16] This opinion, however, was opposed by many authors, most of whom favored the doctrine that the children of heretics were by the very fact of their particular status irregular.[17] Some authors maintained that the prohibition from the reception of Orders was based neither on infamy nor on an irregularity as such, but on the similarity between the duties of a public ecclesiastical office and the functions of Sacred Orders.[18]

All were in agreement that the children of heretics were not to be ordained. This prohibition or irregularity *ex defectu natalium ob haeresim parentum* was held to extend also to the exclusion from the reception of tonsure.[19] If the children were born before the parent or parents fell into heresy, they were not impeded from the reception of Orders according to some authors,[20] but according to other authors they were barred.[21]

It was held that this irregularity or impediment did not extend to children born of pagans.[22] The irregularity affecting the heretic

---

[14] Cf. Boenninghausen, Fasc. III, p. 143.

[15] Cf. Petra, *ibid.*, nn. 44–46.

[16] Peña (1540–1612), Simancas (fl. 1550), and others cited by Petra, *ibid.*, n. 45; Schmier, *Iurisprudentia Canonico-civilis* (2 vols., Venetiis, 1754), I, lib. I, tr. 4, c. 6, n. 515 (hereafter cited as Schmier).

[17] Maioli, lib. V, c. 46, n. 5; Reiffenstuel, lib. V, tit. 7, n. 268; Pirhing, lib. V, tit. 7, n. 101; Boenninghausen, Fasc. III, p. 145.

[18] Petra, *ibid.*, n. 55: "Hinc non sunt inhabiles ad Ordines, ut Ordines sunt, et ratione sanctitatis illorum: sed solum ut sunt ministeria publica, adeoque proprie non sunt irregulares." Cf. also Gasparri, *De Sacra Ordinatione*, n. 473.

[19] S. C. S. Off., decr. 5 dec. 1906—*ASS*, XL (1907), 25.

[20] Pirhing, lib. V, tit. 7, n. 101; Schmalzgrueber, lib. V, tit. 7, n. 115; Gasparri, *De Sacra Ordinatione*, n. 472; Wernz, II, n. 139.

[21] Barbosa, *Collectanea*, lib. V, tit. 2, c. 15, n. 3; Reiffenstuel, lib. V, tit. 7, n. 286; Petra, tom. III, n. 22; Boenninghausen, Fasc. III, n. 146.

[22] Benedictus XIV, *De Synodo Dioecesana*, lib. XII, c. 1, n. 4; Gasparri, *De Sacra Ordinatione*, n. 474.

himself was held to remain even after his conversion, but his conversion was held to obviate the irregularity which had affected his children. If the heretical parent persisted in his error, or even if he died in his error, the irregularity which affected the children still continued.[23]

In Germany there arose a custom in the light of which the children of a heretic were not considered as irregular. This was based on the opinion that the prohibition existed in consequence of the note of infamy, and the authorities in Germany maintained that there was no infamy involved for the children of heretics in their localities.[24] The appeal to this custom was overruled by a decree of the Sacred Congregation of the Holy Office.[25]

Regardless of the arguments among authors as to the prerequisites for the delict of heresy with its consequent disability as affecting the culprit, it was fairly well agreed that the delict of heresy had to be accompanied with some degree of notoriety, either of fact or of law, before it affected the children.[26]

An apostate from the faith and his offspring were held to be subject to the same penalties and prohibitions as the heretic and his offspring.[27] The children of such as were simply suspected of heresy were considered as not falling under this irregularity.[28]

In the event that a heretic after his conversion relapsed and then once more returned to the faith, some authors regarded his children as irregular irrespective of the second conversion.

---

[23] S. C. S. Off., 4 dec. 1890: "Haereticos ad fidem catholicam conversos, ac filios haereticorum qui in haeresi *persistunt vel mortui sunt,* ad primum et secundum gradum per lineam paternam, per maternam vero ad primum dumtaxat, esse irregulares, etiam in Germania, et in aliis locis de quibus petitur; ideoque dispensatione indigere ut ad Tonsuram et Ordines promoveantur."—*Fontes,* n. 1129; *Collectanea Sacrae Congregationis de Propaganda* (2 vols., Romae: Typographia Polyglotta S. C. de Propaganda Fide, 1907), n. 1744 (hereafter cited as *Coll. S. C. P. F.*); *ASS,* XXIII (1890), 700. The italics in the quoted text are inserted by the writer.

[24] Laymann, lib. I, tract. V, pars V, c. IV, n. 12; Pirhing, lib. III, tit. 7, n. 101.

[25] S. C. S. Off., 4 dec. 1890—*Fontes,* n. 1129; *ASS,* XXIII (1890), 700.

[26] Boenninghausen, Fasc. III, p. 151.

[27] Pirhing, lib. V, tit. 9, n. 2; Boenninghausen, Fasc. III, p. 133.

[28] Petra, tom. III, n. 20.

But there were also other authors who regarded the second conversion as equally effective as the first in its removal of the irregularity as affecting the children.[29]

There was no general law which prohibited the ordination of the sons of infidels or the sons of Jews. In some localities particular laws forbade the ordination of the descendants of Jews.[30] It was not permitted to extend to the descendants of Jews and pagans the irregularity affecting the children of heretics. The statutes of any diocesan synod which forbade the ordination of the descendants of infidels or of Jews were considered to have no force whatsoever except on the basis that the descendant in a particular case was a neophyte,[31] although the exercise of great care and caution in the ordination of the descendants of Jews and other non-baptized persons was praised as a commendable procedure.[32] In support of the non-inclusion of the descendants of infidels and of Jews authors[33] referred to two responses of the Sacred Congregation of the Council, in which the descendants of non-baptized non-Catholics were considered relative to their capacity to hold certain offices.[34]

Whenever this impediment or irregularity existed, it was maintained that one could be ordained only if a dispensation had been obtained, and that this could be granted only by the Holy See.[35]

B. Canonical Commentary—" Filii acatholicorum, quandiu parentes in suo errore permanent "

The preceding historical study attests to the gradual change in

[29] Cf. Wernz, II, n. 141; Boenninghausen, Fasc. III, p. 146.

[30] Pope Sixtus V in an apostolic letter dated January 15, 1588. This was confirmed by Pope Clement VIII, on December 18, 1600. These two letters are referred to in Benedictus XIV, *De Synodo Dioecesana,* lib. XII, cap. 1, n. 4. Cf. also Boenninghausen, Fasc. III, p. 156; Gasparri, *De Sacra Ordinatione,* n. 474.

[31] Cf. Benedictus XIV, *De Synodo Diocesana,* lib. XII, cap. 1, nn. 4-6.

[32] *Ibid,* n. 6.

[33] Cf. Boenninghausen, Fasc. III, p. 154.

[34] S. C. C., *Milevitana,* 13 aug. 1718—*Fontes,* n. 3173; S. C. C., *Pragen.,* 12 maii 1759—*Fontes,* n. 3685.

[35] S. C. S. Off., 28 nov. 1688—*Coll. S. C. P. F.,* n. 170; *ASS,* XL (1906), 25.

the law which became the foundation for the legislation expressed in canon 987, 1°. In the beginning both the sons and the grandsons were affected by the impediment. Later the grandsons in the maternal line were excluded from the comprehension of the law. Under the present law the term "*filii*" is used in such manner that only the sons and not the grandsons, as grandsons, in either the maternal or the paternal line are affected with the simple impediment of canon 987, 1°.[36]

1. FILII ACATHOLICORUM

a. The Meaning of the Term "Filii"

The term "*filii*" points to the relationship which exists between the parents and their offspring. Maternity and paternity originate through the fact of conception, but they receive their full external expression at the time of the birth of the child, for it is only upon the birth of the child that the fact of parenthood is predicated of the parents. Nevertheless, if it could be conclusively shown that a son was conceived of one union, although he was born during a later union, then the real parents of the child are the parties of the first union. The presumption in law, which must be overthrown if its opposite is to be admitted and acknowledged, is that the father is he to whom the woman was united at the time of the birth of the child. If it can be conclusively shown that the man and woman of the second union are not the parents of the child, but that those of the first union are, then the religious status of the parties of the first union will be the determining factor for deciding whether an impediment to the reception of Orders affects their son.[37]

The sonship which is expressed in the term "*filii*" refers to the natural offspring, and not to a child which is recognized as a son through the process of adoption. In the pre-Code legislation the irregularity, which now is enacted as a simple impediment, extended to the grandsons, that is, to the second generation in the paternal line. No form of legal adoption gives rise to a relationship either of affinity or of consanguinity between the

[36] P. C. I., 14 Iul. 1922—*AAS*, XIV (1922), 528.
[37] Cf. canon 1114.

adopted son and the father of the adopting father. The use of the phrase "*ad secundam generationem*" plainly indicates that the process of generation, and not of adoption, was the determining factor in this consideration.[38]

This conclusion was supported by the common opinion that those sons and grandsons who were born before the father or mother fell into heresy could be ordained.[39] Legal adoption cannot have its external effect until after the child is born. Yet it is before birth that real parentage is already inherently determined. Thus, if the child is born of Catholic parents, but is later adopted by someone who is not a Catholic, then as far as the impediment is concerned, the adopted son would be in the same condition as a son who was born before his real parents fell into heresy. The term "*filii,*" therefore, refers to male children whose parents are presumed to be those who ordinarily are united in marriage at the time of the birth of the child.

There exists no reason which could raise any justified assumption that there has been a change in the law of the Code in relation to the concept of paternity. The term "*filii*" refers to natural, and not adopted, sons.[40] When the Pontificial Commission for the Interpretation of the Code was asked if the term "*filii*" in canon 987, 1°, refers only to the descendants of the paternal line in the first degree, the Commission replied in the affirmative.[41] Although the main point at issue was whether grandsons were included in the term "*filii,*" still the choice of such words as "descendants" and "in the first degree" favors the view that the term "*filii*" does not include adopted sons.

The illegitimate child is born of parents who live either outside of wedlock or in unlawful wedlock. If the identity of the father is established and he is at the same time a non-Catholic, then the child comes within the scope of canon 987, 1°. An

[38] Cf. S. C. S. Off., decr., 5 dec. 1906—*ASS,* XL (1907), 25; also Boenninghausen, Fasc. III, p. 146, where the following terms are used: "*ex coitu natos,*" "*nepos ab ipso genitus,*" "*filii a patre catholico geniti,*" "*filios natos.*"

[39] Cf. Gasparri, *De Sacra Ordinatione,* n. 472.

[40] The term "natural" is here used exclusively to designate the relationship of the parents to the son through birth.

[41] P. C. I., 14 iul. 1922—*AAS,* XIV (1922), 528.

illegitimate child is not to be treated more favorably than a legitimate child.[42]

All illegitimate sons are comprehended under the term "*filii.*"[43] If they are born of non-Catholic parentage, but the non-Catholic status of the parentage does not persist in the present, then they are not under the impediment in canon 987, 1°. If there exists a doubt as to whose son a particular individual is, or whether the known father is a non-Catholic, the ordinary can grant a dispensation in virtue of the rule of law established in canon 15.[44]

Those who through the power of generation have effected the conception and birth of a child are the parents. If one or both of the parents are non-Catholics at the time of the birth of the child, then there exists a basis for the impediment. Conception establishes parenthood, but the moment of birth marks the time at which the non-Catholicity of the parents remains to be determined. At the time of the child's conception both parents may have been Catholic, but at the time of the child's birth one or both of the parents may have become non-Catholics. In such a case the child is *born* of non-Catholic parents, and will correspondingly come under the impediment. If, however, the parents are Catholics at the time of the birth of the son, and only later on one or both become non-Catholics, then the child does not come under the impediment.[45] This was the more common opinion prior to the Code, and there does not seem to be any reason to recede from this benign interpretation of the law.[46]

Unless one accept the principle that a son who was *born* before either of the parents became a non-Catholic is not under the impediment, it would follow that an ordained son could no longer exercise the Orders he had licitly received, given the simple fact

[42] Boenninghausen, Fasc. III, p. 146; Gasparri, *De Sacra Ordniatione*, n. 472; Cappello, *De Sacra Ordinatione*, n. 519.

[43] "Filii censentur seu legitimi seu illegitimi."—Cappello, *De Sacra Ordinatione*, n. 519.

[44] Cf. Cappello, *De Sacra Ordinatione*, n. 519.

[45] "Vicissim filii nati ex parentibus catholicis non videntur fieri irregulares, si unus parentum vel uterque in haeresim labatur et per evidentiam facti constet esse haereticum."—Wernz-Vidal, IV, pars I, n. 256; cf. also Ayrinhac, *Legislation on the Sacraments*, p. 372.

[46] Cf. Gasparri, *De Sacra Ordinatione*, n. 472 and footnote.

that after the ordination either one of his parents has fallen into the classification of non-Catholics.[47] This does not seem to be the intention of the legislator.

The use of the words, "*quandiu parentes in suo errore permanent,*" seems to support the opinion that it is at the time of the birth of the child that the religion of the parents becomes a determining factor. The term "*permanent*" denotes "continue" or "persevere." Continuation or perseverance necessarily points to the past inception of an act, and therefore denotes a status which up to the present has been in existence since the time of its inception. The moment of inception must be established at some point of time in the past. Since the term "*permanent*" is predicated of "*parentes,*" it is but logical to conclude that the point of inception of the externally expressed status of the parents, that is, the moment of the child's birth, must also be the point of time at which will be determined the religious status of the parents, since it is the particular status and character of their religion through which is effected the condition postulated for the arising of the impediment.

The pertinent question therefore is: What was the religious status of the parents at the time of the birth of their son? Now, with reference to any general ecclesiastical law there can be cases which are comprehended under the law in virtue of the wording of the law itself, but which are not comprehended under the law also in virtue of the end which the law desires to attain. Conversely, there can be cases which are not comprehended under the law in virtue of the wording of the law itself, but which are comprehended under the law *solely* in virtue of the end which the law desires to attain. As a source of interpretation the end of the law is to be resorted to in obtaining its authentic meaning only when there is doubt regarding the meaning of the words in the law itself as contemplated in its text and context.[48]

When one can, without doing violence to the text and context,

---

[47] Cf. canon 968, § 2.

[48] Canon 18; cf. Schmidt, *The Principles of Authentic Interpretation in Canon 17 of the Code of Canon Law,* The Catholic University of America Canon Law Studies, n. 141 (Washington, D. C.: The Catholic University of America Press, 1941), pp. 122–153 (hereafter cited as Schmidt).

interpret the words of the ecclesiastical law in such a manner that the law will be recognized as accomplishing the desired end in the particular case, then one must rely upon the text and context for the proper interpretation. According to the legal principle set forth in canon 19, a law which establishes impediments is subject to a strict interpretation. Now, since the end of the present law is identical with the purpose of the pre-Code law, and since under the former law it was the common opinion that no irregularity arose for those upon whose birth the parents subsequently fell into heresy, there seems to be no ground for any change from the former interpretation.

In an individual case the son of Catholic parents may be far weaker in his faith than the son of non-Catholic parents, whether one or both of them be non-Catholics. The former will be debarred from Orders, not in view of the impediment of canon 987, 1°, but because of his lack of the necessary qualities which are demanded in the candidate for the clerical life.[49] The latter will be debarred from the reception of Orders by reason of the impediment of canon 987, 1°, although he may be well qualified subjectively to attain the desired end for the safeguarding of which the impediment was established.

b. *The Meaning of the Term "Acatholicorum"*

The term "*acatholicorum*" is used in canon 987, 1°, with the unexpressed but implied term "*parentum*" serving as a substantive with which that term must be linked. Although the plural number is used, the impediment still is applicable to the son if simply one of his parents is a non-Catholic . This is true even if a dispensation from the matrimonial impediment of mixed religion or of disparity of cult was granted in preparation for the marriage after the required guarantees had been duly furnished.[50]

---

[49] Cf. canons 973, § 3; 974, § 1, 2°.

[50] The Pontifical Commission for the Interpretation of the Code was asked: "Whether one is to be considered among those impeded when only his father or his mother is non-Catholic, the other parent being Catholic. And if so, whether this would be true even where the mixed marriage was contracted with a dispensation, and the *cautiones* were given." The response

The meaning of parenthood as it is understood in the present law has been explained previously, so that it remains necessary only to determine the meaning of the term "*acatholicorum*."

1. The Etymological Meaning of the Term "*Acatholicorum*"

The word "*acatholicus*" is the result of a union of two terms. The one term, *a*, has the force of a complete negative; the other term, *catholicus*, refers in a positive manner to those who upon receiving the gift of faith and of baptism profess that faith as members of the true Church. Therefore anyone who is not a member of the true Church through faith and baptism is an *acatholicus* or a non-Catholic.[51] Under the term *acatholicus*, then, are included heretics, schismatics, apostates, infidels, Jews, Mohammedans, etc. This is the etymological meaning of the term. Is this the meaning of the term "non-Catholic" as it is used in canon 987, 1°, or is the meaning to be restricted so as to designate simply certain groups or categories of individuals who are not members of the Church, e.g., heretics, schismatics and apostates?

2. The Historical Usage of the Term "*Acatholicorum*"

The term "*acatholicus*" cannot be found in the collection of Gratian or in the decretal collections. The first time, at least in canon law, that the term "*acatholicus*" appears is in a question which was directed to the Sacred Congregation of the Holy Office and answered on November 29, 1764.[52]

---

was in the affirmative to all.—16 oct. 1919—*ASS*, XI (1919), 478. Translation taken from Bouscaren, I, 487. That the same would not be true if the granted dispensation related to the impediment of disparity of cult cannot be argued from the response, for the submitted question and given answer were not such as to exclude the case of a marriage contracted with a dispensation from the impediment of disparity of cult.

[51] Cf. Schmid, "De vi verborum 'acatholicus, secta acatholica, minister acatholicus' in Iure Canonico"—*Apollinaris*, IV (1931), 552-567); V (1931), 69-85 (hereafter this article will be referred to under its author's name).

[52] "An presbyteri catholici licite extra mortis periculum baptizare possint acatholicorum filios a patrinis catholicis oblatos, quibus tamen nullo affulgeat spes illos de catholica religione imbuendi." "R. Negative; sed minister catholicus caute se geret in danda repulsa, ne patrini aut parentes pueri oblati scandalum patiantur."—*Fontes*, n. 815.

Although this response is referred to in the annotations listed under canon 751, which deals with the baptism of the children of heretics, schismatics and apostates, reference to the response could very appropriately have been placed under canon 750, § 2, which deals with the baptism of the children of infidels. However, since it is placed under canon 751, one can argue that by reason of its relation to that canon the term "*acatholicus*" refers in this instance to heretics, schismatics and apostates.

In many of the official documents of the Holy See prior to the Code the term "*acatholicus*" was used to designate infidels.[53] For instance, the decree "*Ne temere*" issued by the Sacred Congregation of the Council on August 2, 1907, very definitely contains the term "*acatholicus.*"[54] The term there includes infidels within its meaning.[55] Thus prior to the Code the term "*acatholicus*" was used both in a restricted and in a general sense.

3. The Use of the Term "*Acatholicorum*" in the Code

In the Code the term "*acatholicus*" is used to refer to all those who are not Catholics, whether or not they are baptized. There seems to be no place for doubt concerning the meaning of the term "*acatholicus*" in canon 1350. The lawmaker intends to include all non-Catholics, the non-baptized as well as the baptized.[56] The same can be said of canon 1149.[57] In the legislation regarding those who may receive the blessings of the Church in order to obtain the light of faith and bodily health, certainly all

[53] Schmid—*Apollinaris,* IV (1931), 554.

[54] *ASS,* XL (1907), 525–530; *Fontes,* n. 4340.

[55] Cf. XI, §§ 2–3, of the decree. The corresponding texts read: "Vigent [leges statutae] quoque pro iisdem de quibus supra catholicis, si cum *acatholicis sive baptizatis sive non baptizatis* . . . sponsalia vel matrimonium contrahunt . . ." and "*Acatholici sive baptizati sive non baptizati,* si inter se contrahunt, nullibi ligantur ad catholicam sponsalium vel matrimonii formam servandam." (Italics inserted by the present writer.)

[56] Canon 1350, § 1—"Ordinarii locorum et parochi acatholicos, in suis dioecesibus et paroeciis degentes, commendatos sibi in Domino habeant."

§ 2—"In aliis territoriis universa missionum cura apud acatholicos Sedi Apostolicae unice reservatur."

[57] "Benedictiones, imprimis impertiendae catholicis, dari quoque possunt cathechumenis, imo, nisi obstet Ecclesiae prohibitio, etiam acatholicis ad obtinendum fidei lumen vel, una cum illo, corporis sanitatem."

baptized and non-baptized non-Catholics are referred to by the lawmaker. Many other canons of the Code evidence the fact that the term "*acatholicus*" refers to all non-members of the true Church, e.g., canons 1062, 1071, 1099, § 3, 1102, § 1, 1109, § 3, 1132, 1152, 1258, § 1, 1325, § 3, 1399, 1°, 4°, 1657, § 1, 1964, and others. In these canons there seems to be no justification for the exclusion of Jews and infidels from the comprehension of the term "non-Catholic."

If the term "*acatholicus*" was intended by the lawmaker to refer only to heretics, schismatics and apostates, as Cappello contends,[58] why was the term not used in canons 751, 731, § 2, and others? The objection thus proposed in this counterquestion may not have a fully convincing value, but it at least shows that the lawmaker may have realized the possibility of misinterpretation had he simply used the term "*acatholicus.*" From internal arguments it seems proper to state the rule: If the lawmaker wishes to exclude some particular group of non-Catholics, he generally makes an express mention of this exclusion by the addition of some restricting word or phrase. With reference to canon 987, 1°, did the lawmaker make use of the general term *acatholicus* without intending to include all non-Catholics, baptized and not baptized alike?

In canon 987, 1°, so it seems, there is no alternative but to adhere to the letter of the text. This may be argued from the authority of the glossator of the law "*Ad audientiam*" of the Decretals.[59]

Can there be an appeal to the pre-Code law, from which the

[58] "Legislator autem quando sub ea voce [acatholico] etiam *infideles* comprehendere voluit, id expresse enuntiavit, v. g. in can. 1099, § 1, 2°."—*De Sacra Ordinatione,* n. 504. (Cappello's text refers to canon 1098, § 1, 2°, which reference is evidently a printing mistake.)

[59] "Argumentum quod a forma verborum sine certa scientia non est recedendum." *Glossa* ad v. *Intelligeremus,* c. 12, X, *de decimis,* II, 30: cf. Schmidt, pp. 149–153. Cf. also Cardinal Gasparri's preface to the text of the present Code: "III. Ut in canonibus redigendis Consultor, aliusve operis ordinator, e documentis excerpta verba, quantum posset, fideliter referret, brevitati simul et perspicuitati studeret . . ."—Quite explicitly canon 18 calls for an understanding of the Church's law "secundum propriam verborum significationem in textu et contextu consideratam."

law of canon 987, 1°, has been derived? In the pre-Code law the phrase "*filii haereticorum,*" and not "*filii acatholicorum,*" was used. For a just cause the Pontiffs in pre-Code times had excluded from Orders the descendants of Jews. This exclusion was enacted by way of particular law, *e.g.*, in Portugal.[60] It is true that synods were explicitly forbidden to make statutes which debarred descendants of Jews, except on the basis that such descendants were neophytes. However, the use of great care and caution in the ordination of the descendants of Jews was praised.[61]

Has the Code made a universal law of that which in pre-Code times was a particular law for localities as determined by the Holy See? Has the lawmaker in the Code enacted a law based on the care and caution which was praised, but which at the same time was not permitted to have the force of a law to establish an irregularity? Or has the lawmaker retained the pre-Code law without any change, at least with reference to any more comprehensive extension of its phrase *filii haereticorum?* If the pre-Code law has been retained, then the phrase *filii haereticorum* is identical in meaning with the phrase *filii acatholicorum,* and the sons of infidels, Jews, etc., are not included in the terminology of canon 987, 1°.

4. An Evaluation of the Arguments of Those Who Favor a Restricted Interpretation of the Phrase "*Filii Acatholicorum*"

Among the authors who maintain that the present law in its use of the phrase *filii acatholicorum* presents but a restatement of the pre-Code law are Cappello, Vidal, Creusen, Ayrinhac and Beste. Cappello in his commentary on canon 987, 1°,[62] refers back to his commentary on canon 985, 2°.[63] There he states:

> Nomine *acatholicorum* hic intelligi debent haeretici, schismatici et apostatae, non autem infideles. Versamur

[60] Cf. Benedictus XIV, *De Synodo Dioecesana,* lib. XII, cap. 1, nn. 4–5; also *supra,* p. 110.

[61] Benedictus XIV, *ibid.,* nn. 4–6.

[62] *De Sacra Ordinatione,* n. 519.

[63] *Ibid.,* n. 504.

> in odiosis. Nam vox *acatholici* presse sumpta haereticos, schismaticos et apostatas significat. Legislator autem quando sub ea voce etiam *infideles* comprehendere voluit id expresse enuntiavit, v. g. in can. 1099, § 1, 2°.

Against this opinion it may be argued that canon 985, 2°, deals with an irregularity arising *ex delicto,* while canon 987, 1°, concerns itself with an impediment which for the efficacy of its juridical effects in no way depends on any delict on the part of the one impeded from the reception of Orders. Then, too, any one who would be prepared to baptize an individual outside the case of extreme necessity could well be presumed to be a member of a sect which confers baptism on its members.[64] An infidel, a Jew of a Mohammedan in all probability would not be prepared under ordinary circumstances to administer the sacrament of baptism. If he were prepared to do so his readiness would in general be occasioned by the petitioner of the baptism. So it seems that only some extreme necessity would prompt the petitioner to instruct an infidel, a Jew, etc., to confer the baptism. Yet in such circumstances nothing is done that gives occasion for the irregularity to arise. Thus by reason of that which ordinarily occurs Cappello may indeed justify his statement on the meaning of the term *acatholicus* in canon 985, 2°, but not by reason of the term itself. If there were found a non-baptized non-Catholic who outside the case of extreme necessity confers baptism, although he be not an apostate, a heretic or a schismatic, it seems that he too would come within the comprehension of the term " non-Catholic " of canon 985, 2°.

Cappello asserts: " *Versamur in idiosis.*" This assertion makes an appeal to the axiom " *Odiosa sunt restringenda.*" But, with reference to canon 987, 1°, one may well ask: Just who is the bearer of the odium in this case? Is it the Church, or is it the prospective candidate for Orders? [65]

In the light of the internal arguments which have been previously submitted, it seems that Cappello reverses the general

---

[64] Canon 985, 2° states: [" Sunt irregulares ex delicto:] Qui praeterquam in casu extremae necessitatis, baptismum ab *acatholicis* quovis modo sibi conferri siverunt." (Italics are inserted by the present writer.)

[65] Cf. Schmidt, p. 150.

principle. He maintains that when the legislator wishes to include infidels under the term "*acatholicus*" he expressly states it. In view of the many canons which have been previously cited,[66] it seems that the principle should read: When the legislator wishes to exclude infidels from the comprehension of the term "*acatholicus*" he expressly states it. However, in an endeavor to support his assertion Cappello gives as an example, canon 1099, § 1, 2°.

Canon 1099 has for the most part been taken from the decree "*Ne temere.*"[67] Prior to the decree "*Ne temere,*" except where the decree "*Tametsi*" was promulgated,[68] a marriage contracted before a civil magistrate or a non-Catholic minister was valid.[69] It seems that if the "*Ne temere*" decree had used the term *acatholici* without any qualification, then there could have been some occasion for the term to be interpreted as referring only to those who were not baptized. Prior to the decree, as now, non-baptized non-Catholics in contracting marriage with Catholics were indirectly bound to contract that union before a priest. A dispensation from the impediment of disparity of cult was necessary. It cannot be thought that such a dispensation would have been granted if the parties intended to go before a non-Catholic minister or a justice of the peace.

It appears, then, that the legislator qualified the term "*acatholici*" in the "*Ne temere*" decree in order that baptized non-Catholics would certainly be included under its comprehension. To the writer it accordingly does not seem correct to appeal to canon 1099, § 1, 2°, in support of the statement that when the legislator wishes to include non-baptized persons under the term "non-Catholic" he expressly states this inclusion.

Cappello admits that there has been a change in the law in many

---

[66] Cf. *supra*, pp. 117–118.

[67] Cf. *supra*, p. 117.

[68] Conc. Trident., sess. XXIV, *de ref. matrim.*, c. 1. Cf. Schroeder, *Canons and Decrees of the Council of Trent* (St. Louis: Herder, 1941), pp. 183–185, for an English translation of the decree *Tametsi*.

[69] For a study on the form of marriage, cf. Carberry, *The Juridical Form of Marriage*, The Catholic University of America Canon Law Studies, n. 84 (Washington, D. C.: The Catholic University of America, 1934).

other regards, but at the same time he contends that the present employment of the term *acatholicorum* in place of the former use of the term *haereticorum* does not imply any change with regard to the class of persons subject to the impediment. There has been a change in the extension of the impediment. It now affects only the sons, and no longer the grandsons as such. If the parents have died in their heresy the impediment no longer binds the son, whereas in pre-Code law the irregularity continued even after the death of the heretical parent.[70]

Now, in making such changes the legislator was well aware of the pre-Code law, and it seems that he likewise contemplated a change when he introduced the use of the new term *acatholicus*. There can of course be no denial of the fact that the law of the Code may retain at least a part of the previous law.[71] And if there is a real doubt whether that part has been retained, then an identity between the earlier and later law must be assumed. However, the doubt of law as affecting the meaning and extent of the impediment here considered depends, not on the number of authors who acknowledge the doubt, but on the weight of the reasons which are deduced from the law itself.[72]

Vidal (1867–1938) rewords canon 987, 1º, to make it read as follows:

> Filii haereticorum, quamdiu parentes in suo errore permanent.

By such a restatement of the canon all readily apparent difficulty is avoided. However, no explanation is given for the substitution of the term "*haereticorum*" in place of the term "*acatholicorum.*"[73] Vidal admits that there have been departures from the previous law in the same things that Cappello singles out as changes in the law.

Vermeersch-Creusen state:

---

[70] *De Sacra Ordinatione*, n. 519.

[71] Cf. canon 6, 3º.

[72] "Non ex auctorum numero, sed ex rationum pondere, et in praesenti materia ex verbis iurium recte expensis et ponderatis colligendum est."—Suarez, *De Censuris*, disp. XL, sect. 5, n. 7.

[73] Wernz-Vidal, IV, pars I, n. 256.

> Contra AUGUSTINE, *A Commentary* IV, p. 498, acatholicis etiam infideles designari non censemus. Ipsa S. C. *Concilii* filium e iudaica stirpe ortum non impederi censuit.[74]

Historically it is true that the sons born of Jews were not under the irregularity in the general legislation before the Code.[75] In the pre-Code law the term "*haereticorum*" was used. The term "*haereticus*" does not include Jews. But the question really is: Would the term "*acatholicorum*" have included them had it been used in the pre-Code legislation? Would the Sacred Congregation have given the same responses, if the term "*acatholicus*" had been used in the pre-Code legislation? It does not seem correct to appeal to the pre-Code response of the Sacred Congregation of the Council, when the term "*haereticus*" was used,

---

[74] *Epitome,* II, n. 259. The response to which Augustine and Vermeersch-Creusen refer is contained in Richter, *Canones et Decreta Concilii Tridentini* (Lipsiae, 1853), p. 339, n. 3. This text together with the text in numbers 4 and 5 is as follows: "Hominem ex Iudaica stirpe ortum a clericali tonsura repulerat episcopus Palmensis propterea, quod licet ab incunabulis Christianam fidem professus esset, infamia tamen facti laboraret . . . S. C. vero impedimentum ab episcopo allegatum non constare censuit. *Maioricen.* 24 ian. 1749. N. 4—Franciscus Bolowski a Capitulo Pragensi ad Beneficium cum cura animarum nominatus fuerat. Quum autem a parentibus Iudaeis originem duxisset et in aetate duorum annorum ad fidem catholicam pervenisset, *petiit dispensationem ab irregularitate.* S. C. respondit: *Non indigere dispensatione.*—S. C. C., *Pragen.*, 12 maii 1759 [*Fontes,* n. 3685]. Contra vero, cum ageretur de oratore in Hebraismo orto et quinque abhinc annis baptizato, qui in seminario Adriensi per duos annos moratus erat, licet de moribus eius et pietate episcopus testaretur eumque dignum haberet qui clericali militiae adscriberetur et ad sacros etiam ordines promoveretur, ad dubia: I An constet de irregularitate in casu? et quatenus affirmative. II An sit locus dispensationi in casu etc? S. C. resp. ad I affirmative, ad II affirmative, nempe esse locum dispensationi arbitrio episcopi. *Adrien.* 31 maii 1783. N. 5—Sacerdotem, natum a parentibus Turcis, in aetate infantili baptizatum, absolutione non indigere cum rehabilitatione ad ordines, neque indigere nova provisione beneficiorum censuit S. C. in *Melevitana* 13 aug. 1718 [*Fontes*, n. 3173]." (It may be noted that these texts are contained under Sess. XXIV, *de ref.*, c. 6 which was speaking of the power of bishops to dispense.)

[75] Cf. *supra,* p. 110.

in order to determine the meaning of the term "*acatholicus,*" which is the term now used in the Code.

The edition of the *Epitome* in which Vermeersch-Creusen make their statement is the fifth (1934). Perhaps in view of the response which was given on July 30, 1934, by the Pontifical Commission for the Interpretation of the Code, this expression of opinion may have been changed. In this response it is stated that any person who belongs to an atheistic sect is to be considered, as regards all legal effects, even those which concern sacred ordination and marriage, the same as persons who belong to a non-Catholic sect.[76]

Ayrinhac (1867–1930), who in view of the same response could well have changed his opinion had he still been alive, stated:

> Some canonists interpret it [the term *acatholicorum*] as thereby including likewise infidels, but others refuse to admit without stronger evidence such an aggravation of the law in odious matters. In other places when the Code designates infidels with the term non-Catholics, it adds some other qualification.[77]

It is hoped that stronger evidence has been offered in accordance with Ayrinhac's desire. The application of the axiom "*Odiosa sunt restringenda*" as a principle for solving the present difficulty does not seem indicated as apropos.[78]

Beste treats the difficulty as follows:

> Utrum vox *acatholicorum* comprehendat haereticos et schismaticos tantum, an etiam extendatur ad infideles (paganos, iudaeos, mahumetanos), non una est doctorum sententia nec certo erui potest, donec authentica declaratio hac super re prodierit.[79]

This statement presupposes that the doubt is one which concerns the meaning of the law itself. If such is the case, then the writer is in perfect agreement with the statement of Beste. If,

---

[76] *AAS,* XXVI (1934), 494. This response will later be considered more at length.

[77] *Legislation on the Sacraments,* p. 372.

[78] Cf. *supra,* p. 120.

[79] *Introductio in Codicem,* p. 534.

however, the doubt is occasioned only by the difference of opinions among the authors, whose reasons for considering the issue as doubtful are unsupported in law, then it follows that any eventual authentic interpretation will be but a declaration of what is certain as far as the law is concerned.[80]

It seems, indeed, that any eventual authentic interpretation may be expected to be simply declarative, rather than extensive in its character. The official interpretation may well follow along the same legal channels as the interpretation which was rendered by the Pontifical Commission for the Interpretation of the Code concerning the phrase "*ab acatholicis nati,*" contained in canon 1099, § 2.[81]

Prior to the given responses there was indeed a difference of opinion among the authors on the meaning of the phrase "*ab acatholicis nati.*" The responses gave a greater extension to the phrase than had been given by many, if not most, of the authors. When asked, the Pontifical Commission stated that its initial response was simply declarative, and not extensive in character. These responses are here referred to in order to show what may well become the Pontifical Commission's authentic interpretation of canon 987, 1°, if and when the Commission is called on to give a response. In themselves, of course, these responses do not offer any direct aid in the matter of determining the meaning of the term "*acatholicus*" as employed in canon 987, 1°.

5. The Term "*Acatholica*" when Joined with the Term "*Secta*"

The term "*acatholicus*" of canon 987, 1°, is not to be considered as equivalently pointing simply to any member of a *secta acatholica*. The member of a non-Catholic sect belongs to a

[80] Canon 17, § 2.

[81] 20 iul. 1929—"D. An *ab acatholicis nati,* de quibus in canone 1099, § 2, dicendi sint etiam nati ab alterutro parente acatholico, cautionibus quoque praestitis ad normam canonum 1061 et 1071. R. Affirmative."—*AAS,* XXI (1929), 573. "D. Utrum interpretatio diei 20 iulii 1929 ad canonem 1099, § 2, sit declarativa, an extensiva. R. Affirmative ad primam parten, negative ad secundam."—*AAS,* XXIII (1931), 388. Cf. Schmidt, pp. 149-153, for a discussion regarding these two responses. Cf. also a response on February 17, 1930, which put apostates in the class of *acatholici.*—*AAS,* XXII (1930), 195.

more restricted category than the person whom the Code calls an *acatholicus*. Some of the authors who regard the term "*acatholicus*" now used in the Code as an equivalent for the term "*haereticus*" as used in the pre-Code law nevertheless admit that a public apostate or schismatic is to be included under the term "*acatholicus*." These authors generally make no demand that the apostate or the schismatic be affiliated with a heretical sect in order to be classed as *acatholicus*.[82] Vidal, however, seems to demand that the schismatic or the apostate belong to a heretical sect before his son becomes subject to the impediment listed in canon 987, 1°.[83]

Thus, those who refused to admit that the term "non-Catholic" includes infidels are at variation among themselves. They do not agree on the extension of the term. Vidal seems to exclude from the meaning of non-Catholic, as used in canon 987, 1°, all apostates and heretics who have not joined a heretical sect, and all apostates and heretics who have joined a sect such as a Jewish, Mohammedan, or atheistic sect. To Vidal a heretical sect is one in which the reception of baptism can alone constitute the rite of initiation. Cappello and Beste exclude infidels, Jews, etc., if they have been such from birth, from the category of the non-Catholics mentioned in canon 987, 1°. Logically, then, they must include in that category any baptized Catholic who has publicly become a Jew, a Mohammedan, or an atheist. Certainly such a Catholic has become an apostate, or at least a heretic.

It is evident that the doctrine which leads to this conclusion lays emphasis on the past reception of baptism as a condition which must be fulfilled in the life of a person if he is to be regarded as an *acatholicus*. The reception of baptism does not seem to be an essential factor in the determination of who is

82 "Nam vox presse sumpta haereticos, schimaticos et apostatas significat . . . Necesse est ut *publici* seu *notorii* acatholici, sive per se sectae haereticae aut schismaticae sint adscripti sive non."—Cappello, *Da Sacra Ordinatione*, n. 504. Beste includes heretics and schismatics under the term "*acatholici*." He does not distinguish between schismatics who have joined a heretical sect and schismatics who have not joined a sect."—*Introductio in Codicem*, p. 534.

83 "*Practice* etiam filius scismatici non puri, et apostatae qui ad sectam haereticam transierit comprehenditur."—*Ius Canonicum*, IV, pars I, n. 256.

to be regarded as an *acatholicus* according to the wording of canon 987, 1°. This can be argued from a response of the Pontifical Commission for the Interpretation of the Code, which was given on July 30, 1934.[84] The son of parents of a Christian sect definitely is under the impediment. According to the aforementioned response, membership in an atheistic sect begets the same juridical consequences in relation to ordination as does membership in a Christian sect. Thus, the son of parents of an atheistic sect is under the impediment even though the parents have not been baptized.

In virtue of this response, by the equation which it sets up between Christian and atheistic sects in the juridical consequences following from the sectarian membership, the children born of parents who belong to an atheistic sect are impeded from the reception of Orders. This response makes it clear that all atheistic sects fall within the category of the *secta acatholica.* However, it is not evident from the response that the false religions of Mohammedans and Judaism are similarly classified. Nor has the response made clear whether the *secta acatholica* is equivalent to a *secta haeretica seu schismatica.*[85] If the *secta acatholica* in the law were the equivalent of the *secta haeretica seu schismatica,* then this response would imply an extension of the law. This does not seem to be the case, and there seems to be no justification for any conclusion which would emphasize baptism as a requisite for one's inclusion under the term "*acatholicus.*" Certainly no such conclusion for future application would be permissible.[86]

[84] The Commission was asked: Whether according to the Code of Canon Law, persons who belong or have belonged to an atheistic sect are to be considered, as regards all legal effects, even those which concern sacred ordination and marriage, the same as persons who belong or have belonged to a non-Catholic sect. The reply was in the affirmative.—*AAS,* XXVI (1934), 494. Translation is taken from Bouscaren (II, 286–287). Non-Catholic sect here means a Christian sect.

[85] Heneghan, *The Marriage of Unworthy Catholics: Canons 1065 and 1066,* The Catholic University of America Canon Law Studies, n. 188 (Washington, D. C.: The Catholic University of America Press, 1944), p. 76 (hereafter cited as Heneghan).

[86] For a discussion on this response in relation to canon 1060–1065 the reader is referred to Heneghan, pp. 69–82.

6. Conclusions from the Preceding Discussion

In accordance with the etymology of the term *acatholicus,* and in consequence of the solidly juridical reasons which oppose the acceptance of a restricted meaning of it, it seems a warranted statement that the lawmaker has made a general law of that which prior to the enactment of the present Code was only a particular law for certain localities, as then determined by the Holy See. It appears that through the agency of canon 987, 1°, the lawmaker has established an obligatory norm of law, derived from what formerly stood commended as the exercise of a laudable care and caution, but at the same time was acknowledged as not having the force of a law in giving rise to an irregularity for the reception of Orders. And thus it can be assumed that the law of canon 987, 1°, is not simply a restatement of the pre-Code law. The concept of the *filii acatholicorum* as mentioned in canon 987, 1°, is not identical with the concept of the *filii haereticorum* as mentioned in the pre-Code law. The category of the *filii acatholicorum* is sufficiently comprehensive to include not only public heretics, schismatics and apostates, but also infidels, Jews, Mohammedans, etc.

There is indeed a number of authors who are of the opinion that the term " non-Catholic " as used in canon 987, 1°, is not to be restricted in its meaning in such manner as to refer only to heretics, schismatics and apostates. Blat, arguing from the word itself, holds that the term " non-Catholic " includes pagans.[87] Woywod (1880–1941) favored the literal meaning of *acatholicus* in canon 987, 1°.[88] Augustine included pagans and Jews under the term " non-Catholic " of canon 987, 1°.[89]

Schmid, who explicitly treats of the term "*acatholicus,*" and

[87] "*Acatholicorum* . . . parentum, qui vel pagani, vel in haeresi aut schismate fuerunt semper, vel in alterutrum prolapsi, vel apostatae a fide, quia proprie non sunt catholici, . . ."—*Commentarium,* III, pars I, n. 355.

[88] *A Practical Commentary,* I, 537.

[89] *A Commentary,* IV, 498.—Augustine refers to a response of the Sacred Congregation of the Council as contained in Richter, *Canones et Decreta Concilii Tridentini* (Lipsiae, 1853), p. 339, n. 3. Cf. *supra,* p. 123, footnote. This response does not prove his point, for from the historical study already submitted (cf. *supra,* pp. 118–119) it is evident that it was a *particular* law which forbade the ordination of the descendants of Jews.

then manifests the application of his doctrine to canon 987, 1°, concludes that the term "*acatholicus*" embraces all who are not Catholics.[90] Heneghan, after a discussion regarding the meaning of the phrase "*secta acatholica*" in canon 1065, § 1, concludes that all non-Catholic sects or religions, whether Christian or non-Christian, are comprehended under the term "*secta acatholica.*"[91] This term includes every kind of non-Catholic religious sect, whether it represents a belief in God or a denial of His existence. It can imply a profession of apostasy, of atheism, of pantheism or of polytheism.[92]

c. *Application of the Phrase "Filii Acatholicorum"*

In the application of the phrase "*filii acatholicorum*" of canon 987, 1°, whatever be the conclusions that are enunciated, they apply even if only one of the parents is a non-Catholic. The impediment can arise only if at least one of the parents was a non-Catholic at the time of the birth of the child. If one or both of the parents come to belong to the category of non-Catholics only after the birth of their son, then the impediment will not affect him. The factor of the conversion of the parents after the birth of their son will be studied later.

1. The Son of a Heretic

There are two classes of heretics. The one class, which is by far the larger group, consists of all those who were validly baptized in a non-Catholic sect and then were reared outside of the Church.[93] A son of such heretical parents is impeded from the

---

[90] Cf. "De vi verborum 'acatholicus, secta acatholica, minister acatholicus' in Iure Canonico"—*Apollinaris*, IV (1931), 552–567; V (1932), 69–85. On page 567 of the earlier part of the article Schmid states: "Si codex aliquam classem 'non-Catholicorum' excludere vult generatim expresse enumerat. Quare ergo hic adhibetur verbum generale, nisi legislator vellet omnes 'non-Catholicos' sumere?" Cf. also Claeys Bouuaert-Simenon, II, n. 205.

[91] *The Marriage of Unworthy Catholics*, pp. 75–80.

[92] Larraona, "Commentarium Codicis"—*Commentarium pro Religiosis* (Romae, 1920– ; from 1935: *Commentarium pro Religiosis et Missionariis*), XVI (1935), 430; Heneghan, *loc. cit.*

[93] Heneghan, p. 93.

reception of Orders according to the norms of canon 987, 1°. The other class consists of all those who were at one time members of the Catholic Church, either through infant baptism, or through later conversion, but have become heretics by a personal act of denial or doubt. By such an act they abandon their relations with the Catholic Church, to which they previously belonged.[94] The act of denial or of doubt posited by this second group must be not only external but also public, if they are to be reputed as non-Catholics whose son, born after their abandonment of relations with the Catholic Church, will come under the comprehension of the law enacted in canon 987, 1°. This, of course, supposes that the parents continue in this heretical state. It is not necessary that the parents have joined a heretical sect.[95] The law of canon 987, 1°, is enacted in and for the external forum. Unless the heretical belief of the parent is publicly manifest, such a parent cannot be reputed as a non-Catholic in the sense that his son comes within the scope of the law of canon 987, 1°.

Prior to the Code it was held that, unless the heresy of the parent was a thing of public knowledge, the son was not irregular.[96] There does not seem to be any reason for departing from this interpretation. It is in the opinion of the people that the person must be reputed to be a non-Catholic. An official condemnation by the Church is not necessary. If the parent has affiliated with a heretical sect, then it is evident that the newly born son is bound by the impediment.[97]

The son is not subject to the impediment when his parent is simply under the suspicion of heresy.[98] However, those who

---

[94] MacKenzie, *The Delict of Heresy in Its Commission, Penalization, Absolution,* The Catholic University of America Canon Law Studies, n. 77 (Washington, D. C.: The Catholic University of America, 1932), pp. 17–18 (hereafter cited as MacKenzie).

[95] Cappello, *De Sacra Ordinatione,* nn. 504, 519.

[96] Petra, II, n. 20; Boenninghausen, Fasc. III, p. 151.

[97] Cf. MacKenzie, pp. 33–53, for a treatment of heresy and affiliation with a heretical sect.

[98] Canon 2316—"Qui quoquo modo haeresis propagationem sponte et scienter iuvat, aut qui communicat in divinis cum haereticis contra praescriptum can. 1258, suspectus de haeresi est." Can. 2319, § 2, "Ii de quibus in § 1,

are considered by the law as suspected of heresy, and who show no signs of amendment within a period of six months after they have been debarred from the exercise of ecclesiastically authorized acts in punishment of their non-heeding of the warning then administered, are to be considered as heretics,[99] and any son born to them after that will come under the law of canon 987, 1°.

2. The Son of an Apostate

An apostate is officially defined by the Code as a person who, after receiving baptism, has completely abandoned the Christian faith.[100] Since heretics are guilty of only a *partial* defection from the Catholic faith, what has been said of the sons of heretics certainly applies to the sons of apostates. Therefore, a son born of apostate parents is impeded from the reception of Orders in virtue of canon 987, 1°.

3. The Son of a Schismatic

A schismatic is officially defined by the Code as one who, after receiving baptism, refuses to remain subject to the Supreme Pontiff or to communicate with the members of the Church who are subject to the Supreme Pontiff. The definition as given by the Code refers to formal schism.[101] It applies, in the strict

---

nn. 2–4 [§ 1: Subsunt excommunicationi latae sententiae Ordinario reservatae catholici: 2°. Qui matrimonio uniuntur cum pacto explicito vel implicito ut omnis vel aliqua proles educetur extra catholicam Ecclesiam; 3°, Qui scienter liberos suos acatholicis ministris baptizandos offerre praesumunt: 4°. Parentes vel parentum locum tenentes qui liberos in religione acatholica educandos vel instituendos scienter tradunt.] sunt praetera suspecti de haeresi." Canon 2320:—"Qui species consecratas abiecerit vel ad malum finem abduxerit aut retinuerit, est suspectus de haeresi . . ." Canon 2332—"Omnes et singuli cuiuscunque status, gradus seu conditionis etiam regalis, episcopalis vel cardinalitiae fuerint, a legibus decretis, mandatis Romani Pontificis pro tempore existentis ad Universale Concilium appellantes, sunt suspecti de haeresi . . ." Canon 2340, § 1, "Si quis, obdurato animo, per annum insorduerit in censura excommunicationis, est de haeresi suspectus." Canon 2371—"Omnes, etiam episcopali dignitate aucti, qui per simoniam ad ordines scienter promoverint vel promoti fuerint aut alia Sacramenta ministraverint vel receperint, sunt suspecti de haeresi; . . ."

[99] Canon 2315.

[100] Canon 1325, § 2.

[101] Coronata, II, n. 911.

sense of the term, only to those who are guilty of pure schism. Pure schism is not a sin against the faith, but a sin against obedience and charity.[102] A pure schismatic can be classified as a disobedient or uncharitable Catholic.[103] The son of a pure schimatic is not under the impediment of canon 987, 1°.

Pure schism is now not very common. Pure schism tends to become mixed schism, that is, pure schism mixed with heresy. Under the present discipline of the Church it is almost impossible to continue to profess belief in the dogmas of the infallibility and of the primacy of the Roman Pontiff the while one refuses to acknowledge subjection to this authority or communion of association with his subjects as subordinates of a common spiritual father.[104] This refusal to acknowledge subjection to the Holy Father or communion of association with his subjects must be an established principle of action inspired by the mental directive of a habitual conviction. Unless this is public, the schismatic's son will not come within the law of canon 87, 1°. If the schism is public, then, in practice, the son of the one guilty of this schism is to be considered as coming within the scope of canon 987, 1°.

4. The Son of a Non-Christian

By the term " non-Christian " is understood a person who has not been baptized. As a member of this category he may be one who denies the existence of God, or one who professes a belief in God's existence. The profession of this belief may in turn be centered in the one true God, or it may be referred to a false god or gods. Placed in the category of non-Christians are infidels, atheists, pantheists, polytheists, Mohammedans and Jews. The special case of the son of a Jew will be treated separately after a general consideration of all other non-Christians.

---

[102] Noldin-Schmitt, *Summa Theologiae Moralis* (3 vols., Oeniponte: Typis et Sumptibus Fel. Rauch [Vol. II, 25. ed., 1938; Vol. III, 26. ed., 1940]), II, n. 32.

[103] The presence of the disobedience or uncharitableness is to be established within the compass of the definition of a pure schismatic. Not every disobedient or uncharitable Catholic is a schismatic. It is the converse of this statement that holds true.

[104] Cf. MacKenzie, p. 17; Heneghan, p. 96.

If a baptized person becomes a member of any of the groups to which the aforementioned persons belong, he becomes an apostate. That case has already been treated. It is the one who has been an infidel, Mohammedan, etc., from birth who constitutes the present consideration. In view of the interpretation which has been attached by the writer to the term "non-Catholic," as used in canon 987, 1°, a son born of parents who belong to any of the aforementioned groups is impeded from the reception of Orders. If, however, the arguments which have been proposed for such a conclusion were not to be accepted as cogent, and in consequence it were held that in reality a doubt of law exists, then in virtue of canon 15 the sons born of infidels, Mohammedans, etc., would not come within the scope of canon 987, 1°. But until there are presented better reasons than the ones alleged, the writer proposes the doctrine that such sons do come within the scope of canon 987, 1°. Sons born of atheistic parents who belong to an atheistic sect certainly are subject to the law enacted in canons 987, 1°. In view of the response of the Pontifical Commission for the interpretation of the Code as given on July 30, 1934,[105] it appears not only warranted, but even necessary, to acknowledge that all doubt in the law has been removed in relation to the sons of atheistic parents who belong to a sect which denies the existence of God.

5. The Son of a Jew

It seems that the best argument for the non-inclusion of the sons born of Jewish parents [106] derives from a pre-Code decision of the Sacred Congregation of the Council.[107] This decision is referred to in the footnote to canon 987, 1°. The Sacred Congregation was asked to grant a dispensation from his irregularity in order that a son of Jewish parents might obtain a certain

[105] *AAS*, XXVI (1934), 494. Cf. *supra*, p. 127.

[106] The adjective "Jewish" refers to their religion and not to their nationality.

[107] *Pragen.*, 12 maii 1759—"Franciscus Bolowski a Captulo Pragensi ad Beneficium cum cura animarum nominatus fuerat. Quum autem a parentibus Iudaeis originem duxisset et in aetate duorum annorum ad fidem catholocam pervenisset, *petiit dispensatione ab irregularitate.* S. C. C. respondit: *Non indigere dispensatione.*"—*Fontes*, n. 3685.

benefice. It seems that the individual in this case had already been ordained. There was no question of a son born of heretical parents. Nor was the question of the reception of Orders involved. There was no dispensation from any irregularity needed in the case proposed to the Sacred Congregation.

There immediately arise the following questions: Was it the consideration of the religious beliefs of his parents, or was it his status of a neophyte, that prompted the request? Would the Sacred Congregation have answered in the same manner if there was question of the receiving of Orders, and not simply question of the receiving of a benefice? Relative to the first question it seems that it was the consideration of the religious belief of the parents that prompted the petition for a dispensation. A neophyte is one who has been baptized in adult age. But the individual in question had been baptized while he was still an infant. Thus, it does not seem that his status of a neophyte was involved. However, if it is the status of a neophyte that was intended to be emphasized by the reference to this response in the footnote to canon 987, then it has no bearing on the present question.

Posited, however, that the reason which prompted the petition was the consideration of the religious belief of the parents, there remains the necessity of finding a plausible answer to the question: Why was the request for a dispensation from any irregularity presented to the Sacred Congregation? The answer seems to rest with the possible fact that in the locality there was a particular law which forbade the ordination of the son of a Jew.

There was no question of the reception of any Orders, but only of the appointment to a benefice. Posited that there had been question of the receiving of Orders, what would have been the answer of the Sacred Congregation? Would a dispensation have been granted? None of the authors attempts to answer this question.[108]

The reference which the annotations to canon 987 make to this response furnishes the main argument in favor of the exclusion of the sons of Jews from the scope of canon 987, 1°. If that reference be sufficient to warrant a prudent doubt regard-

---

[108] Cf. Schmid—*Apollinaris,* IV (1931), 567, footnote.

ing the intent of the law itself, then in virtue of canon 15 the sons of Jews are not impeded from the reception of Orders by the law as contained in canon 987, 1°. The writer, in his own mind, finds it impossible for himself to acknowledge the existence of any prudent doubt of law. In practice, dispensations from the impediment of canon 987, 1°, have been requested and have been granted for the sons of Jews.[109] The writer holds that the sons born of Jews come within the scope of the prohibitive law contained in canon 987, 1°.

6. The Son of an Unworthy Catholic

An unworthy Catholic is not a non-Catholic. He may have been excommunicated or interdicted, but, unless the penalty has been incurred or inflicted for a publicly made denial or manifestly expressed doubt of one, several or all the dogmas of the Church, he is still a Catholic. An unworthy Catholic may be a public sinner. He may have joined a condemned society, e.g., that of the Masons.[110] But membership in a condemned society, or the condition occasioned by one's being a public sinner, does not change the status of an individual from that of a Catholic to that of a non-Catholic.

The son of parents who are unworthy Catholics is not included within the scope of the law enacted in canon 987, 1°. The son may however be debarred from the reception of Orders because of his lack of the necessary qualities for the clerical life.[111] The refusal in such a case to ordain an individual results simply from the exercise of a prudent judgment on the part of the ordinary, who has discovered in the individual a lack of the requisite qualities

[109] Cf. canon 20—"Si certa de re desit expressum praescriptum legis sive generalis sive particularis, norma sumenda est . . . a stylo et praxi Curiae Romanae . . ."

[110] For a treatment of condemned societies consult—Quigley, *Condemned Societies,* The Catholic University of America Canon Law Studies, n. 46 (Washington, D. C.: The Catholic University of America, 1927). Cf. Heneghan, pp. 104–108, for a treatment of Excommunicated and Interdicted Catholics; pp. 109–120, for a treatment of Public Sinners; pp. 97–101, for a treatment of Catholics enrolled in condemned societies.

[111] Canons 968, § 1; 973, § 3; 974, § 1, 2°.

for the reception of Orders. It does not arise in view of any *defectus natalium ob acatholicitatem parentum.*

It may be noted that the status of a person who was baptized a Catholic but who was reared without any religious training is juridically identical with the canonical status of a Catholic who is ignorant of the truths of the faith. The retention of the status of a Catholic postulates of course that the person shall not have joined a non-Catholic sect. If his lack of education in the Catholic religion is due to his own neglect, then he is a sinner, but not a non-Catholic.[112]

C. Cessation of the Impediment—"Quandiu Parentes in Suo Errore Permanent"

1. The Effect of Conversion

A son born of non-Catholic parents can be freed from his subjection to the impediment of canon 987, 1°, through the conversion of his non-Catholic parents or parent. As long as one of the parents remains in the status of a non-Catholic, which status he had at the time of his son's birth, the son may not receive ordination, unless a dispensation has been obtained. The conversion of the non-Catholic to the Catholic faith must be external and public.[113] When the non-Catholic parent has been converted, the condition for the continued existence of the effects of the impediment on the son—*quandiu in suo errore permanent*—has ceased.

If at any time after the son's birth both of his parents have been Catholics, the impediment of canon 987, 1°, will thereafter no longer extend to him. The son is equivalent canonically to a son born of Catholic parents. As a son born of Catholic parents does not come within the scope of the prohibitive law of canon 987, 1°, so, too, the son of converted parents does not fall under the prohibition. If the parents were non-Catholics at the time of the birth of their son, and then later became converts to the true faith, but still later, prior to the ordination of their son, lapse into their former error, the son does not fall under

---

[112] Heneghan, pp. 91–92.

[113] Cappello, *De Sacra Ordinatione*, n. 519.

the prohibitive law of canon 987, 1°. The term *permanent* supposes a continued action or status. Once the status or action has been broken, then the requisite strict interpretation which the law itself demands [114] in relation to the term "*permanent*" can no longer find application.[115]

Unless this conclusion is accepted, it would follow that the son would likewise be forbidden to exercise the Orders he already had received, once his father or mother lapsed or relapsed into the status of a non-Catholic.[116] But in the pre-Code law a cleric was not to be deprived of his benefice, nor was he to be prohibited from the exercise of his Orders, if his parents fell into heresy after his ordination or after his reception of a benefice.[117] It is to be presumed that the lawmaker wished to obtain the same effect under the present law. In virtue of canon 987, § 2, the only interpretation which makes possible the gaining of this effect is the one which holds that the relapse of the parent into the status of a non-Catholic will not bring the son under the prohibitive law of canon 987, 1°.

The lawmaker intended to legislate for the ordinary and usual circumstances. Ordinarily the parents retain the religious belief they had at the time of the birth of the child. If they turn away from it by means of a conversion to the Catholic faith, they then ordinarily retain their newly found faith. However, there can arise a situation which does not come within the scope of the law itself as expressed in canon 987, 1°, but which does come within the scope of the end for the attainment of which the law was enacted.

The law was enacted in order to insure worthy candidates for the clerical life. The ordinary is obliged to achieve this end which prompted the enactment of the law. Therefore, even though a candidate for Orders has not contracted the impedi-

---

[114] Canon 19.

[115] Cf. Vermeersch-Creusen, II, n. 259. Under the pre-Code law this point was disputed among authors.

[116] Canon 968, § 2.

[117] ". . . haereticorum filii ss. ordinibus insigniti et beneficiis praediti, antequam parentes in haeresim inciderint, neque exercitio ordinum iam susceptorum interdicuntur neque beneficiis legitime obtentis privantur." Boenninghausen, Fasc. III, p. 150.

ment enacted in canon 987, 1°, he still must prove his fitness to accept the responsibilities of the clerical life before he may be admitted to the reception of Orders.

2. THE EFFECT OF DEATH

Will the death of the non-Catholic parents do away with the existence of the condition expressed in the words, *quandiu in errore permanent?* In the pre-Code legislation the irregularity remained if the parent died in his heresy. Under the present law the prohibition affecting the children of non-Catholics is an impediment, and not an irregularity. Authors are in disagreement regarding the effect of the death of the parents on this impediment.

Blat maintains that the pre-Code interpretation is to be retained in this matter. He holds that if the parent dies as a non-Catholic, then the impediment continues to exist. He admits that the law has been changed through the use of the phrase "*filii acatholicorum,*" but contends that the law has remained unchanged in the effect of the parental death on the status of the son in relation to canon 987, 1°. He states:

> *Permanent* "vel mortui sunt" congruentur iuri praecedenti (can 6, 2°), quia permanentia per mortem, quando in errore persistunt, firmatur in aeternum.[118]

The pre-Code law has in many cases been retained. At times, however, the present law has retained only a part of the pre-Code law. If the pre-Code law has been retained, then in virtue of canon 6, 2° and 3°, the death of the parents will not free the son from the impediment enacted in canon 987, 1°. The fundamental question, then, is whether or not the pre-Code law has been retained.

The pre-Code law in dealing with the children of heretics was restated by the Sacred Congregation of the Holy Office on December 4, 1890, in the following manner:

> Sacer consessus Eminentissimorum . . . resolvit: Haereticos ad fidem catholicam conversos, ac filios haereti-

[118] *Commentarium,* III, pars I, n. 355.

> corum qui in haeresi ***persistunt vel mortui sunt,*** ad primum et secundum gradum per lineam paternam, per maternam vero ad primum dumtaxat, esse irregulares, etiam in Germania, et in aliis locis de quibus petitur; ideoque dispensatione indigere ut ad Tonsuram et Ordines promoveantur.[119]

For the text itself it seems that the phrase "*vel mortui sunt*" was employed inasmuch as the lawmaker felt that the term "*persistunt*" was not of sufficient force to include also the concept of what is contained in the phrase "*mortui sunt.*"

There was no clear distinction between a temporal and a perpetual impediment in pre-Code legislation. If there had been the clear distinction which now is manifest in the Code, and if the son of heretics had been considered as temporally impeded, and not as irregular, it may be asked whether the lawmaker would have added the phrase "*vel mortui sunt*" to the term "*persistunt.*" The phrase "*mortui sunt*" seems to have put emphasis on the consideration that the condition of the *filii haereticorum* was intended as a perpetual impediment, that is, as an irregularity arising *ex defectu natalium.*

The complete juridical basis of a simple impediment, in its precise nature as an impediment and not as an irregularity, does not rest solely in the fact that there is given a possibility of the cessation of the impediment without a dispensation. If it did, then the irregularity *ex defectu* mentioned in canon 984, 1°, should be listed as a simple impediment. The juridical basis for the simple impediment rests also in the fact of the possible cessation of the cause *qua causa.* Certainly death removes the parents as a cause *qua causa.*[120] If this additional basis be denied, then the sole reason for the impediment inheres in the *defectus natalium.* Those who espouse the opinion that the death of the non-Catholic parents does not free the son from the impediment enacted in

[119] *Fontes,* n. 1129; *Coll. S. C. P. F.,* n. 1744; *ASS,* XXIII (1890), 700. Italics are inserted by the present writer.

[120] The parents are considered as a cause, *qua causa,* in this that as non-Catholics they gave birth to a son, and that in the continuation of their non-Catholic status there lurks the danger that they will exert a non-Catholic influence on the child.

canon 987, 1°, must necessarily come to this conclusion, for by the death of the parents the impediment would then become an irregularity *ex defectu.* This is precisely the argument stressed by the opponents in their refusal to admit that the death of the non-Catholic parent does not free the son from the impediment listed in canon 987, 1°.[121]

The term "*persistunt*" in the pre-Code law seems to be the equivalent of the term "*permanent*" in the law of canon 987, 1°.[122] Since the phrase "*vel mortui sunt*" has not been retained in the Code, it seems fully warranted to conclude that the pre-Code law has not been retained. Inasmuch as the word *persistunt* did not include the concept of *mortui sunt,* so now it seems logically consequent to conclude that the word *permanent* does not include the idea of *mortui sunt.*

Blat maintains that death brings an eternal permanency to the error of the parents—*firmatur in aeternum.*[123] Against this it may be argued that the Code seems to take into account the present condition of the candidate,[124] and seems to speak of the living only.[125] Can the permanency of the parents' error be said to be eternally established by their death? The permanency of their error for the time that they were *homines viatores* can never, it is true, be changed. Therefore the fact of the retention of the error by them while they were alive can never undergo a change. But in the case as contemplated they are now among the deceased. Once they are deceased it cannot be said that as dead persons they still remain in their error.[126] Among those who hold that the death of the non-Catholic parent does away

---

[121] Cappello, *De Sacra Ordinatione,* n. 519; Wernz-Vidal, IV, pars I, n. 256.

[122] Blat uses the two terms interchangeably.—*Commentarium,* III, pars I, n. 355.

[123] *Commentarium, loc. cit.* This opinion is also contained in the work of Noldin-Schmitt (*Summa Theologica Moralis,* III, n. 499). The word *videtur* is used, but no reasons are offered for the conclusion adopted by these authors.

[124] Ayrinhac, *Legislation on the Sacraments,* p. 371.

[125] Woywod, I, 538.

[126] Augustine, IV, 497; Beste, p. 535.

with the effect of the impediment on the son are: Cappello,[127] Vidal,[128] Augustine,[129] Vermeersch-Creusen,[130] Woywod [131] and Ayrinhac.[132]

At any rate the negation of any effect through the death of the non-Catholic parents relative to the question of the son's continuation under the impediment listed in canon 987, 1°, is of doubtful cogency. That makes of the issue a *dubium iuris*. But in virtue of canon 15 even such laws as establish a personal incapacity are no longer binding when the meaning and intent of the law are involved in doubt. Hence the son of a deceased non-Catholic father or mother, or also the son whose deceased parents were both non-Catholics, is no longer subject to the impediment which stands enacted in canon 987, 1°.[133]

D. Dispensation from the Impediment

A dispensation from this impediment can be obtained. However, the granting of such a dispensation will not free the ordinary from the obligation of making sure that the candidate for Orders is firm in his faith.[134] This obligation is incumbent upon the ordinary when he confers Orders on any candidate.

The dispensation is to be requested from the Sacred Congregation of the Sacraments.[135] Prompted no doubt by the consideration that the impediment was enacted because of the danger of weakness in the *faith* of the son, Beste maintains that this dispensation should be requested from the Holy Office.[136] However, before the Code this impediment was classified as an irregularity *ex defectu*. And since prior to the Code the Sacred Congregation of the Sacraments was the competent Congrega-

127 *De Sacra Ordinatione*, n. 519.

128 *Ius Canonicum*, IV, pars I, n. 256.

129 *A Commentary*, IV, 497.

130 *Epitome Iuris Canonici*, II, n. 259.

131 *A Practical Commentary*, I, 538.

132 *Legislation on the Sacraments*, p. 371.

133 Cf. Raus, "Weihehindernis der Söhne von Nichtkatholiken"—*Theologisch-praktische Quartalschrift* (Linz, 1832–), LXXVI (1923), 122–127.

134 Cf. canons 968, § 1; 973, § 3; 974, § 1.

135 Cf. *supra*, pp. 14–17.

136 Beste, p. 535.

tion in this matter, there seems to be no reason to depart from this procedure.[137]

---

[137] On November 28, 1911, the Sacred Congregation of the Consistory indicated that the Holy Father ordered the following response: "Dispensationem ex defectu reservari ad S. Congregationem de Sacramentis, ex delicto autem ad S. Congregationem Concilii."—*AAS,* III (1911), 658; *Fontes,* n. 2082.

PART IV

THE IMPEDIMENT BASED ON ONE'S EVIL ACTS

CHAPTER VI

INFAMY OF FACT

A. Historical Synopsis

One raised to the dignity of Orders is ordained for men in the things that appertain to God. If men, whose needs he is to serve, hold him in ill-repute, his ministry would be far from effective. St. Paul said that a candidate for the episcopate must be blameless, and must have a good reputation with those who are outside.[1] This also applies to candidates for Orders other than the episcopate.[2] All candidates must have a good name, *bona fama*.

Ioannes Andreae (1272–1348) said that opinion, esteem and repute were the same. Repute or *fama* he defined as the state of untainted dignity attested to both by custom and law.[3] The lack of *fama* was known as *infamia*. A person suffered under *infamia facti* when he was considered offensive and disgraceful among good and sound-thinking people.[4] The opinion of right-minded people was the *causa essendi* of *infamia facti*, while the law itself was the *causa essendi* of *infamia iuris*.

No one could dispense from infamy of fact.[5] All those who were empowered with the acceptance or rejection of candidates

[1] I Tim., III, 2 and 7.

[2] Gratian on c. 1, D. LXXXI; *Glossa Ordinaria* on the comments of Gratian to c. 1, D. LXXXI, s. v. *haec de ordinandis; Glossa Ordinaria*—Casus—c. 1, D. LXXXI, s. v. *Apostolus*.

[3] *Glossa Ordinaria* ad c. 2, C. III, q. 7, s. v. *Infamia*.

[4] *Loc. cit.*: "Infamia facti est quando quis aggravatur vel infamatur apud bonos et graves."

[5] *Loc. cit.*

for Orders agreed that the infamous were not to be ordained.[6] It remains to investigate some of the more important legislation on this point.

The loss of one's good name could be occasioned in many and divers ways.[7] To list completely those evil actions which occasioned an *infamia facti* would be impossible, since it depends on the opinion of the people which could vary according to time, place and circumstances. Pope Stephen I (254–257) allegedly listed some of the crimes which bring about infamy. No distinction was made between *infamia iuris* and *infamia facti*. There was simply a general statement which declared that they who were infamous were not to be promoted to Sacred Orders.[8] In the IV Provincial Council of Toledo (633) there was drawn up another partial list of crimes which were recognized as capable of bringing about infamy both of fact and of law.[9] But the fact that a crime was found mentioned in the lists referred to previously did not in itself bring about an *infamia facti*. The very definition of infamy of fact argues against such a conclusion. Although the legislation of the Council was enacted primarily with reference to candidates for the episcopate, yet it had application also with regard to candidates for any other dignity, and hence also with regard to aspirants to the clerical life.[10]

Anyone who ordained an unworthy candidate was to be punished and even deposed if the circumstances warranted it.[11] That there were individuals who were not to be admitted to Orders because of their sins can be gathered from the comments

[6] *Summa* of St. Raymond, lib. III, tit. 25, p. 313: "Generaliter ergo et sine exceptione tenendum est, quod omnis infamis tam de iure, quam de facto, repellitur a promotione, quia portae dignitatum, vel ordinum infamibus et suspectis personis patere non debet." In the foregoing statement one cannot but note the force of jurisprudence in shaping the later well known *Regula Iuris:* "Infamibus portae non pateant dignitatum."—Reg. 87, R. I., in VI°.

[7] *Glossa Ordinaria* ad c. 2, C. III, q. 7, s. v. *Infamia.*

[8] C. 17, C. VI, q. 1; JK, n. 130 (spurious).

[9] Can. 19—Mansi, X, 624; c. 5, D. LI.

[10] *Glossa Ordinaria*—Casus—c. 5, D. LI, s. v. *Qui in aliquo.*

[11] C. 3, D. LXXXI; JK, n. 369.

of Bernard of Pavia (+1213).[12] Occult sins could not effect infamy of fact, but the bishop could exclude those who committed certain sins, whether occult or public, from the reception of Orders until they had been reconciled with the Church.[13] The effecting of this reconciliation rested with the judgment of the bishop.[14] It is reasonable to suppose that the judgment of the bishop was to be consulted when there existed a prudent doubt whether *infamia facti* still endured.

There had to be some notoriety connected with the evil act before one could be excluded from the reception of Orders.[15] If one was accused of a crime he was not to be ordained until the case was settled.[16] This positive legislation was enacted in view of the possible emergence of infamy, whether of fact or of law.

All legislation governing the impediment of infamy was epitomized in the *Regular Iuris* of Boniface VIII (1294–1303). "*Infamibus portae non pateant dignitatum.*" [17] The dignity referred to in this rule could be either ecclesiastical or secular, and certainly the clerical state then as now ranked as an ecclesiastical dignity.[18] The main conclusion to be drawn from all the legislation regarding this impediment was that one had to be in good repute before he could be ordained.[19]

The Council of Trent did not consider it necessary to legislate on infamy in its effect on the reception of Tonsure and of Orders. The notion of infamy is a concept fundamentally inherent in the natural law, and has therefore undergone no change with the

---

[12] Cf. *Glossa*, c. 6, D. XXV, s. v. *Primum*.

[13] *Loc. cit.; Glossa Ordinaria*, c. 38, C. II, q. 7, s. v. *nec esse*.

[14] C. 4, C. XXVI, q. 6.

[15] C. 17, X, *de temporibus ordinationum et qualitate ordinandorum*, I, 11: "Respondemus quod si proposita crimina ordine iudiciario comprobata, vel alias notoria non fuerint, non debent hi, praeter reos homicidii, post poenitentiam in iam susceptis vel suscipiendis ordinibus impediri . . ." Potthast, n. 9550.

[16] C. 56, X, *de testibus cogendis*, II, 20; Potthast, n. 9603; c. 4, X, *de accusationibus*, V, 1; JE, n. 1352.

[17] Reg. 87, R. I., in VIo.

[18] *Glossa Ordinaria* ad Reg. 87, R. I., in VIo, s. v. *infamibus*.

[19] *Summa* of St. Raymond, lib. III, tit. 25, p. 313.

succeeding generations. It has always been considered as implying or entailing the loss of one's good name or reputation.[20]

The division of infamy into that of law (*iuris*) and that of fact (*facti*), already in existence before the Council of Trent, has retained its place throughout the years,[21] and also in present day legislation.[22] Infamy of law was known also as legal infamy (*legalis*), while the term "popular" (*popularis*) in connection with infamy was used at times to refer to infamy of fact.[23] To this twofold division of infamy there was added by some authors a third, which was known as canonical infamy. It was defined as that which arises in consequence of some mortal sin, and continues in existence for the duration of the sin itself.[24] The concern of this study, as stated before, centers upon infamy of fact.

The existence both of one's good name and of one's bad name hinges on the opinion of upright and respectable men.[25] The opinion of upright and respectable men is based on the external acts revealed in an individual's life. If these acts are of an incontrovertibly evil character, then infamy of fact can result.[26]

Secret delicts, crimes, moral deficiencies, etc., could not lead to any extant infamy of fact. They had to be public with a note

---

20 Laymann, lib. I, tract. V, pars IV, n. 3; Pignatelli, *Consultationes Canonicae* (10 vols. in 4, Coloniae Allobrogum, 1700), VII, consult. 19, n. 7 (hereafter cited as Pignatelli); Wernz, II, n. 130.

21 Ferraris, *Prompta Bibliotheca Canonica, Iuridica, Moralis, Theologica, necnon Ascetica, Polemica, Rubricistica, Historica* (ed. Migne, 8 vols., Parisiis, 1860–1863), s. v. *irregularitas* (hereafter cited as Ferraris); Boenninghausen, Fasc. III, p. 158.

22 Canon 2293, § 1.

23 Cf. Boenninghausen, Fasc. III, p. 158, footnote.

24 Gonzalez-Tellez, *Commentaria Perpetua in singulos textus Quinque Libros Decretalium Gregorii IX* (5 vols. in 4, Venetiis, 1699), lib. III, tit. 20, c. 54, n. 2 (hereafter cited as Gonzalez-Tellez).

25 Schmier, lib. I, tract 4, cap. 6, n. 515; Wernz, II, n. 130.

26 Leurenius, *Forum Ecclesiasticum in quo Ius Canonicum Explanatur* (5 vols. in 3, Venetiis, 1729), lib. V, tit. 37, q. 508: ". . . ex quocumque enormi crimine . . ." (hereafter cited as Leurenius); Schmier, *loc. cit.:* ". . . ex facto turpi . . ."; Wernz, *loc. cit.:* ". . . ex delicto vel defectu ignominioso et publico . . ."

of notoriety.[27] Many authors held that the very suspicion of the people that an individual had committed a crime or misdeed was sufficient to constitute infamy of fact, provided that this suspicion was based on probable reasons. Some authors, however, without positing any distinction maintained that the basis for infamy of fact was verified only on the supposition that a public sin had been committed.[28]

There had to be present a well founded suspicion of the commission of a delict, or of a crime, or of the appearance of some moral deficiency, acknowledged by a majority of the good and earnest-minded people of the community, who manifested their opinion by external actions, particularly by word of mouth.[29] Any loss of good name which arose from an arbitrary opinion of men, based on a fact which itself was not a sin, or which furnished no rightful presumption for the presence of sin, was not admitted as a foundation for infamy of fact.[30]

The very definition of infamy of fact runs counter to the idea that the commission of any act prohibited to a cleric necessarily entailed his infamy. Even if legislators and commentators drew up lists of crimes which occasion infamy, a crime would not by the mere fact that mention of it was thus inserted in the list give rise to infamy of fact. Conversely, the fact that mention of a specific crime was not inserted in the list would not exclude the possible emergence of infamy of fact, since such infamy could readily result from any external morally disreputable action or omission whatsoever.[31]

Infamy of fact excluded from the reception of Orders any one who bore the moral stigma connoted by it. All authors agreed on this exclusion, but some taught that it followed upon an irregularity as arising from infamy,[32] while others, basing

[27] Laymann, *ibid.*, n. 4; Ferraris, s. v. *irregularitas,* n. 48; Gasparri, *De Sacra Ordinatione,* n. 305; Wernz, II, n. 130.

[28] Cf. Schmier, *ibid.*, n. 523; Boenninghausen, Fasc. III, p. 164, footnotes.

[29] Schmier, *loc. cit.*

[30] S. C. C., *Caputaquen.*, 26 apr., 10 maii 1755—*Fontes,* n. 2650; *Thesaurus Resolutionum,* XXIV, 29, 36; Boenninghausen, Fasc. III, p. 159; Gasparri, *De Sacra Ordinatione,* n. 306.

[31] Gasparri, *De Sacra Ordinatione,* n. 305; Wernz, II, n. 130.

[32] Boenninghausen, Fasc. III, p. 164; Wernz, II, n. 130.

their arguments on the temporary nature of the impediment, maintained that the exclusion was occasioned not by any irregularity but in consequence of the very nature of the infamy itself.[33]

It was admitted that the cessation of this impediment could be effected by an amendment of one's life, which in turn had altered the reaction of those whose opinion determined one's *fama* or *infamia*. As to the length of time during which the amendment of life had to endure, the authors disagreed. Some were of the opinion that it had to last for a definite length of time,[34] while others maintained that the determination of this time-period should be left to the prudent judgment of the ordinary.[35] It was held that this amendment of life had to be public and continued,[36] and that it had to be manifest in the place where the crime or crimes which brought about the infamy of fact had been committed.[37]

The Sacred Congregation of the Council held that the effect of the public suspicion of an ignominious deed which entailed infamy could not be removed by the mere absolution of a superior, but that one's innocence had to be established publicly by sufficient proof.[38] This was formerly known as the canonical purgation,[39] which moved the judge to render a sentence of innocence with no restricting clauses attached.[40] If there was a restricting clause in the sentence—*sententia liberatoria vel absolutoria*—then the accused was still subject to the infamy of fact.[41] The state-

[33] Laymann, *ibid.*, n. 10; Pirhing, lib. I, tit. 11, n. 19.

[34] Pirhing, *loc. cit.;* Schmier, *ibid.*, n. 549; Leurenius, *loc. cit.*

[35] Schmalzgrüeber, lib. V, tit. 37, n. 174; Boenninghausen, Fasc. III, p. 164; Gasparri, *De Sacra Ordinatione,* n. 310.

[36] Wernz, II, n. 130.

[37] S. C. C., *Ferrarien.,* 25 ian. 1851—*Fontes,* n. 4116; Gasparri, *De Sacra Ordinatione,* n. 310.

[38] S. C. C., *Vigilien.,* 23 sept. 1673—*Thesaurus Resolutionum,* IX, 174 (under *Capuan.,* 21 nov. 1739); S. C. C., *Nullus Montis Virginis,* 16 febr., 5 apr. 1788—*Fontes,* n. 3858; Boenninghausen, Fasc. III, p. 164.

[39] Boenninghausen, *ibid.*, footnote: "purgatio canonica."

[40] S. C. C., *Beneventana,* 6 aug. 1763—*Fontes,* n. 3730.

[41] S. C. C., *Nullius Montis Virginis,* 16 febr., 5 apr. 1788—restricting clause—"*Novis supervenientibus*"—*Fontes,* n. 3858; S. C. C., *Vigilien.,* 23 sept. 1673—restricting clause—"*Ex hactenus deductis*"—*Thesaurus Resolutionum,* IX, 174 (under Capuan., 21 nov. 1739).

ment that one remained under infamy of fact until a sentence of innocence had been rendered was however disputed among the authors.[42] As long as a doubt persisted, it was held that there was no need of obtaining a dispensation from the Holy See,[43] although at times a dispensation was granted "*ad cautelam*" when it had been sought under circumstances which made the granting of it only doubtfully imperative.[44]

In the strict sense of the term there is not possible any dispensation from the real existence of infamy of fact.[45]

B. Canonical Commentary—"Qui Infamia Facti Laborant, Dum Ipsa Iudicio Ordinarii, Perdurat"

One who was marked with the stigma of infamy was always barred from the clerical state. The preceding historical synopsis has offered a cursory study regarding the truth of this statement. Any individual who suffers from infamy of law is irregular,[46] and may not be ordained until this infamy has been removed. Likewise, any individual who is affected with infamy of fact may not be ordained as long as this infamy rests upon him.[47] But unlike the infamy of law, which constitutes an irregularity, the latter species of infamy (*infamia facti*) constitutes a simple impediment to the reception of Orders. *Infamia facti*, then, and not *infamia iuris*, forms the basis for the present consideration.

1. Definition of Infamy of Fact

Infamia facti has been defined in the present Code of Canon Law. The definition is a description of the manner in which infamy of fact can arise. Infamy of fact is contracted when, because of a crime which he has committed, or because of his wicked mode of life, a person has lost his good name with upright

---

42 Cf. Pignatelli, VII, consult., 93, n. 3.

43 Wernz, II, n. 130.

44 S. C. C., *Melphicten.*, 30 mart. 1833—*Thesaurus Resolutionum*, XCIII, 131–133.

45 Gasparri, *De Sacra Ordinatione*, n. 310.

46 Canon 984, 5º.

47 Canon 987, 7º.

and serious-minded Catholics, concerning all of which the ordinary is to judge.[48]

The definition as it is given in the Code lists two general causes which may effect infamy. The one is the commission of a crime, and the other is a wicked mode of life. The "*delictum patratum*" is an external and morally imputable violation of the law.[49] The law which is violated may be the divine or the ecclesiastical law. The violation of the law must be not only external but also public, that is, already known to the people of the community, or sure to be divulged in consequence of the concomitant local and personal circumstances.[50] The existence of infamy necessarily involves the judgment of the people of the community. Therefore an occult violation of the law [51] cannot form the basis for infamy of fact. The actual defamation among upright and serious-minded persons cannot be thought of as arising from an occult cause.[52]

Is the term *delictum* as it is used in the definition of infamy of fact to be considered in the strict sense of canon 2195, § 1? [53] Infamy of fact is not a true penalty which is inflicted by the law for some delict; rather, it is but the natural consequence of some delict.[54] The exclusion from the reception of Orders because of the presence of an impediment is not a penalty in the strict sense, even though its effect is such as could derive from a penalty. As an impediment it implies the simple existence of a juridical entity which has the effect of depriving one of the right to receive Orders as long as it exists.

The delict is to be considered in the strict sense of canon 2195, § 1. The canonical sanction invoked by the law is the privation

---

[48] Canon 2293, § 3.

[49] Canon 2195, § 1.

[50] Canon 2197, 1o.

[51] Canon 2197, 4o.

[52] Gasparri, *De Sacra Ordinatione*, n. 287; Sole, *De Delictis et Poenis* (Romae: Pustet, 1920), n. 275 (hereafter cited as Sole); Wernz-Vidal, IV, pars I, n. 264.

[53] "Nomine delicti, iure ecclesiastico, intelligitur externa et moraliter imputabilis legis violatio cui addita sit sanctio canonica saltem indeterminata."

[54] Gasparri, *De Sacra Ordinatione*, n. 287; Sole, n. 275; Cocchi, V, pars II, n. 194.

of the right to perform certain ecclesiastically authorized acts and to receive Orders. This sanction does not become operative *ipso facto,* but depends for its efficacy on factual infamy, which derives as a natural consequence from a public delict. With reference, then, to the postulated condition of a *patratum delictum,* as long as the crime which has been committed is not a delict in the strict sense of the term, the infamy of fact which results is not of itself sufficient to deprive one of the right to receive Orders. The infamy can, however, be sufficient to prohibit the exercise of the right one already has acquired, even though the juridical basis for the impediment, that is, the removal of the right, be not verified. As long as an appeal is not made to the second phrase of canon 2293, § 3, "*ob pravos mores,*" the prohibition which affects the exercising of one's right is based, not on the wording of the law, but on the desired end of the law, which is the preservation of the sanctity and dignity of the sacred ministry.

The phrase "*ob pravos mores*" is rather generic in its import. It is referable to every sinful action insofar as that action has become a usual public occurrence in an individual's life. Since infamy of fact necessarily presupposes the judgment of others, a complete listing of those actions which will effect infamy of fact is impossible. The practice of a particular virtue may in a given community be so highly developed that certain acts contrary to that virtue may result in infamy, whereas in another community similar acts will not beget a similar effect.

A wicked mode of life (*pravi mores*) simply denotes the practise of sin. It need not necessarily be construed as involving the perpetration of a delict in the strict sense of canon 2195, § 1. Much less is it to be understood as implying any and every lowly occupation or menial service in life.[55] The attitude of the people toward certain occupations has changed. In the past certain forms of employment were considered as unbecoming, and correspondingly occasioned an unfavorable opinion on the part of the people. Such, for example, were the forms of employment engaged in by tavern proprietors, by executioners, by actors, by

[55] Hickey, p. 83.

musicians, by policemen, etc. Even prior to the Code not all authors were in agreement that such occupations gave rise to factual infamy for those who held or exercised them. Some maintained that in view of the changed attitude of the people infamy of fact could arise only when the occupation was sinful.[56] Ferraris (+ca. 1763), however, had held the opposite opinion.[57]

Under the present law such occupations are no longer considered as in themselves occasioning a basis for any consequent effect of infamy of fact. The "*delictum patratum*" and the "*pravi mores*" presuppose a criminal act or at least a sinful practice. If anything less objectionable than this is involved in a person's life, then the conditions contemplated by these two phrases in canon 2293, § 3, are no longer verified, since the facts in the case fall outside the purview as set by the all-inclusive intent of these phrases. The second phrase, however, admits of a varied application. Even though a certain occupation may not constitute a canonical impediment, the occupation may present a sufficient cause for the bishop to refuse to admit one to the clerical state.

Subjective culpability in the evil actions from which infamy of fact has resulted is not absolutely postulated for the status of ill-fame. But when upright and serious-minded Catholics have judged a person to be infamous, their judgment must of course be construed as pointing to at least a presumption of subjective guilt. Thus, infamy of fact can arise not merely from the public knowledge of the commission of a crime, but also from the public knowledge which is had of the punishment that was inflicted by a civil court.[58] This latter knowledge makes of the commission of the crime a thing of publicity. Hence serious-minded and upright Catholics who are convinced of the justice of the inflicted penalty presume the guilt of the offender.

This presumption, however, remains of a nature which allows its juridically consequent effect to be countervailed in the face

---

[56] Suarez, *De Censuris*, disp., XLVIII, sect. III, n. 1; Gasparri, *De Sacra Ordinatione*, n. 307; Hollweck, *Die kirchlichen Strafgesetze* (Mainz, 1899), p. 150.

[57] *Bibliotheca*, s. v. *irregularitas*, n. 12.

[58] Hickey, p. 83.

of conclusive proof to the contrary. It can happen that an innocent person may be affected with infamy of fact.[59] Among upright and serious-minded Catholics the innocent person has been judged to be guilty, and unless their judgment is proved to be erroneous, the subjectively innocent person still incurs factual infamy. If the loss of a person's good name results from the public suspicion that one has committed a serious crime, the presumption is that the judgment of serious-minded and upright Catholics is correct as long as the person's innocence has not been established by a sufficient and conclusive proof.[60] Ordinarily the presumption militates in favor of one's good name. However, when there is a question of choosing between one's good name, on the one hand, and the sanctity of and the reverence for the sacred ministry, on the other hand, the latter consideration prevails over the former. As will be pointed out later, not every suspicion effects infamy.

Notoriety, as it is defined in canon 2197, 3°, is not necessarily postulated for infamy of fact. A delict is called notorious when the imputability of a public delict is so certain that it cannot be concealed in any way.[61] It is not necessary that a delict be absolutely manifest, that is, known with complete certainty by certain individuals. Suspicion can be sufficient to make a delict public in the sense that it will result in infamy of fact.[62]

Through historical development *fama* has come to mean the good estimation that others have of an individual. Thus *infamia* is now considered as the loss of that good opinion which was formerly enjoyed in view of one's dignity and good behaviour.

---

[59] Cappello, *De Sacra Ordinatione*, n. 525; Merkelbach, III, n. 745.

[60] "Accidere potest aliquando ut infamia facti laborent etiam *innocentes*, si ut rei habeantur: qui idcirco arcentur ab ordinibus suscipiendis, donec eorum innocentia cognita fuerit." Cappello, *De Sacra Ordinatione*, n. 525.

[61] "Quare delictum dicitur notorium quando factum est publicum qua est delictum et ita certa est moralis imputabilitas delinquentis ut nulla possit tergiversatione celari."—Sole, n. 11.

[62] "Manifestum illud est quod pluribus certo cognitum est atque ab iisdem divulgatum."—Boenninghausen, Fasc. I, p. 41; ". . . proprie tamen fama quandoque procedit ex scientia, quandoque ex suspicione, quandoque ex certo, quandoque ex incerto auctore . . . et in hoc differt a manifesta."—Durandus [Durantis], *Speculum Iuris* (Venetiis, 1577), lib. III, p. 46.

The Code in defining infamy of fact uses the words *bonam aestimationem amisit.*

This good opinion or esteem comes from the judgment of others regarding an individual's character. Not every one is qualified to judge regarding the character of an individual. Not everyone has a correct appreciation of virtue, or a definite objective criterion for judging what is worthy of praise and what is deserving of condemnation. Too many people are rumormongers and easy preys for the ofttimes insidious force of propaganda. They believe what they wish, with little regard for the truth. They are governed in their judgments by the emotions rather than by an intellectual appreciation of the facts and a cautious disregard for fiction.

The ever solicitous lawmakers of the Church have always realized the injustice of rash and false judgments. The law has in effect made certain individuals relatively incompetent to judge on one's *fama* or on one's lack of it. The law states that the loss of one's good name is to be determined by an appeal to the judgment of upright and serious-minded Catholics. The present law is quite explicit. Under the present law one's good name is to be determined by what the faithful, and not by what those who are outside the Church, think of an individual.[63] Thus there has been added a specific ecclesiastical element to the notion of infamy of fact.

In the pre-Code law little or no emphasis was placed on the particular type of upright and serious-minded people of a community. The specific designation of the people as the faithful is proper to the Code. It is altogether fitting that the faithful be the ones to whom anyone would appeal to discover the esteem with which an individual has been endowed. Although the judgment of those outside the Church can serve as adminicular proof, primarily it is the matter of what the faithful think of this individual that is significant. One must ask: " Has the person lost his good name among the upright and serious-minded faithful? "

In a particular instance the upright and serious-minded Catholics may be wrong in their judgment, but as a general rule they will

---

63 ". . . apud fideles probos et graves . . ."—Canon 2293, § 3.

be well informed of the matters which relate to the good reputation of an individual, and to his fitness for bearing the honor, for enjoying the rights and for assuming the duties of the clerical life.

However, posited that the faithful are mistaken, there is given in the Code a practical possibility for rectifying the error. The final judgment concerning the presence of infamy of fact is left to the ordinary—"*de quo iudicium spectat ad Ordinarium.*"[64]

2. THE JUDGMENT OF THE ORDINARY

The fact that the judgment of the ordinary is postulated in the definition of infamy of fact seems to justify a distinction relative to factual infamy. From the wording of the law there seem to be two kinds of infamy of fact, the one a *common* infamy of fact, the other a *canonical* infamy of fact. The common infamy of fact is that infamy which exists among the people. There may be present all the requisites for a justified infamy of fact, but of itself such a situation will not of necessity beget the juridical effects which the law of the Code attaches to infamy of fact.[65] The juridical effects of factual infamy depend for their operative efficacy on the judgment of the ordinary. His judgment raises *common* infamy of fact to the status of *canonical* infamy of fact. The term "*canonical*" is employed to distinguish the infamy of fact which has not been judged to be present by the ordinary from that infamy of fact which has been judged to be present by the ordinary. This *canonical* infamy of fact is not to be confused with infamy of law.

The declaration of the ordinary seems to be so necessary that, unless his declaration has taken place, the individual in question is not to be considered liable to the juridical effects of infamy of fact.[66] Yet, though a canonical infamy of fact will not result

[64] Canon 2293, § 3.

[65] Canon 2294, § 2, recounts the various effects consequent upon the contraction of factual infamy.

[66] "Declaratio autem Ordinarii necessaria omnino videtur ita ut nunquam quis infamia facti laborare censendus sit nisi haec declaratio praecesserit." —Coronata, *Institutiones Iures Canonici* (5 vols., Taurini: Marietti, 1928–1936), IV (*De Delictis et Poenis*, 1935), n. 1826 (hereafter cited as Coronata, *De Delictis et Poenis*).

apart from a declaration of the ordinary, neither the individual nor those who know of his infamous character are ever justified in remaining silent about the common infamy of fact. They have a grave obligation of making known anything that would detract from the honor and dignity due to the sacred ministry.[67] An individual who has managed to conceal the common infamy of fact to which he is subject certainly commits a grave sin in entering the clerical state.

Granted that the judgment of the ordinary is necessary before infamy of fact will beget its juridical effects, the question arises: "On what basis will the ordinary make his judgment?" He will need the help of the people and of the parish priest of the locality in which the individual has resided long enough for contracting the impediment.[68] This help will be solicited by means of a faithful observance of the instruction of the Sacred Congregation of the Sacraments.[69]

With the aid of the pastor of the locality the ordinary can decide on the right of the people to pass judgment on the infamy in question. Are they upright and serious-minded Catholics? If some of the people are non-Catholics,[70] what is their status in the community, particularly among the Catholic members? Of the Catholics who have formed a judgment regarding the presence of infamy, the question must be asked: On what do they base their judgment? Is the crime or wicked mode of life a matter of public knowledge? How large a number of the faithful of the community have judged the person infamous?[71] How

---

[67] S. C. de Sacr., instr., 27 dec. 1930, nn. 6, 7, 8, and Appendix, Modus I, II, III—*AAS,* XXIII (1931), 121 ss.

[68] Canon 993, 4o.

[69] 27 dec. 1930, esp. Appendix, Modus I, II, III.

[70] It is here to be recalled that whatever proof they can furnish will have no more than an adminicular import.

[71] If a delict is known to only a few who have not divulged and do not intend to divulge the fact, then the delict is occult. Cf. Sole, n. 9.

How large may the number be when one can rightfully refer to them as only a "few"? Gasparri is of the opinion that 10 people in a large community would still be only a few.—*De Sacra Ordinatione,* n. 222. In effect, since "few" is a relative term, it is to be left to the prudent judgment of the ordinary to determine the matter in each case.

many actually saw the crime or the sins committed? What is the reliability of the source from which the people have learned of the sinful practice or the criminal deed? If the infamy is the result of a suspicion that the infamous person has committed an evil act, or has been living a wicked mode of life, does a firm basis exist for the suspicion? Can the effect of the suspicion be offset through the furnished proof of the innocence of the individual, so that no future harm will come to the sacred ministry?

All of these questions, and perhaps others, the ordinary must consider when he forms his judgment. Even though the ordinary judges that real infamy of fact is not present, yet prudence may dictate that he bar a person even when he is only suspected of infamy. The refusal in this case, however, is not based on the impediment, for real infamy must be present before the impediment can exist. And if the impediment does not exist for lack of real infamy, then the case clearly lies outside the scope of the present study.

When the ordinary has judged an individual to be under infamy of fact, his judgment does not affect the delinquent outside the limits of his territory or jurisdiction.[72] Thus a delinquent who has been judged infamous by an ordinary in a European country is not simply in view of that fact to be treated as canonically infamous in a diocese in the United States. If the major superior in an exempt clerical institute has judged an individual to be under infamy of fact, the bishop of a diocese is not obliged to follow the superior's judgment, if the individual seeks ordination in preparation for the secular priesthood.[73] The application of this principle becomes a very relevant matter when an ordinary wishes to decide on the ordination of a delinquent who has lived a very exemplary life since his arrival in the new territory in which he will be assigned to exercise the ministry if he is ordained.

It is not necessary that the ordinary who judges on the presence

[72] "Infamia facti delinquentem non afficit ultra terminos territorii aut iurisdictionis Ordinarii qui eiusdem declarationem emisit."—Coronata, *De Delictis et Poenis,* n. 1826.

[73] In all probability, however, the bishop will follow the judgment of the superior.

of infamy be an "*ordinarius loci.*" The judge can be any ordinary of whom mention is included in canon 198. The power which each ordinary has in this matter can be delegated.[74]

Coronata is of the opinion that the official sentence or declaration of the ordinary need not be made for each and every case. It seems to Coronata that this official declaration would be sufficiently expressed if it were enacted in a diocesan law or statute.[75] This could serve as a guide for those who are called upon to admit or reject individuals when there is question of their exercise of ecclesiastical acts as authorized in law,[76] but to use a diocesan statute which is anticipative in its import in place of a specifically formulated declaration of the presence of infamy of fact seems to go contrary to the very notion of infamy of fact. The attitude of people toward certain crimes, the judgment of the people in an individual case, the number of people who know of the crime, all of these factors are so relative in character that it is very difficult to legislate on the effects of them with reference to any and every emergent case of infamy of fact. It is not the ordinary's judgment alone that gives rise to the juridical concept of infamy of fact. Hence his judgment may not be arbitrary. It must be based on the presence or the absence of the elements which are necessary to constitute *common* infamy of fact.

It is possible in a limited way to justify Coronata's statement on the score of a judgment which is exercised through delegated power. The ordinary's power to pass judgment on the presence of infamy can be delegated. Thus the ordinary may delegate every pastor with the power to pass judgment on the presence of *canonical* infamy of fact. Again, he may delegate the pastors with the power to judge only regarding the presence of the

[74] Cf. S. C. de Sacr., instr., 27 dec. 1930, n. 2: cf. also the discussion on pages 102–103 of the present work.

[75] "Infamia vero facti, cum de ea ad Ordinarium, non necessario Ordinarium loci, iudicium pertineat, etiam iure particulari aut speciali statui potest. Nec necessaria videtur singulis in casibus sententia aut declaratio Ordinarii, sed sufficere declaratio lege dioecesana aut statuto lata."—Coronata, *De Delictis et Poenis*, n. 1826.

[76] Canon 2294, § 2.

elements necessary for constituting *common* infamy of fact. If the granted delegation is of the latter kind, then the ordinary's ultimate judgment could receive its specification from a diocesan law or statute. The law could read: "The pastor having judged that the necessary elements for *common* infamy of fact are present, the judgment of the ordinary is that *canonical* infamy of fact has ensued, and that its juridical effects are in force."

The law could also list certain crimes, or continued sinful modes of life, which are judged by the ordinary to effect *canonical* infamy of fact when and if the pastor has judged that *common* infamy of fact is present. The law could read: "When in the judgment of the pastor *common* infamy of fact is present, then the judgment of the ordinary is that such infamy of fact will have the juridical effects of canon 2294, § 2, if the crime is murder, robbery, public concubinage, continued refusal to attend Sunday mass, or a continued habit of drunkenness. All other cases are to be submitted to the ordinary for his particular judgment." Merely to recount a list of crimes or of sinful actions in a diocesan law or statute, and to legislate that whoever is guilty of such crimes or sinful actions is subject to the juridical effects of infamy of fact does not seem to be justifiable.

If a person (1) has committed a crime or is living a wicked life on account of which (2) he has lost his good name among upright and serious-minded Catholics and (3) the ordinary has judged that these facts are true, then the person is under *canonical* infamy of fact and is subject to its juridical effects. He cannot be ordained because there exists an impediment. This juridical effect of *canonical* infamy of fact extends only to the individual himself, and not to his relatives.[77]

C. Cessation of the Impediment

The impediment which arises from *canonical* infamy of fact can cease. This cessation can be effected by the effacement of the infamy itself. The Code itself indicates in which manner the infamy can become effaced. The law states that infamy of fact ceases when one has regained his good reputation in the eyes

[77] Canon 2293, § 4.

of upright and serious-minded Catholics. However, it is the ordinary who after considering the particular circumstances, especially the prolonged amendment of the guilty person, is to judge whether the lost reputation has been recovered.[78]

1. PROLONGED AMENDMENT

All upright and serious-minded Catholics must admit that a sinner can repent, and that his repentance can merit not only his forgiveness but can vindicate for him also the recovery of his good reputation. In the law no definite time is set for the duration of this repentance.[79] The reaching of a decision in this matter is left to the prudent judgment of the ordinary. The length of the requisite time will depend upon the nature of the crime or sinful actions, upon the degree of publicity attaching to the acts, upon the former status of the delinquent, upon the excellence of the virtues of the community in which the repentance takes place, and upon the outward expression of the excellence of the penitent's virtues.[80]

The amendment as recognized and acknowledged by the faithful must continue at least until the ordinary has judged that the penitent has recovered his good name.[81] The Code gives the ordinary the complete authority to decide on the requisite duration of the amendment. This settles the pre-Code dispute regarding the duration of the time required for the amendment. The duration of time can no longer be identified with a definite number of years. However, in forming his judgment the ordinary may be guided by the legislation of canon 672, § 1,[82] so that three years of continuous amendment would be sufficient to meet the requirement expressed in the phrase "*diuturna rei emendatione.*" [83]

This prolonged amendment must be of such a nature that it

[78] Canon 2295.

[79] Cocchi, V, 194; Wernz-Vidal, IV, pars I, n. 264.

[80] Cf. Blat, III, pars I, n. 262.

[81] Canons 2295, 987, 7o; Wernz-Vidal, IV, pars I, n. 264.

[82] ". . . et si argumenta plenae emendationis per triennium dederit religio tenetur eum [religiosum dimissum] recipere; . . ."

[83] Cf. Coronata, *De Delictis et Poenis,* n. 1828.

will restore one's good name among those who were considered competent to judge on the loss of one's good name. Just as the judgment of the ordinary in determining the presence of infamy of fact is based on what upright and serious-minded Catholics think about the offender, so too in determining the recovery of an individual's good name the ordinary's decision is to be based on the favorable reactions of serious-minded and upright Catholics. If these Catholics have been convinced by the prolonged amendment of the offender that he is deserving of his good name, then *common* infamy of fact, the basis for *canonical* infamy of fact, ceases.

2. THE JUDGMENT OF THE ORDINARY

Before infamy of fact entails its juridical effects the judgment of the ordinary is necessary. So, too, before the canonical infamy of fact will cease to be present, and its contracted juridical effects will cease to bind, the judgment of the ordinary is necessary. Just as the judgment of the ordinary furnishes a necessary element for the contraction of canonical infamy of fact, so his judgment must accede if the contracted infamy is to be fully effaced.

It is necessary that the prolonged amendment be manifested in the place where one has lost his good name. For the cessation of *common* infamy of fact the prolonged amendment must have become known to those through whose judgment the erstwhile *common* infamy of fact was made a reality. They could not judge that a person has recovered his good name if they did not know of his amendment either by actual observation or by some reliable report of the amendment.

From the testimonial letters gathered in accordance both with the norms of canon 993, 4°, and with the directions of the Instruction of the Sacred Congregation of the Sacraments,[84] the ordinary will learn of the character of the individual who is seeking ordination. If the candidate has been judged infamous by an extraneous ordinary, the ordinary in whose service the candidate is to be admitted will not strictly be required to consider the candidate as continuing subject to the impediment of infamy of fact. If

[84] 27 dec. 1930—*AAS,* XXIII (1931), 121 ss.

in the territory of the ordinary who is accepting the candidate the crime or the wicked mode of life is unknown, and moreover will not become known, then in that locality the crime or the wicked mode of life is occult, and as such does not give rise to infamy of fact.[85] The judgment of the ordinary of the place in which the person has lost his good name does not have any binding effect in reference to that person outside the territory of the ordinary's jurisdiction. Therefore, if an ordinary judges that a person who is subject to canonical infamy in another locality is not infamous (*infamia facti*) in his own locality, he is not obligated to concern himself about the impediment of infamy of fact.

Unless this conclusion is accepted, the offender who has moved away from the scene of his crime would be obliged to go back and prove his amendment. An individual who has committed a crime but later moved away and led an exemplary life for many years would be perpetually barred from Orders unless he returned and began a new prolonged amendment for the observation of those who had judged him infamous, or else his amendment would have to be publicized in some manner so that the people could reach a judgment concerning the amendment.

If in the judgment of the later ordinary the crime will remain occult in his territory, and there is no likelihood that the ordination of the erstwhile offender will ever become known in the place of his offense, and moreover the ordinary does not judge the offender to be under infamy of fact, then the simple impediment is not present in the case. It is not the purpose of the present work to decide on what would be the more prudent course to follow when an infamous person has moved to a different locality. The sole aim is to determine when and where the simple impediment of infamy of fact exists.

Prior to the Code *common* infamy of fact was considered as an irregularity or an impediment to Orders. The judgment of the ordinary was not given the importance that is accorded to it in the Code for determining the emergence of the juridical

---

85 "Item delictum quamvis in uno loco sit publicum, in alio potest esse occultum, dummodo eius notitia non facile eo sit perventura."—Sole, n. 10.

effects of infamy of fact. Whether because of the lack of emphasis on the judgment of the ordinary relative to infamy of fact, or because of the failure to consider the possibility of an infamous person's moving to another locality and living there a exemplary life, it is difficult to determine the basis for the pre-Code necessity of a delinquent's performing his amendment in the place of the committed crime or perpetrated evil actions.[86]

If the prolonged amendment has taken place, must the ordinary's judgment regarding the cessation of *common* infamy of fact be manifested explicitly? Is the ordinary obliged in each and every case to state explicitly: "This individual is no longer under the impediment of infamy of fact?" The judgment of the ordinary will be sufficiently expressed by his faithful observance of canon 968, § 1. In virtue of this canon he is obliged to pass judgment on the necessary qualities of a candidate for Orders. This judgment proves sufficient, so that a candidate for Orders will not be obliged to recall to the mind of the ordinary that he had at one time judged him to be canonically infamous.[87]

Since every impediment renders illicit not only the reception of Orders, but also the exercise of the Orders received, the assignment of some particular exercise of the sacred ministry, or the conferring of an ecclesiastical office or of a benefice by the ordinary which demands the exercise of Orders, would be a sufficient expression of his judgment that *common* infamy of fact is no longer present, as long of course as a prolonged amendment has preceded.[88]

---

86 "Necesse est ad tollendam infamiae notam ut poenitentia peragatur in loco commissi delicti."—Gasparri, *De Sacra Ordinatione*, n. 310.

87 "Licit forte ad infamiam facti incurrendam, ut supra diximus, necessaria sit positiva Ordinarii declaratio, attamen ad ipsam infamiam facti auferendam positivum Ordinarii iudicium non requiri videtur, quia in poenis benignior est interpretatio facienda, et nimis grave videretur delinquenti qui diuturna emendatione delictum redemit Superiorem adire debere eique antiquum et forte oblitum ex diuturna emendatione delictum in memoriam revocare."—Coronata, *De Delictis et Poenis*, n. 1828.

88 "Dicemus proinde implicitum iudicium Ordinarii, quo clerico conferuntur ab eodem Ordinario ordines, officia aut beneficia aut exercitium sacri ministerii, sufficere ad recuperandam famam, dummodo habeatur diuturna emendatio." Coronata, *loc. cit.*

D. Dispensation from the Impediment

There can be no dispensation from infamy of fact.[89] If in the judgment of the ordinary an individual is under infamy of fact, the Holy See will never dispense from the juridical effects of this infamy. This denial of the dispensation follows as a natural consequence from the aims and purposes inherent in the clerical state. A cleric, especially the priest, is ordained for promoting the spiritual good and well-being of man. But if men held the cleric or priest in ill-repute, the ordination would occasion harm instead of good. The honor and the dignity due the sacred ministry would be endangered by the ordination of an infamous person. Hence the Holy See will in no way countenance the granting of a dispensation in consequence of which it would be no longer unlawful for a person to receive Orders when he continues at the same time subject to factual infamy.

[89] Wernz-Vidal, IV, pars I, n. 264.

CONCLUSIONS

1. The term *uxor,* as employed in canon 987, 2°, is to be considered as referring to a woman *lawfully* united to a man by the bond of a valid marriage which in its nature is perpetual and exclusive.

2. If the invalidity of a given marriage is doubtful in the eyes of the Church, inasmuch as it has not been proved with certitude, the marriage is to be considered as valid. Until the presumption of the law for the validity of the marriage has been overthrown, the man will be impeded from the reception of Orders in virtue of canon 987, 2°. Therefore the husband of a presumptively valid marriage is impeded until a declaration of nullity has been given by the ecclesiastical court.

3. The basis for the impediment listed in canon 987, 2°, is constituted by the extant bond of marriage which exists between the married parties. Therefore a convert, in lieu of entering a second mariage through the use of the Pauline Privilege, cannot in the same condition or status receive Orders. He will need a dispensation from the impediment which is based on the extant bond of marriage.

4. The religious profession of the wife is not absolutely required for a dispensation from the impediment listed in canon 987, 3°; however, on the possibility that it might be demanded, it will be a matter of prudent foresight to try to discover beforehand how much time must elapse before a wife can be admitted to a solemn profession in a religious order, or a perpetual simple profession in a congregation of women religious.

5. Absolute and full liberty or freedom is not a necessary postulate for the removal of a slave properly so called from the category of persons subject to the impediment listed in canon 987, 4°.

6. The effect of ordination on the status of a slave can be determined only by a consultation of the civil law of the country which permits the institute of slavery properly so called to exist.

7. Service in the National Guard will not cause one to fall

within the comprehension of the law of canon 987, 5°, unless it becomes an organization in which national compulsory ordinary military service can be fulfilled.

8. The directions of the decree "*Redeuntibus*" of the Sacred Congregation of the Consistory, which was issued on October 25, 1918, for soldiers returning from *extraordinary* military service, should be followed by the ordinary when he deals with soldiers returning from compulsory *ordinary* military service.

9. The prohibitions of canon 139 and 142 are likewise contemplated under canon 987, 3°, insofar as there is connected with the position which is forbidden by these two canons (139 and 142) the obligation of rendering an account.

10. The *antecedent* permission of the authorities competent to grant permission to accept a position forbidden to clerics in canons 139 and 142 removes the holder of such positions from the prohibition enacted in canon 987, 3°. This permission obviates the prohibition inherent in the term "*vetita,*" and consequently precludes the possibility of the emergence of an impediment.

11. A true *clinicus,* although it can happen that he too must be subjected to a period of probation in his faith, is not a neophyte and does not come under the comprehension of the law as enacted in canon 987, 6°.

12. If conditional baptism has been conferred on an individual because the invalidity of his earlier baptism, which was conferred at least three years previous to the candidate's request for Orders, is not certain, then the earlier baptism which may have been valid removes the recipient from the comprehension of the term "neophyte," although in virtue of canons other than 987, 6°, he may need to be subjected to a period of probation in his faith.

13. A child born of Catholic parents, but later adopted by parents of whom one is a non-Catholic, does not come within the scope of canon 987, 1°.

14. The term "*acatholicus*" of canon 987, 1°, includes all non-Catholics, i.e., heretics, apostates, Jews, atheists, Mohammedans, etc.

15. A son whose parents at the time of his birth were Catholics and only later became non-Catholics is not affected by the im-

pediment enacted in canon 987, 1°; nor is a son impeded from the reception of Orders in consequence of the law enacted in canon 987, 1°, when he was born of non-Catholic parents who were later converted, but then fell back into their previous status of non-Catholics.

16. A child born of non-Catholic parents who are now deceased is not subject to the prohibition enacted in canon 987, 1°.

17. *Canonical* infamy of fact postulates the judgment of the ordinary for its existence.

18. *Canonical* infamy of fact, and not *common* infamy of fact, subjects the infamous person to the impediment enacted in canon 987, 7°.

19. The judgment of the ordinary of the place in which an individual has lost his good name does not in reference to that person have any juridical value outside the territory of the ordinary's jurisdiction.

BIBLIOGRAPHY

SOURCES

Acta Apostolicae Sedis, Commentarium Officiale, Romae, 1909–

Acta de Decreta Concilii Plenarii Baltimorensis Tertii, A. D. *MDCCCLXXXIV,* Baltimorae, John Murphy, 1886.

Acta Sanctae Sedis, 41 vols., Romae, 1865–1908.

Bouscaren, T. Lincoln, *The Canon Law Digest,* 2 vols., Milwaukee: Bruce, 1934–1943.

Canones et Decreta Sacrosancti Oecumenici Concilii Tridentini, Parisiis, 1856.

Codex Iuris Canonici Pii X Pontificis Maximi iussu digestus Benedicti XV auctoritate promulgatus, Romae: Typis Polyglottis Vaticanis, 1917.

Codicis Iuris Canonici Fontes cura Emi Petri. Card. Gasparri editi, 9 vols., Romae (postea Civitate Vaticana): Typis Polyglottis Vaticanis, 1923–1939. (Vols. VII–IX ed. cura et studio Emi Iustiniani Card. Serédi.)

Collectanea Sacrae Congregationis de Propaganda Fide, 2 vols., Romae: Typographia Polyglotta S. C. de Propaganda Fide, 1907.

Concilii Plenarii Baltimorensis II, in Ecclesia Metropolitana Baltimorensi, a die VII ad diem XXI Octobris, A. D. *MDCCCLXVI, habiti, et a Sede Apostolica Recogniti, Acta et Decreta,* Baltimorae, John Murphy, 1868.

Corpus Iuris Canonici, editio Lipsiensis secunda post Aemilii Ludovici Richteri curas instruxit Aemilius Friedburg, 1879–1881. Editio anastatice repetita, Lipsiae: Tauchnitz, 1928.

Corpus Iuris Civilis, 3 vols., Berolini: apud Weidmannos, 1928–1929.

Vol. I, *Institutiones,* quas recognovit et retractavit P. Krueger.

Digesta, quae recognovit et retractavit P. Krueger.

Vol. II, *Codex Iustinianus,* quem recognovit et retractavit P. Krueger.

Vol. III, *Novellae,* quas recognovti R. Schoell, et absolvit G. Kroll.

Decretales D. Gregorii Papae IX, una cum Glossis Restitutae, Romae, 1582.

Decretum Gratiani, una cum Glossis Gregorii XIII Pont. Max. isuus editum, Romae, 1582.

Enchiridion Fontium Historiae Ecclesiasticae Antiquae, ed., C. Kirch, 4. ed., Friburgi Brisgoviae: Herder & Co., 1923.

Jaffé, Philippus, *Regesta Pontificium Romanorum ab condita Ecclesia ad annum post Christum natum MCXCVIII,* ad. 2. correctam et auctam auspiciis Gulielmi Wattenbach curaverunt S. Loewenfeld, F. Kaltenbrunner, P. Ewald, 2 vols. in 1, Lipsiae: 1885–1888.

Liber Sextus Decretalium D. Bonifacii Papae VIII suae integritati una cum Clementinis et Extravagantibus earumque Glossis restitutis, Romae: 1582.

Mansi, Ioannes Dominicus, *Sacrorum Conciliorum Nova et Amplissima Collectio,* 53 vols. in 60, Paris-Leipzig-Arnhem, 1901–1927.

Potthast, A., *Regesta Pontificum Romanorum inde ab anno post Christum natum 1198 ad annum 1304,* 2 vols. in 1, Berolini, 1874–1875.

Richter, A., *Canones et Decreta Sacrosancti Concilii Tridentini,* Lipsiae, 1853.

Schroeder, H. J., *Canons and Decrees of the Council of Trent: Original Text with English Translation,* St. Louis: B. Herder Book Co., 1941.

Thesaurus Resolutionum Sacrae Congregationis Concilii, 167 vols., Romae: 1718–1908.

AUTHORS

Ayrinhac, H. A., *Legislation on the Sacraments,* New York: Longmans Green and Co., 1928.

[Bachofen], Charles Augustine, *A Commentary on the New Code of Canon Law,* 8 vols., Vol. IV, 1. ed., Vol. V, 2. ed., St. Louis: Herder, 1919–1924.

Barbosa, A., *Collectanea Doctorum tam Veterum quam Recentiorum in Ius Pontificium Universum,* 6 vols. in 3, Lugduni, 1656.

———, *Summa Apostolicarum Decisionum,* Lugduni, 1645.

Benedictus XIV, *De Synodo Dioecesana,* 2 vols., Typographia S. C. de Propaganda Fidei: Romae, 1806.

Berardi, C., *Commentaria in Ius Ecclesiasticum Universum,* Taurinorum Augustae, 1766.

Beste, U., *Introductio in Codicem,* Collegeville, Minn.: St. John's Abbey Press, 1944.

Blat, A., *Commentarium Textus Codicis Iuris Canonici,* 5 vols. in 7, Romae: Collegio "Angelico," 1920–1927.

Boenninghausen, F. E. von, *Tractatus Iuridico-Canonicus de Irregularitatibus,* 3 fasc., Monasterii: Typis et Sumptibus Theissingianis, 1863–1866.

Bonacina, M., *De Morali Theologia,* 3 vols., Venetiis, 1867.

Borgasio, P., *Tractatus de Irregularitatibus et Impedimentis Ordinum, Officiorum et Beneficiorum Ecclesiasticorum,* Venetiis, 1574.

Brunini, J., *The Clerical Obligations of Canons 139 and 142,* The Catholic University of America Canon Law Studies, n. 103, Washington, D. C.: The Catholic University of America, 1937.

Buckland, W., *Roman Law of Slavery,* Cambridge: University Press, 1908.

Caponi, I., *Institutiones Canonicae,* 2 vols., Coloniae Allobrogum, 1734.

Cappello, F., *Tractatus Canonicus de Sacramentis,* 3 vols., Vol. II, pars III, *De Sacra Ordinatione,* 1. ed., Vol. III, *De Matrimonio,* 4. ed., 1939, Romae: Marietti, 1932–1939.

Carberry, J., *The Juridical Form of Marriage,* The Catholic University of America Canon Law Studies, n. 84, Washington, D. C.: The Catholic University of America, 1934.

Catholic Dictionary, A, Donald Attwater, general editor, The Catholic Action Society of the College of St. Robert Bellarmine, Heythrop: New York: Macmillan Co., 1941.

Cavagnis, F., *Institutiones Iuris Publici Ecclesiastici,* 2. ed., 2 vols., Romae, 1888.

Claeys Bouuaert, F.–Simenon, G., *Manuale Iuris Canonici,* 3 vols., Vol. I, 3. ed., 1930, Vol. II, 2. ed., 1935, Gandae et Leodii: Seminarium Gandavense et Leodiense.

Cocchi, G., *Commentarium in Codicem Iuris Canonici ad usum scholarum,* 5 vols. in 8, Vol. I, 4. ed., 1931, Taurinorum Augustae: Marietti.

Coronata, M. Conte a, *Institutiones Iuris canonici,* 5 vols., Taurini: Marietti, 1928–1936, Vol. IV, *De Delictis et Poenis,* 1935.

D'Annibale, I., *Summula Theologiae Moralis,* 5. ed., 3 vols., Romae, 1908.

De Meester, A., *Iuris Canonici et Iuris Canonico-Civilis Compendium,* 3 vols. in 4, nova editio, Brugis, 1921–1928.

Devoti, I., *Ius Canonicum Universum Publicum et Privatum,* 3 toms., ed. nova, Romae, 1837.

Downs, J., *The Concept of Clerical Immunity,* The Catholic University of America Canon Law Studies, n. 126, Washington, D. C.: The Catholic University of America Press, 1941.

Durandus [Durantis], G., *Speculum Iuris,* Venetiis, 1577.

Encyclopedia Americana, The, 30 vols., ed. 1943, New York: Americana Corporation.

Fagnanus, P., *Commentaria in Quinque Libros Decretalium,* 4 vols., Venetiis, 1697.

Fargna, F., *Commentaria in Canones de Iurepatronatus,* 3 vols., Romae, 1717–1719.

Ferraris, L., *Prompta Bibliotheca Canonica, Iuridica, Moralis, Theologica, necnon Ascetica, Polemica, Rubricistica, Historica,* ed. Migne, 8 vols., Parisiis, 1860–1863.

Galganettus, L., *De Tutela et Cura,* Venetiis, 1618.

Gasparri, P., *Tractatus de Sacra Ordinatione,* 2 vols., Parisiis, 1893.

Gibalinus, I., *De Universa Rerum Humanarum Negotiatione,* Lugduni, 1663.

Giraldi, U., *Expositio Iuris Pontificii iuxta Recentiorem Ecclesiae Disciplinam,* 2 vols., Romae, 1829.

Gonzalez-Tellez, M., *Commentaria Perpetua in singulos textus Quinque Libros Decretalium Gregorii IX,* 5 vols. in 4, Venetiis, 1699.

Goodwine, J.. *The Reception of Converts,* The Catholic University of America Canon Law Studies, n. 198, Washington, D. C.: The Catholic University of America Press, 1944.

Gregory, D., *The Pauline Privilege,* The Catholic University of America Canon Law Studies, n. 68, Washington, D. C.: The Catholic University of America, 1931.

Guilfoyle, M., *Custom,* The Catholic University of America Canon Law Studies, n. 105, Washington, D. C.: The Catholic University of America, 1937.

Heneghan, J., *The Marriage of Unworthy Catholics: Canons 1065–1066,* The Catholic University of America Canon Law Studies, n. 188, Washington, D. C.: The Catholic University of America Press, 1944.

Hickey, J., *Irregularities and Simple Impediments in the New Code of Canon Law,* The Catholic University of America Canon Law Studies, n. 7, Washington, D. C.: The Catholic University of America, 1920.

Hollweck, J., *Die kirchlichen Strafgesetze,* Mainz, 1899.

Hostiensis, Cardinalis (Henricus de Segusio), *Commentaria in Quinque Decretalium Libros,* 5 vols. in 3, Venetiis, 1581.

Kearney, R., *The Principles of Delegation,* The Catholic University of America Canon Law Studies, n. 55, Washington, D. C.: The Catholic University of America, 1929.

Kirchenlexikon, Hergenröther, J.–Kaulen, F., 2. ed., 13 vols., Freiburg im Breisgau: Herder, 1882–1903.

Leage, R.–Ziegler, C., *Roman Private Law,* 2. ed., New York: Macmillan and Co., Ltd., 1937.

Leurenius, P., *Forum Ecclesiasticum in quo Ius Canonicum Explanatur,* 5 vols. in 3, Venetiis, 1729.

Lexicon Totius Latinitatis, Forcellini–Furlanetti, 4 vols. in 8, Patavii, 1864–1887.

Liguori, St. Alphonsus Maria de, *Theologia Moralis,* 4 vols., ed. Gaudé, Romae, 1905–1912.

MacKenzie, E., *The Delict of Heresy in its Commission, Penalization, Absolution,* The Catholic University of America Canon Law Studies, n. 77, Washington, D. C.: The Catholic University of America, 1932.

Maioli, S., *De Irregularitatibus,* Romae, 1575.

McDevitt, G., *Legitimacy and Legitimation,* The Catholic University of America Canon Law Studies, n. 138, Washington, D. C.: The Catholic University of America Press, 1941.

Manning, J., *Presumption of Law in Matrimonial Procedure,* The Catholic University of America Canon Law Studies, n. 94, Washington, D. C.: The Catholic University of America, 1935.

Maroto, P., *Institutiones Iuris Canonici ad Normam Novi Codicis,* 2 vols., Vol. I, 3. ed., Romae, 1921.

Merkelbach, B., *Summa Theologiae Moralis,* ed. altera, 3 vols., Parisiis: Typis Desclée De Brouwer, 1935–1936.

Navarrus (Martinus de Azpilcueta), *Consiliorum seu Responsorum in Quinque Libros iuxta Numerum et Titulos Decretalium Distributorum Tomi Duo,* Venetiis, 1621.

Noldin, H.–Schmitt, S., *Summa Theologiae Moralis,* 3 vols., Oeniponte: Typis et Sumptibus Fel. Rauch, Vol. II, 25. ed., 1938, Vol III, 26. ed., 1940.

Payen, G., *De Matrimonio in Missionibus et Potissimum in Sinis Tractatus Practicus et Casus,* 2. ed., 3 vols., Zi-ka-wei: in Typographia T'ou-sè-wè, 1935–1936.

Petrovits, J., *The New Church Law on Matrimony,* The Catholic University of America Canon Law Studies, n. 6, Washington, D. C.: The Catholic University of America, 1919.

Pignatelli, I., *Consultationes Canonicae,* 10 vols. in 4, Coloniae Allobrogum, 1700.

Pirhing, E., *Ius Canonicum Nova Methodo Explicatum,* 5 vols. in 4, Dilingae, 1674–1678.

Quigley, J., *Condemned Societies,* The Catholic University of America Canon Law Studies, n. 46. Washington, D. C.: The Catholic University of America, 1927.

Raymond of Peñafort, St., *Summa,* ed. nova, Veronae, 1744.

Reiffenstuel, A., *Ius Canonicum Universum,* 5 vols. in 7, Parisiis, 1864–1870.

Reilly, H., *Compulsory Military Training,* Washington, D. C.: Civilian Military Education Fund, 1940.

Robinson, W., *Elementary Law,* New Edition, Boston: Little, Brown, and Company, 1910.

Roskovány, A., *De Coelibatu et Breviario,* 13 vols., Vols. I–IV, 1861, Pestini.

Sanchez, T., *De Sancto Matrimonii Sacramento Disputationum Tomi Tres,* Lugduni, 1669.

Schmalzgrueber, F., *Ius Ecclesiasticum Universum,* 5 vols. in 12, Romae, 1843–1845.

Schmidt, J., *The Principles of Authentic Interpretation in Canon 17 of the Code of Canon Law,* The Catholic University of America Canon Law Studies, n. 141, Washington, D. C.: The Catholic University of America Press, 1941.

Schmier, F., *Iurisprudentia Canonico-civilis,* 2 vols., Venetiis, 1754.

Sole, I., *De Delictis et Poenis,* Romae: Pustet, 1920.

Suarez, F., *Opera Omnia,* 28 vols., ed. L. Vivès, Parisiis, 1856–1861, Vol. XXIII, *De Censuris in Communi.*

Thomas Acquinas, St., *Summa Theologica,* 5 vols., Taurini: Marietti, 1938.

Van Hove, S., *Prolegomena ad Codicem Iuris Canonici,* Mechliniae–Romae, H. Dessain, 1928.

Verano, G., *Iuris Canonici Universi Commentarius,* 5 vols., Monachii, 1703–1708.

Vermeersch, A.-Creusen, J., *Epitome Iuris Canonici,* 3 vols., Vol. I, 6. ed., 1937, Vols. II et III, 5. ed., 1934–1936, Mechliniae-Romae: H. Dessain.

Wernz, F., *Ius Decretalium,* 6 vols., Romae et Prati, 1898–1905.

Wernz, F.-Vidal, P., *Ius Canonicum,* 7 vols. in 9, Romae: Apud Aedes Universitatis Gregorianae, 1923–1938.

Woywod, S., *A Practical Commentary on the Code of Canon Law,* 2 vols., 4. ed., New York: Wagner, 1932.

PERIODICALS

American Ecclesiastical Review, The (formerly *The Ecclesiastical Review*), Philadelphia, 1889–1943; Baltimore, 1944–

Apollinaris, Romae, 1928–

Archiv für katholisches Kirchenrecht, Innsbruck, 1857–1861; Mains, 1862–

Commentarium pro Religiosis, Romae, 1920– ; from 1935: *Commentarium pro Religiosis et Missionariis.*

Jurist, The, Washington, D. C., 1941–

Periodica de Re Canonica et Morali Utili praesertim Religiosis et Missionariis, Brugis, 1905; ab anno 1927; *Periodica de Re Canonica, Morali, Liturgica.*

Theologisch-praktische Quartalschrift, Linz, 1832–

ARTICLES

Gillman, F., "Die *anni discretionis* im Kanon *Omnis utriusque sexus*"—*AKKR*, CVIII (1928), 556–617.

Larraona, A., "Commentarium Codicis"—*CpR(M)*, XVI (1935), 430.

McKenna, S., "The Mystical Body in the Social and Political Sphere"—*AER*, CIII (1940), 209–218.

Raus, J., "Weihehindernis der Söhne von Nichtkatholiken"—*TpQS*, LXXVI (1923), 122–127.

Schmid, L., "De vi verborum 'acatholicus, secta acatholica, minister acatholicus' in Iure Canonico"—*Apollinaris*, IV (1931), 552–567; V (1932), 69–85.

Vermeersch, A., "Annotationes"—*Periodica*, V (1913), 284–286.

ABBREVIATIONS

AAS—*Acta Apostolicae Sedis.*
AER—*The American Ecclesiastical Review.*
AKKR—*Archiv fur katholisches Kirchenrecht.*
ASS—*Acta Sanctae Sedis.*
C.—Codex Iustinianus.
CpR(M)—*Commentarium pro Religiosis (et Missionariis).*
Coll. S. C. P. F—*Collectanea S. Congregationis de Propaganda Fide.*
D.—Digesta Iustiniana.
Fontes—*Codicis Iuris Canonici Fontes.*
I.—Institutiones Iustinianae.
JE—Jaffé, *Regesta Pontificum Romanorum* (edited by Ewald: from 590 to 882).
JK—Jaffé, *op. cit.* (edited by Kaltenbrunner: from 33 to 590).
JL—Jaffé, *op. cit.* (edited by Loewenfeld: from 882 to 1198).
Mansi—*Sacrorum Conciliorum Nova et Amplissima Collectio.*
N.—Novellae Iustinianae.
P. C. I.—Pontifical Commission for the Authentic Interpretation of the Code.
Periodica—*Periodica de Re Canonica et Morali Utilii praesertim Religiosis et Missionariis.*
Potthast—Potthast, A., *Regesta Pontificum Romanorum.*
R. I.—*Regula Iuris.*
S. C. C.—Sacra Congregatio Concilii.
S. C. de Prop. Fide—Sacra Congregatio de Propaganda Fide.
S. C. de Rel.—Sacra Congregatio de Religiosis.
S. C. de Sacr.—Sacra Congregatio de Sacramentis.
S. Poenit.—Sacra Poenitentiaria Apostolica.
S. C. S. Off.—Sacra Congregatio Sancti Officii.
Thesaurus Resolutionum—*Sacrae Congregationis Concilii Resolutiones.*
TpQS—*Theologisch-praktische Quartalschrift.*

ALPHABETICAL INDEX

BIOGRAPHICAL NOTE

Henry John Vogelpohl was born September 1, 1913, in Cincinnati, Ohio. He received his elementary education at the Parochial Schools of St. Pius in Cincinnati, of the Assumption in Mt. Healthy and of St. Lawrence in Cincinnati, Ohio. After completing his high school and college education at St. Gregory Seminary, Cincinnati, Ohio, he received the degree of Bachelor of Arts from that institution in 1935. He pursued his course in Theology at St. Mary Seminary, Norwood, Ohio, and on June 3, 1939, was ordained to the priesthood. In September, 1942, he enrolled in the School of Canon Law at the Catholic University of America, where he received the degree of the Baccalaureate in Canon Law in May, 1943, and the degree of the Licentiate in Canon Law in May, 1944.

CANON LAW STUDIES*

1. FRERIKS, REV. CELESTINE A., C.PP.S., J.C.D., Religious Congregations in Their External Relations, 121 pp., 1916.
2. GALLIHER, REV. DANIEL M., O.P., J.C.D., Canonical Elections, 117 pp., 1917.
3. BORKOWSKI, REV. AURELIUS L., O.F.M., J.C.D., De Confraternitatibus Ecclesiasticis, 136 pp., 1918.
4. CASTILLO, REV. CAYO, J.C.D., Disertacion Historico-Canonica sobre la Potestad del Cabildo en Sede Vacante o Impedida del Vicario Capitular, 99 pp., 1919 (1918).
5. KUBELBECK, REV. WILLIAM J., S.T.B., J.C.D., The Sacred Penitentiaria and Its Relation to Faculties of Ordinaries and Priests, 129 pp., 1918.
6. PETROVITS, REV. JOSEPH J. C., S.T.D., J.C.D., The New Church Law on Matrimony, X-461 pp., 1919.
7. HICKEY, REV. JOHN J., S.T.B., J.C.D., Irregularities and Simple Impediments in the New Code of Canon Law, 100 pp., 1920.
8. KLEKOTKA, REV. PETER J., S.T.B., J.C.D., Diocesan Consultors, 179 pp., 1920.
9. WANENMACHER, REV. FRANCIS, J.C.D., The Evidence in Ecclesiastical Procedure Affecting the Marriage Bond, 1920 (Printed 1935).
10. GOLDEN, REV. HENRY FRANCIS, J.C.D., Parochial Benefices in the New Code, IV-119 pp., 1921 (Printed 1925).
11. KOUDELKA, REV. CHARLES J., J.C.D., Pastors, Their Rights and Duties According to the New Code of Canon Law, 211 pp., 1921.
12. MELO, REV. ANTONIUS, O.F.M., J.C.D., De Exemptione Regularium, X-188 pp., 1921.
13. SCHAAF, REV. VALENTINE THEODORE, O.F.M., S.T.B., J.C.D., The Cloister, X-180 pp., 1921.
14. BURKE, REV. THOMAS JOSEPH, S.T.D., J.C.D., Competence in Ecclesiastical Tribunals, IV-117 pp., 1922.
15. LEECH, REV. GEORGE LEO, J.C.D., A Comparative Study of the Constitution "Apostolicae Sedis" and the "Codex Juris Canonici," 179 pp., 1922.
16. MOTRY, REV. HUBERT LOUIS, S.T.D., J.C.D., Diocesan Faculties According to the Code of Canon Law, II-167 pp., 1922.
17. MURPHY, REV. GEORGE LAWRENCE, J.C.D., Delinquencies and Penalties in the Administration and the Reception of the Sacraments, IV-121 pp., 1923.

* Below n. 100 only numbers 25 and 57 are still available. Beginning with n. 100 only the following numbers are unavailable: Nos. 100–118 inclusive, and also n. 122.

18. O'Reilly, Rev. John Anthony, S.T.B., J.C.D., Ecclesiastical Sepulture in the New Code of Canon Law, II-129 pp., 1923.
19. Michalicka, Rev. Wenceslas Cyril L., O.S.B., J.C.D., Judicial Procedure in Dismissal of Clerical Exempt Religious, 107 pp., 1923.
20. Dargin, Rev. Edward Vincent, S.T.B., J.C.D., Reserved Cases According to the Code of Canon Law, IV-103 pp., 1924.
21. Godfrey, Rev. John A., S.T.B., J.C.D., The Right of Patronage According to the Code of Canon Law, 153 pp., 1924.
22. Hagedorn, Rev. Francis Edward, J.C.D., General Legislation on Indulgences, II-154 pp., 1924.
23. King, Rev. James Ignatius, J.C.D., The Administration of the Sacraments to Dying Non-Catholics, V-141 pp., 1924.
24. Winslow, Rev. Francis Joseph, O.F.M., J.C.D., Vicars and Prefects Apostolic, IV-149 pp., 1924.
25. Correa, Rev. Jose Servelion, S.T.L., J.C.D., La Potestad Legislativa de la Iglesia Catolica, IV-127 pp., 1925.
26. Dugan, Rev. Henry Francis, A.M., J.C.D., The Judiciary Department of the Diocesan Curia, 87 pp., 1925.
27. Keller, Rev. Charles Frederick, S.T.B., J.C.D., Mass Stipends, 167 pp., 1925.
28. Paschang, Rev. John Linus, J.C.D., The Sacramentals According to the Code of Canon Law, 129 pp., 1925.
29. Piontek, Rev. Cyrillus, O.F.M., S.T.B., J.C.D., De Indulto Exclaustrationis necnon Saecularizationis, XIII-289 pp., 1925.
30. Kearney, Rev. Richard Joseph, S.T.B., J.C.D., Sponsors at Baptism According to the Code of Canon Law, IV-127 pp., 1925.
31. Bartlett, Rev. Chester Joseph, A.M., LL.B., J.C.D., The Tenure of Parochial Property in the United States of America, V-108 pp., 1926.
32. Kilker, Rev. Adrian Jerome, J.C.D., Extreme Unction, V-425 pp., 1926.
33. McCormick, Rev. Robert Emmett, J.C.D., Confessors of Religious, VIII-266 pp., 1926.
34. Miller, Rev. Newton Thomas, J.C.D., Founded Masses According to the Code of Canon Law, VII-93 pp., 1926.
35. Roelker, Rev. Edward G., S.T.D., J.C.D., Principles of Privilege According to the Code of Canon Law, XI-166 pp., 1926.
36. Bakalarczyk, Rev. Richardus, M.I.C., J.U.D., De Novitiatu, VIII-208 pp., 1927.
37. Pizzuti, Rev. Lawrence, O.F.M., J.U.L., De Parochis Religiosis, 1927. (Not Printed.)
38. Bliley, Rev. Nicholas Martin, O.S.B., J.C.D., Altars According to the Code of Canon Law, XIX-132 pp., 1927.
39. Brown, Mr. Brendan Francis, A.B., LL.M., J.U.D., The Canonical Juristic Personality with Special Reference to its Status in the United States of America, V-212 pp., 1927.

40. Cavanaugh, Rev. William Thomas, C.P., J.U.D., The Reservation of the Blessed Sacrament, VIII-101 pp., 1927.
41. Doheny, Rev. William J., C.S.C., A.B., J.U.D., Church Property: Modes of Acquisition, X-118 pp., 1927.
42. Feldhaus, Rev. Aloysius H., C.PP.S., J.C.D., Oratories, IX-141 pp., 1927.
43. Kelly, Rev. James Patrick, A.B., J.C.D., The Jurisdiction of the Simple Confessor, X-208 pp., 1927.
44. Neuberger, Rev. Nicholas J., J.C.D., Canon 6 or the Relation of the Codex Juris Canonici to the Preceding Legislation, V-95 pp., 1927.
45. O'Keefe, Rev. Gerald Michael, J.C.D., Matrimonial Dispensations, Powers of Bishops, Priests, and Confessors, VIII-232 pp., 1927.
46. Quigley, Rev. Joseph A. M., A.B., J.C.D., Condemned Societies, 139 pp., 1927.
47. Zaplotnik, Rev. Johannes Leo, J.C.D., De Vicariis Foraneis, X-142 pp., 1927.
48. Duskie, Rev. John Aloysius, A.B., J.C.D., The Canonical Status of the Orientals in the United States, VIII-196 pp., 1928.
49. Hyland, Rev. Francis Edward, J.C.D., Excommunication, Its Nature, Historical Development and Effects, VIII-181 pp., 1928.
50. Reinmann, Rev. Gerald Joseph, O.M.C., J.C.D., The Third Order Secular of Saint Francis, 201 pp., 1928.
51. Schenk, Rev. Francis J., J.C.D., The Matrimonial Impediments of Mixed Religion and Disparity of Cult, XVI-318 pp., 1929.
52. Coady, Rev. John Joseph, S.T.D., J.U.D., A.M., The Appointment of Pastors, VIII-150 pp., 1929.
53. Kay, Rev. Thomas Henry, J.C.D., Competence in Matrimonial Procedure, VIII-164 pp., 1929.
54. Turner, Rev. Sidney Joseph, C.P., J.U.D., The Vow of Poverty, XLIX-217 pp., 1929.
55. Kearney, Rev. Raymond A., A.B., S.T.D., J.C.D., The Principles of Delegation, VII-149 pp., 1929.
56. Conran, Rev. Edward James, A.B., J.C.D., The Interdict, V-163 pp., 1930.
57. O'Neill, Rev. William H., J.C.D., Papal Rescripts of Favor, VII-218 pp., 1930.
58. Bastnagel, Rev. Clement Vincent, J.U.D., The Appointment of Parochial Adjutants and Assistants, XV-257 pp., 1930.
59. Ferry, Rev. William A., A.B., J.C.D., Stole Fees, V-136 pp., 1930.
60. Costello, Rev. John Michael, A.B., J.C.D., Domicile and Quasi-Domicile, VII-201 pp., 1930.
61. Kremer, Rev. Michael Nicholas, A.B., S.T.B., J.C.D., Church Support in the United States, VI-136 pp., 1930.
62. Angulo, Rev. Luis, C.M., J.C.D., Legislation de la Iglesia sobre la intencion en la application de la Santa Misa, VII-104 pp., 1931.

63. FREY, REV. WOLFGANG NORBERT, O.S.B., A.B., J.C.D., The Act of Religious Profession, VIII-174 pp., 1931.
64. ROBERTS, REV. JAMES BRENDAN, A.B., J.C.D., The Banns of Marriage, XIV-140 pp., 1931.
65. RYDER, REV. RAYMOND ALOYSIUS, A.B., J.C.D., Simony, IX-151 pp., 1931.
66. CAMPAGNA, REV. ANGELO, PH.D., J.U.D., Il Vicario Generale del Vescovo, VII-205 pp., 1931.
67. COX, REV. JOSEPH GODFREY, A.B., J.C.D., The Administration of Seminaries, VI-124 pp., 1931.
68. GREGORY, REV. DONALD J., J.U.D., The Pauline Privilege, XV-165 pp., 1931.
69. DONOHUE, REV. JOHN F., J.C.D., The Impediment of Crime, VII-110 pp., 1931.
70. DOOLEY, REV. EUGENE A., O.M.I., J.C.D., Church Law on Sacred Relics, IX-143 pp., 1931.
71. ORTH, REV. CLEMENT RAYMOND, O.M.C., J.C.D., The Approbation of Religious Institutes, 171 pp., 1931.
72. PERNICONE, REV. JOSEPH M., A.B., J.C.D., The Ecclesiastical Prohibition of Books, XII-267 pp., 1932.
73. CLINTON, REV. CONNELL, A.B., J.C.D., The Paschal Precept, IX-108 pp., 1932.
74. DONNELLY, REV. FRANCIS B., A.M., S.T.L., J.C.D., The Diocesan Synod, VIII-125 pp., 1932.
75. TORRENTE, REV. CAMILO, C.M.F., J.C.D., Las Procesiones Sagradas, V-145 pp., 1932.
76. MURPHY, REV. EDWIN J., C.PP.S., J.C.D., Suspension Ex Informata Conscientia, XI-122 pp., 1932.
77. MACKENZIE, REV. ERIC F., A.M., S.T.L., J.C.D., The Delict of Heresy in its Commission, Penalization, Absolution, VII-124 pp., 1932.
78. LYONS, REV. AVITUS E., S.T.B., J.C.D., The Collegiate Tribunal of First Instance, XI-147 pp., 1932.
79. CONNOLLY, REV. THOMAS A., J.C.D., Appeals, XI-195 pp., 1932.
80. SANGMEISTER, REV. JOSEPH V., A.B., J.C.D., Force and Fear as Precluding Matrimonial Consent, V-211 pp., 1932.
81. JAEGER, REV. LEO A., A.B., J.C.D., The Administration of Vacant and Quasi-Vacant Episcopal Sees in the United States, IX-229 pp., 1932.
82. RIMLINGER, REV. HERBERT T., J.C.D., Error Invalidating Matrimonial Consent, VII-79 pp., 1932.
83. BARRETT, REV. JOHN D. M., S.S., J.C.D., A Comparative Study of the Third Plenary Council of Baltimore and the Code, IX-221 pp., 1932.
84. CARBERRY, REV. JOHN J., PH.D., S.T.D., J.C.D., The Juridical Form of Marriage, X-177 pp., 1934.
85. DOLAN, REV. JOHN L., A.B., J.C.D., The Defensor Vinculi, XII 157 pp., 1934.

86. Hannan, Rev. Jerome D., A.M., S.T.D., LL.B., J.C.D., The Canon Law of Wills, IX-517 pp., 1934.
87. Lemieux, Rev. Delise A., A.M., J.C.D., The Sentence in Ecclesiastical Procedure, IX-131 pp., 1934.
88. O'Rourke, Rev. James J., A.B., J.C.D., Parish Registers, VII-109 pp., 1934.
89. Timlin, Rev. Bartholomew, O.F.M., A.M., J.C.D., Conditional Matrimonial Consent, X-381 pp., 1934.
90. Wahl, Rev. Francis X., A.B., J.C.D., The Matrimonial Impediments of Consanguinity and Affinity, VI-125 pp., 1934.
91. White, Rev. Robert J., A.B., LL.B., S.T.B., J.C.D., Canonical Ante-Nuptial Promises and the Civil Law, VI-152 pp., 1934.
92. Herrera, Rev. Antonio Parra, O.C.D., J.C.D., Legislacion Ecclesiastica sobra el Ayuno y la Abstinencia, XI-191 pp., 1935.
93. Kennedy, Rev. Edwin J., J.C.D., The Special Matrimonial Process in Cases of Evident Nullity, X-165 pp., 1935.
94. Manning, Rev. John J., A.B., J.C.D., Presumption of Law in Matrimonial Procedure, XI-111 pp., 1935.
95. Moeder, Rev. John M., J.C.D., The Proper Bishop for Ordination and Dimissorial Letters, VII-135 pp., 1935.
96. O'Mara, Rev. William A., A.B., J.C.D., Canonical Causes for Matrimonial Dispensations, IX-155 pp., 1935.
97. Reilly, Rev. Peter, J.C.D., Residence of Pastors, IX-81 pp., 1935.
98. Smith, Rev. Mariner T., O.P., S.T.Lr., J.C.D., The Penal Law for Religious, VII-169 pp., 1935.
99. Whalen, Rev. Donald W., A.M., J.C.D., The Value of Testimonial Evidence in Matrimonial Procedure, XIII-297 pp., 1935.
100. Cleary, Rev. Joseph F., J.C.D., Canonical Limitations on the Alienation of Church Property, VIII-141 pp., 1936.
101. Glynn, Rev. John C., J.C.D., The Promoter of Justice, XX-337 pp., 1936.
102. Brennan, Rev. James H., S.S., M.A., S.T.B., J.C.D., The Simple Convalidation of Marriage, VI-135 pp., 1937.
103. Brunini, Rev. Joseph Bernard, J.C.D., The Clerical Obligations of Canons 139 and 142, X-121 pp., 1937.
104. Connor, Rev. Maurice, A.B., J.C.D., The Administrative Removal of Pastors, VIII-159 pp., 1937.
105. Guilfoyle, Rev. Merlin Joseph, J.C.D., Custom, XI-144 pp., 1937.
106. Hughes, Rev. James Austin, A.B., A.M., J.C.D., Witnesses in Criminal Trials of Clerics, IX-140 pp., 1937.
107. Jansen, Rev. Raymond J., A.B., S.T.L., J.C.D., Canonical Provisions for Catechetical Instruction, VII-153 pp., 1937.
108. Kealy, Rev. John James, A.B., J.C.D., The Introductory Libellus in Church Court Procedure, XI-121 pp., 1937.

109. McManus, Rev. James Edward, C.SS.R., J.C.D., The Administration of Temporal Goods in Religious Institutes, XVI-196 pp., 1937.
110. Moriarty, Rev. Eugene James, J.C.D., Oaths in Ecclesiastical Courts, X-115 pp., 1937.
111. Rainer, Rev. Eligius George, C.SS.R., J.C.D., Suspension of Clerics, XVII-249 pp., 1937.
112. Reilly, Rev. Thomas F., C.SS.R., J.C.D., Visitation of Religious, VI-195 pp., 1938.
113. Moriarty, Rev. Francis E., C.SS.R., J.C.D., The Extraordinary Absolution from Censures, XV-334 pp., 1938.
114. Connolly, Rev. Nicholas P., J.C.D., The Canonical Erection of Parishes, X-132 pp., 1938.
115. Donovan, Rev. James Joseph, J.C.D., The Pastor's Obligation in Prenuptial Investigation, XII-322 pp., 1938.
116. Harrigan, Rev. Robert J., M.A., S.T.B., J.C.D., The Radical Sanation of Invalid Marriages, VIII-208 pp., 1938.
117. Boffa, Rev. Conrad Humbert, J.C.D., Canonical Provisions for Catholic Schools, VII-211 pp., 1939.
118. Parsons, Rev. Anscar John, O.M.Cap., J.C.D., Canonical Elections, XII-236 pp., 1939.
119. Reilly, Rev. Edward Michael, A.B., J.C.D., The General Norms of Dispensation, XII-156 pp., 1939.
120. Ryan, Rev. Gerald Aloysius, A.B., J.C.D., Principles of Episcopal Jurisdiction, XII-172 pp., 1939.
121. Burton, Rev. Francis James, C.S.C., A.B., J.C.D., A Commentary on Canon 1125, X-222 pp., 1940.
122. Miaskiewicz, Rev. Francis Sigismund, J.C.D., Supplied Jurisdiction According to Canon 209, XII-340 pp., 1940.
123. Rice, Rev. Patrick William, A.B., J.C.D., Proof of Death in Prenuptial Investigation, VIII-156 pp., 1940.
124. Anglin, Rev. Thomas Francis, M.S., J.C.D., The Eucharistic Fast, VIII-183 pp., 1941.
125. Coleman, Rev. John Jerome, J.C.D., The Minister of Confirmation, VI-153 pp., 1941.
126. Downs, Rev. Joseph Emmanuel, A.B., J.C.D., The Concept of Clerical Immunity, XI-163 pp., 1941.
127. Esswein, Rev. Anthony Albert, J.C.D., Extrajudicial Penal Powers of Ecclesiastical Superiors, X-144 pp., 1941.
128. Farrell, Rev. Benjamin Francis, M.A., S.T.L., J.C.D., The Rights and Duties of the Local Ordinary Regarding Congregations of Women Religious of Pontifical Approval, V-195 pp., 1941.
129. Feeney, Rev. Thomas John, A.B., S.T.L., J.C.D., Restitutio in Integrum, VI 169 pp., 1941.
130. Findlay, Rev. Stephen William, O.S.B., A.B., J.C.D., Canonical

Norms Governing the Deposition and Degradation of Clerics, XVII-279 pp., 1941.

131. Goodwine, Rev. John, A.B., S.T.L., J.C.D., The Right of the Church to Acquire Property, VIII-119 pp., 1941.

132. Heston, Rev. Edward Louis, C.S.C., Ph.D., S.T.D., J.C.D., The Alienation of Church Property in the United States, XII-222 pp., 1941.

133. Hogan, Rev. James John, A.B., S.T.L., J.C.D., Judicial Advocates and Procurators, XIII-200 pp., 1941.

134. Kealy, Rev. Thomas M., A.B., Litt.B., J.C.D., Dowry of Women Religious, IX-152 pp., 1941.

135. Keene, Rev. Michael James, O.S.B., J.C.D., Religious Ordinaries and Canon 198, V-164 pp., 1942.

136. Kerin, Rev. Charles A., S.S., M.A., S.T.B., J.C.D., The Privation of Christian Burial, XVI-279 pp., 1941.

137. Louis, Rev. William Francis, M.A., J.C.D., Diocesan Archives, X-101 pp., 1941.

138. McDevitt, Rev. Gilbert Joseph, A.B., J.C.D., Legitimacy and Legitimation, X-247 pp., 1941.

139. McDonough, Rev. Thomas Joseph, A.B., J.C.D., Apostolic Administrators, X-217 pp., 1941.

140. Meier, Rev. Carl Anthony, A.B., J.C.D., Penal Administrative Procedure Against Negligent Pastors, XI-240 pp., 1941.

141. Schmidt, Rev. John Rogg, A.B., J.C.D., The Principles of Authentic Interpretation in Canon 17 of the Code of Canon Law, XII-331 pp., 1941.

142. Slafkosky, Rev. Andrew Leonard, A.B., J.C.D., The Canonical Episcopal Visitation of the Diocese, X-197 pp., 1941.

143. Swoboda, Rev. Innocent Robert, O.F.M., J.C.D., Ignorance in Relation to the Imputability of Delicts, IX-271 pp., 1941.

144. Dubé, Rev. Arthur Joseph, A.B., J.C.D., The General Principles for the Reckoning of Time in Canon Law, VIII-299 pp., 1941.

145. McBride, Rev. James T., A.B., J.C.D., Incardination and Excardination of Seculars, XX-585 pp., 1941.

146. Król, Rev. John T., J.C.D., The Defendant in Ecclesiastical Trials, XII-207 pp., 1942.

147. Comyns, Rev. Joseph J., C.SS.R., A.B., J.C.D., Papal and Episcopal Administration of Church Property, XIV-155 pp., 1942.

148. Barry, Rev. Garrett Francis, O.M.I., J.C.D., Violation of the Cloister, XII-260 pp., 1942.

149. Bolduc, Rev. Gatien, C.S.V., A.B., S.T.L., J.C.D., Les Études dans les Religions Cléricales, VIII-155 pp., 1942.

150. Boyle, Rev. David John, M.A., J.C.D., The Juridic Effects of Moral Certitude on Pre-Nuptial Guarantees, XII-188 pp., 1942.

151. Canavan, Rev. Walter Joseph, M.A., Litt.D., J.C.D., The Profession of Faith, XII-143 pp., 1942.

152. **Desrochers, Rev. Bruno, A.B., Ph.L., S.T.B., J.C.D., Le Premier** Concile Plénier de Québec et le Code de Droit Canonique, XIV-186 pp., 1942.
153. Dillon, Rev. Robert Edward, A.B., J.C.D., Common Law Marriage, X-148 pp., 1942.
154. **Dodwell, Rev. Edward John, Ph.D., S.T.B., J.C.D., The Time and** Place for the Celebration of Marriage, X-156 pp., 1942.
155. Donnellan, Rev. Thomas Andrew, A.B., J.C.D., The Obligation of the Missa pro Populo, VII-131 pp., 1942.
156. Eltz, Rev. Louis Anthony, A.B., J.C.D., Cooperation in Crime, XII-208 pp., 1942.
157. Gass, Rev. Sylvester Francis, M.A., J.C.D., Ecclesiastical Pensions, XI-206 pp., 1942.
158. Guiniven, Rev. John Joseph, C.SS.R., J.C.D., The Precept of Hearing Mass, XIV-188 pp., 1942.
159. Gulczynski, Rev. John Theophilus, J.C.D., The Desecration and Violation of Churches, X-126 pp., 1942.
160. Hammill, Rev. John Leo, M.A., J.C.D., The Obligations of the Traveler According to Canon 14, VIII-204 pp., 1942.
161. Haydt, Rev. John Joseph, A.B., J.C.D., Reserved Benefices, XI-148 pp., 1942.
162. Huser, Rev. Roger John, O.F.M., A.B., J.C.D., The Crime of Abortion in Canon Law, XII-187 pp., 1942.
163. **Kearney, Rev. Francis Patrick, A.B., S.T.L., J.C.D., The Principles of Canon 1127, X-162 pp., 1942.**
164. Linahen, Rev. Leo James, S.T.L., J.C.D., De Absolutione Complicis In Peccato Turpi, 114 pp., 1942.
165. McCloskey, Rev. Joseph Aloysius, A.B., J.C.D., The Subject of Ecclesiastical Law According to Canon 12, XVII-246 pp., 1942.
166. O'Neill, Rev. Francis Joseph, C.SS.R., J.C.D., The Dismissal of Religious in Temporary Vows, XIII-220 pp., 1942.
167. **Prince, Rev. John Edward, A.B., S.T.B., J.C.D., The Diocesan Chan**cellor, X-136 pp., 1942.
168. Riesner, Rev. Albert Joseph, C.SS.R., J.C.D., Apostates and Fugitives from Religious Institutes, IX-168 pp., 1942.
169. Stenger, Rev. Joseph Bernard, J.C.D., The Mortgaging of Church Property, 186 pp., 1942.
170. Waldron, Rev. Joseph Francis, A.B., J.C.D., The Minister of Baptism, XII-197 pp., 1942.
171. Willett, Rev. Robert Albert, J.C.D., The Probative Value of Documents in Ecclesiastical Trials, X-124 pp., 1942.
172. Woeber, Rev. Edward Martin, M.A., J.C.D., The Interpellations, XII-161 pp., 1942.
173. Benko, Rev. Matthew Aloysius, O.S.B., M.A., J.C.D., The Abbot *Nullius*, XIV-148 pp., 1943.

174. Christ, Rev. Joseph James, M.A., S.T.L., J.C.D., Dispensation from Vindicative Penalties, XIV-285 pp., 1943.
175. Clancy, Rev. Patrick M. J., O.P., A.B., S.T.Lr., J.C.D., The Local Religious Superior, X-229 pp., 1943.
176. Clarke, Rev. Thomas James, J.C.D., Parish Societies, XII-147 pp., 1943.
177. Connolly, Rev. John Patrick, S.T.L., J.C.D., Synodal Examiners and Parish Priest Consultors, X-223 pp., 1943.
178. Drumm, Rev. William Martin, A.B., J.C.D., Hospital Chaplains, XII-175 pp., 1943.
179. Flanagan, Rev. Bernard Joseph, A.B., S.T.L., J.C.D., The Canonical Erection of Religious Houses, X-147 pp., 1943.
180. Kelleher, Rev. Stephen Joseph, A.B., S.T.B., J.C.D., Discussions with Non-Catholics: Canonical Legislation, X-93 pp., 1943.
181. Lewis, Rev. Gordian, C.P., J.C.D., Chapters in Religious Institutes, XII-169 pp., 1943.
182. Marx, Rev. Adolph, J.C.D., The Declaration of Nullity of Marriages Contracted Outside the Church, X-151 pp., 1943.
183. Matulenas, Rev. Raymond Anthony, O.S.B., A.B., J.C.D., Communication, a Source of Privileges, XII-225 pp., 1943.
184. O'Leary, Rev. Charles Gerard, C.SS.R., J.C.D., Religious Dismissed After Perpetual Profession, X-213 pp., 1943.
185. Power, Rev. Cornelius Michael, J.C.D., The Blessing of Cemeteries, XII-231 pp., 1943.
186. Shuhler, Rev. Ralph Vincent, O.S.A., J.C.D., Privileges of Regulars to Absolve and Dispense, XII-195 pp., 1943.
187. Ziolkowski, Rev. Thaddeus Stanislaus, A.B., J.C.D., The Consecration and Blessing of Churches, XII-151 pp., 1943.
188. Heneghan, Rev. John Joseph, S.T.D., J.C.D., The Marriages of Unworthy Catholics: Canons 1065 and 1066, XVI-213 pp., 1944.
189. Carroll, Rev. Coleman Francis, M.A., S.T.L., J.C.L., Charitable Institutions.
190. Ciesluk, Rev. Joseph Edward, Ph.B., S.T.L., J.C.L., National Parishes in the United States.
191. Coburn, Rev. Vincent Paul, A.B., J.C.D., Marriages of Conscience, XII-172 pp., 1944.
192. Connors, Rev. Charles Paul, C.S.Sp., A.B., J.C.D., Extra-Judicial Procurators in the Code of Canon Law, X-94 pp., 1944.
193. Coyle, Rev. Paul Raymond, A.B., J.C.D., Judicial Exceptions, X-142 pp., 1944.
194. Fair, Rev. Bartholomew Francis, A.B., S.T.L., J.C.L., The Impediment of Abduction.
195. Gallagher, Rev. Thomas Raphael, O.P., A.B., S.T.Lr., J.C.D., The Examination of the Qualities of the Ordinand, X-166 pp., 1944.
196. Gannon, Rev. John Mark, S.T.L., J.C.D., The Interstices Required for the Promotion to Orders, XII-100 pp., 1944.

197. GOLDSMITH, REV. J. WILLIAM, B.C.S., S.T.L., J.C.D., The Competence of Church and State over Marriage—Disputed Points, X-128 pp., 1944.
198. GOODWINE, REV. JOSEPH GERARD, A.B., S.T.B., J.C.D., The Reception of Converts, XIV-326 pp., 1944.
199. KOWALSKI, REV. ROMUALD EUGENE, O.F.M., A.B., J.C.D., Sustenance of Religious Houses of Regulars, X-174 pp., 1944.
200. McCOY, REV. ALAN EDWARD, O.F.M., J.C.D., Force and Fear in Relation to Delictual Imputability and Penal Responsibility, XII-160 pp., 1944.
201. McDEVITT, REV. VINCENT JOHN, Ph.B., S.T.L., J.C.L., Perjury.
202. MARTIN, REV. THOMAS OWEN, Ph.D., S.T.D., J.C.D., Adverse Possession, Prescription and Limitation of Actions: The Canonical "Praescriptio," XX-208 pp., 1944.
203. MIKLOSOVIC, REV. PAUL JOHN, A.B., J.C.L., Attempted Marriages and Their Consequent Juridic Effects.
204. MUNDY, REV. THOMAS MAURICE, A.B., S.T.L., J.C.D., The Union of Parishes, X—164 pp., 1945.
205. O'DEA, REV. JOHN COYLE, A.B., J.C.D., The Matrimonial Impediment of Nonage, VIII-126 pp., 1944.
206. OLALIA, REV. ALEXANDER AYSON, S.T.L., J.C.D., A Comparative Study of the Christian Constitution of States and the Constitution of the Philippine Commonwealth, XII—136 pp., 1944.
207. POISSON, REV. PIERRE-MARIE, C.S.C., A.B., Ph.L., Th.L., J.C.L., Droits Patrimoniaux des Maisons et des Églises Religieuses.
208. STADALNIKAS, REV. CASIMIR JOSEPH, M.I.C., J.C.D., Reservation of Censures, X-141 pp., 1944.
209. SULLIVAN, REV. EUGENE HENRY, S.T.L., J.C.D., Proof of the Reception of the Sacraments, X—165 pp., 1944.
210. VAUGHAN, REV. WILLIAM EDWARD, J.C.D., Constitutions for Diocesan Courts, X-210 pp., 1944.
211. PARO, REV. GINO, S.T.D., J.C.L., The Right of Apostolic Legation.
212. BALZER, REV. RALPH FRANCIS, C.P., J.C.L., The Computation of Time in a Canonical Novitiate.
213. DOUGHERTY, REV. JOHN WHELAN, A.B., S.T.L., J.C.L., De Inquisitione Speciali.
214. DZIOB, REV. MICHAEL WALTER, J.C.L., The Sacred Congregation for the Oriental Church.
215. EIDENSCHINK, REV. JOHN ALBERT, O.S.B., B.A., J.C.L., The Election of Bishops in the Letters of Pope Gregory the Great.
216. GILL, REV. NICHOLAS, C.P., J.C.L., The Spiritual Prefect in Clerical Religious Houses of Study.

217. Hynes, Rev. Harry Gerard, S.T.L., J.C.D., The Privileges of Cardinals, XII-183 pp., 1945.
218. McDevitt, Rev. Gerald Vincent, S.T.L., J.C.D., The Renunciation of an Ecclesiastical Office, XIV—179 pp., 1946.
219. Manning, Rev. Joseph Leroy, J.C.L., The Free Conferral of Offices.
220. Meyer, Rev. Louis G., O.S.B., A.B., S.T.B., J.C.D., Alms-Gathering by Religious, XII—163 pp., 1946.
221. O'Donnell, Rev. Cletus Francis, M.A., J.C.L., The Marriage of Minors.
222. Prunskis, Rev. Joseph, J.C.D., Comparative Law, Ecclesiastical and Civil, in Lithuanian Concordat, X—161 pp., 1945.
223. Sweeney, Rev. Francis Patrick, C.SS.R., J.C.D., The Reduction of Clerics to the Lay State, X—199 pp., 1945.
224. Vogelpohl, Rev. Henry John, J.C.L., The Simple Impediments to Holy Orders.